CW01638813

GWILYM PRICHARD

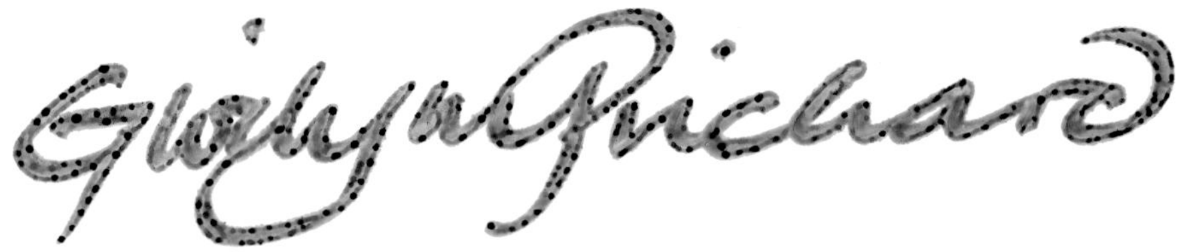

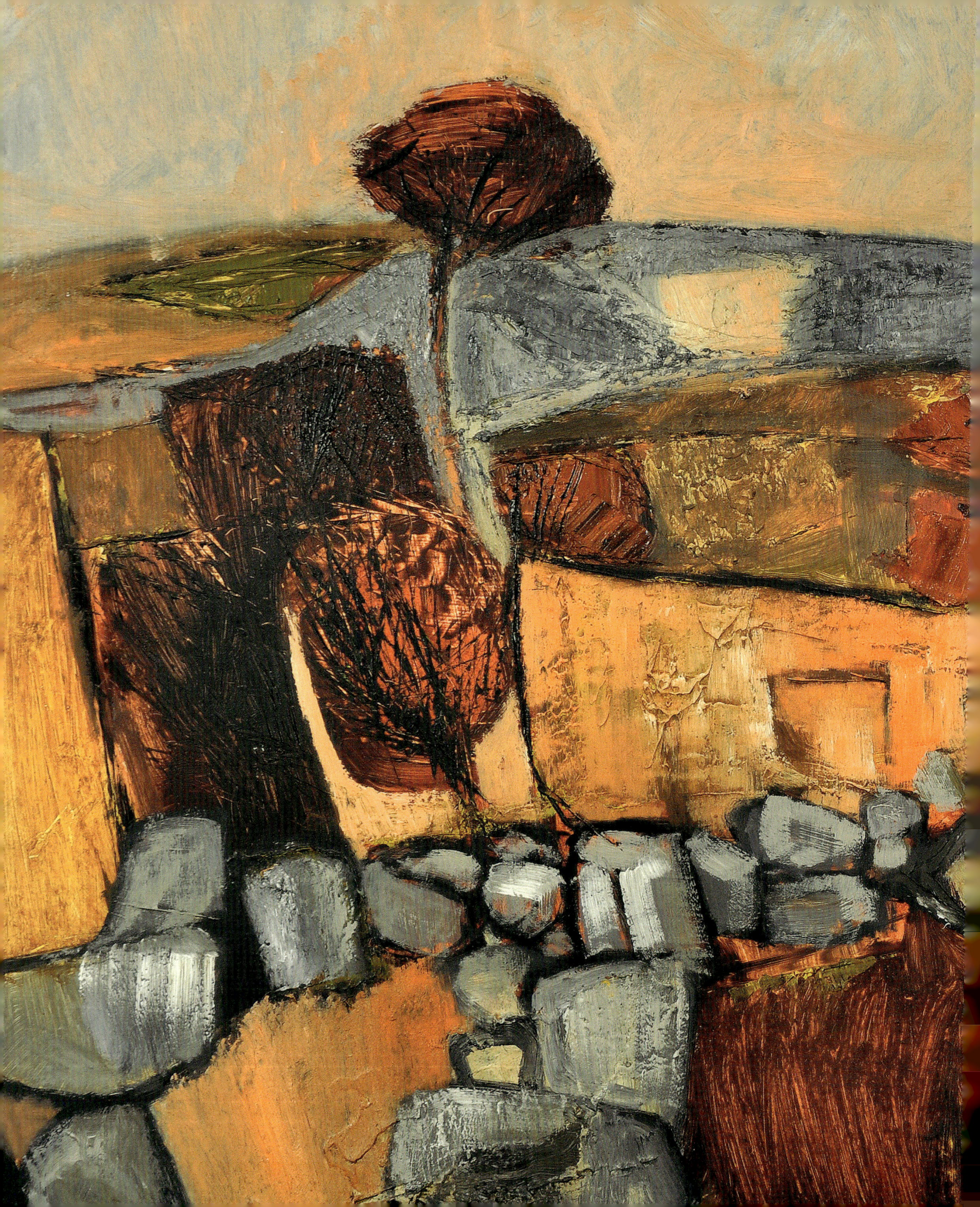

GWILYM PRICHARD

A Lifetime's Gazing

Harry Heuser &
Robert Meyrick

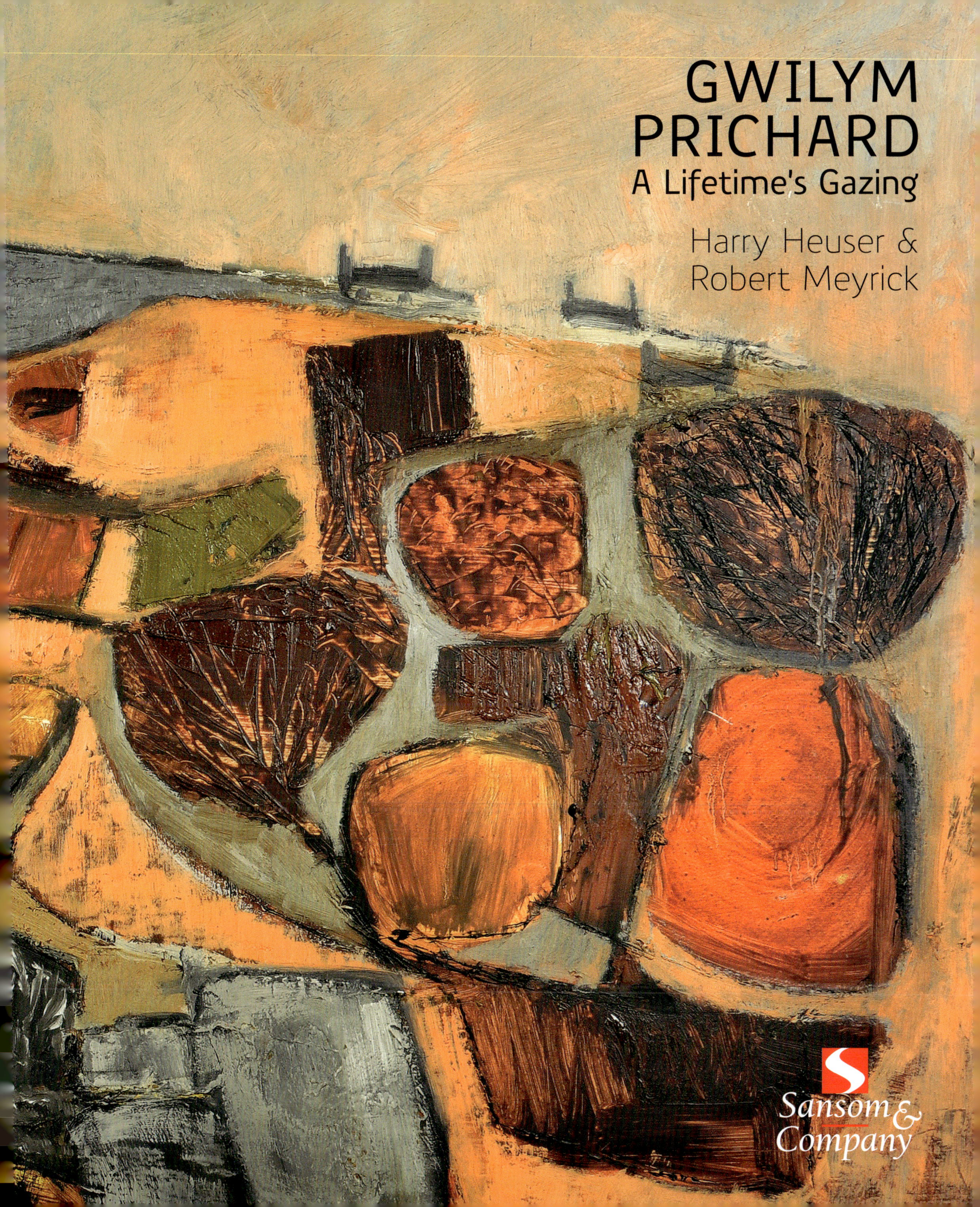

Sansom & Company

To my wife Claudia for her love and help.
To my children Ceri, Ben, Justin and Clare,
and my grandchildren Hannah, Laurie, Rebecca,
Amber, Emily Rachel, Miriam and Emily Josephine.
To Robert and Harry for their patience and understanding.
To the Martin Tinney Gallery for showing my work.
Gwilym Prichard

First published in 2013 by Sansom & Co Ltd,
81G Pembroke Road, Bristol BS8 3EA
www.sansomandcompany.co.uk
info@sansomandcompany.co.uk

© Harry Heuser and Robert Meyrick

ISBN 978-1-908326-15-7
British Library cataloguing-in-publication data
A catalogue record for this book is available from the British Library

All rights reserved. Except for the purpose of review, no part of this
book may be reproduced, stored in a retrieval system, or transmitted,
in any form or by any means, electronic, mechanical, photocopying,
recording or otherwise, without the prior permission of the publishers.

Design and typesetting by E&P Design
Photographs (unless otherwise credited):
Gwilym Prichard; Robert Meyrick; Martin Tinney Gallery, Cardiff
Printed and bound by Zenith Media

CONTENTS

FOREWORD

The evocative power of Gwilym Prichard's landscapes derives from three principal elements, each essentially formal. The first is the precise correspondence of painterly forms – brush stroke, brush scribble, palette-knife slab – to the natural forms of shrubs and trees, clouds and water surfaces, and geological, topographical and architectural structures. It seems that Prichard closely studied and learned what he needed from artists as diverse as early Monet, de Vlaminck and de Stael. The second is the uncanny match of painterly colour to the variations of hue and tone, and the sudden variegations of light, in the natural appearances of farmland, hill and mountainside, meadow and lake, cliff, cove and coastal waters. And finally, there are the rhythms, rhymes, counterpoints and repetitions that set up in every painting a kind of lyrical and witty music, its curved and sinuous melodies quite distinct from the craggy tone-poems of his compatriot Kyffin Williams.

He is, in short, a consummate artist whose every subject is an occasion for a passionate formal engagement with his medium. For Prichard, paint is nothing less than a material means to the joyous revelation of the sensational world he loves for its manifold forms and textures, its turning seasons and its ever-expressive weather.

Mel Gooding

'A LIFETIME'S GAZING'

Though it is a 'very small country', art historian David Bell observed in 1957, Wales is distinguished by such a 'wide variety of scenery' that it would be difficult to conceive of 'any type of landscape' that could not be encountered 'somewhere within her borders'. There are spots of 'unspoiled rural beauty, of wild and untouched desolation', as well as 'areas where the industrial age has lain heavy on the land'. Each having its 'peculiar beauty', these features appealed to 'varying tastes' and sensibilities, from the classical and picturesque painters of the eighteenth century to the 'modern', twentieth-century artist. What distinguishes the latter, as Bell put it, is an attention to 'a single peculiar quality rather than the whole character in landscapes', be it the

> *twisted flotsam of the Pembrokeshire beaches, or the lowering precipices of Eryri, or the sombre tips of the South Wales industrial scene, or the homely coming-out-of-church on a Sunday morning into the quiet, respectable, typically Welsh beauty of Cardiganshire. It has it all, all in the changing seasons of the year, alike in the austerity of winter and the luxury of summer, in the first fine flush of spring and in autumn, when the dying leaves burn in the valleys and flame to the autumn skies.*[1]

One of those 'modern artists' starting out in the 1950s was Gwilym Prichard, for whom seeking out the peculiar qualities of a familiar landscape became a lifetime quest. From the mid-1950s to the present day, parts of his native Wales have remained to him an inexhaustible source of subjects for compositions in oil, gouache, watercolour, pastel and mixed media: remote farmsteads and sandy coves, drystone walls and sinuous roads, lichen-dappled rocks and snow-mantled fields.

For most of his life, Prichard has been working on Anglesey and in the foothills of Snowdonia – on the Llŷn Peninsula, where he grew up, and in Pembrokeshire, where he lives now. His birthplace and his current home are a mere 135 miles apart, and yet the journey, much of which Prichard travelled alongside his wife, painter Claudia Williams, has been a tortuous one. It entailed reconciling his life as an artist with the need to make a living as a teacher; providing a home for his four children without ever settling down for good; setting out anew at midlife in a temperamental old estate car for Greece; setting up studios in Brittany and Provence; and moving house some two dozen times along the way. It is an ongoing narrative whose storyline has been sketched out and redrawn at many a proverbial crossroads. To arrive at the sites that have arrested his gaze, Prichard took paths that he and Williams decided to forge for themselves. 'And that', to borrow a line from one of Prichard's favourite poems, 'has made all the difference'.[2] After all, however inspiring the varied Welsh vistas, they alone could not produce, foster and sustain an artistic career for which Prichard's upbringing and early education provided a less than auspicious start.

'AND CAN YOU PAINT, GWILYM?'

Gwilym Arifor Pritchard was born on 4 March 1931 in Llanystumdwy, a small village on the Llŷn Peninsula in North Wales. Five decades later, he would drop the 't' in his surname after realising that he had been sharing his name with another artist on whose work he alighted in an exhibition catalogue. The adjustment, though slight, was neither trifling nor arbitrary. Consulting the family bible, Pritchard discovered that his great-grandfather had been a Prichard, which meant that in the act of distancing himself from an unknown namesake by letting go of a single letter in the name he had made for himself, he could affirm the ties to his ancestors and the past that shaped him. Prichard grew up in a community that was firmly rooted in tradition and defined by social conventions. As a boy, he was expected to doff his cap to his elders and presumably betters, to respect the vicar and the *crachach*. His father, Hugh Ivor Pritchard, was a diocesan lay reader and church organist. Having served in the Great War, he became a graduate of the University College of Wales, Aberystwyth, and, for 28 years, until his retirement in 1955, was headmaster of the village school in Llanystumdwy. 'Church three times on a Sunday' and 'sermons that seemed to go on and on' – these are among Prichard's earliest memories, along with being handed sweets to keep him quiet during the service (fig. 1).[3]

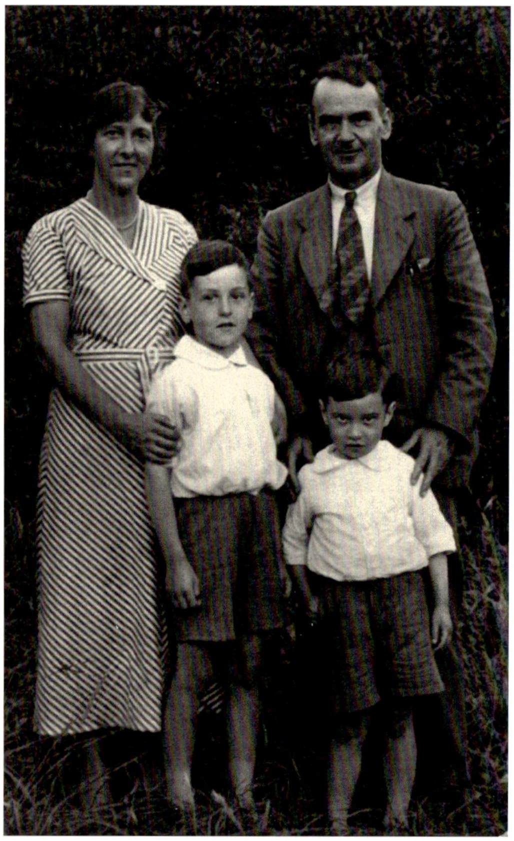

Fig. 1
Rhoda and Hugh Pritchard with Arthur (left) and Gwilym (right), c.1935–36

Although he grew up in a schoolhouse, the son of 'The School,' Prichard cannot recall 'seeing any art books at school or at home'. Damp, dark and without the benefit of electricity to brighten it, the place was downright spooky during the winter months. The child's imagination was fuelled by spoken words rather than printed images: bedtime stories by candlelight – 'all in Welsh, of course' – about the *tylwyth teg*, which came to mind so vividly that the boy 'could see these little people in the flickering shadows of the candle'. The fairies, Cledwyn Hughes insisted in 1949, had remained with the people of North Wales, and at 'heart most of the Northern Welsh' believed in them, as the 'mountains and lakes and the bogs of the North', unlike the 'great cities of the industrial south', were the places that the Little Folk continued to haunt.[4] When Prichard was five or six years old, he, his older brother Arthur and their parents moved into a newly erected house about a quarter of a mile from the old school building. Not only did it feature electric light – an innovation that gave Prichard's mother Rhoda headaches – but the new home, Ael y Bryn, was also brightened by its elevated position. This afforded views of the sea and the River Dwyfor a field away, at whose banks the child learned the shapes of trees, the colours of wild flowers and the song of birds. The life outdoors was immediate, palpable and concrete – a life that mattered. Prichard's childhood was not unlike the 'village boy' experiences that R.S. Thomas contrasts in his poems 'The One Furrow' and 'Farm Child' – days spent sitting on a 'tall stool' at 'learning's gate', '[w]ith pencil and foot-rule / Sponge and slate', or else roaming, wandering, his face freckled by the rays of the sun like a 'finch's egg' under a 'bush of hair / That dares the wind', and his head 'stuffed / With all the nests he knows, his pockets with flowers'.[5] The Dwyfor became increasingly important to young Gwilym as it promised a 'wonderful', 'tranquil' life away from the grammar school that he, for the most part, quite passionately disliked.

'I was brought up by the river', Prichard introduced himself years later in an exhibition catalogue, 'nature and landscape were part of my life; the river my bloodstream'.[6] Indeed, he once went so far as to say that, painting aside, the 'only other thing' he truly enjoyed was fishing.[7] As a boy, he spent many an afternoon fly fishing, and the Dwyfor would become a valuable source of food when wartime rationing came into force. Such restrictions aside, it was a war the child noticed only in passing. He could see and hear German aircraft flying over on their bombing missions to Liverpool. There was a Royal Navy camp at Afonwen and an airfield at Llanbedrog, both near Pwllheli. Looking out onto the sea, where a target had been erected for bombing practice, young Gwilym spent hours drawing spitfires and hurricanes engaged in mock air battles 'with dots coming out of the wings!' If war made its presence felt it was in the games, at times fiercely violent, that the boy played with his brother, Arthur, whom he once shot in the eye with an airgun and who nearly cut Gwilym's thumb off with a knife. The tranquillity and wholesomeness of the river made its banks a welcome retreat.

One evening, walking up from the Dwyfor and returning to the village, the child came across an old man sitting on a rock, his hair long and white and his figure cloaked in a black cape. The elder asked the boy whether he had caught any trout. Dutifully replying in the affirmative, the boy handed the stranger about half a dozen fish on a reed, threaded through the gills. 'He thanked me,' Prichard recalls, 'and said if I ever had any to spare again, he lived in Ty Newydd just up the road.' When he came back home, the child told his father about this chance encounter and learned that the man he had seen – perched on the boulder that is now a monument – was the former prime minister, the Earl Lloyd George of Dwyfor. After the death of Lloyd George, whose March 1945 funeral young Gwilym attended along with thousands of mourners and spectators, two books on fishing were left by Llanystumdwy's most distinguished denizen and were given to Prichard by the Countess Lloyd George. Such were the treasures and wonders of the outdoors that school and home offered comparatively little stimulation, and even less of the visual sort.

When he did happen upon works of art in his immediate environment, the child paid close attention. Aside from the 'many opportunities' he had to examine very closely a print of Millais' *Boyhood of Raleigh*, which hung outside the headmaster's room at Porthmadog Grammar School, young Gwilym first came into contact with the fine arts by turning the pages of *The Book of Knowledge*, an encyclopedia for children. He was intrigued by a reproduction of Picasso's 1938 painting *Maya with Doll*.

Attempting to copy it, he 'was promptly told that it was modern art and rubbish'. It is a prejudicial way of looking – and of not looking – at art that has troubled Prichard ever since. Yet the eye needed training, the mind opening; and with next to no instruction in art appreciation, even a rare childhood visit to the Walker Art Gallery in Liverpool was a lost opportunity; he was taken there once, Prichard recalls, and 'found it very boring'. In the days of wartime and post-war austerity, another such opportunity would not soon present itself; 'travelling', as Prichard recalls, 'was difficult and most things were in short supply'. With little access to art and yet eager to create, Prichard spent a lot of time 'carving wood and just making things'. He describes himself as a 'practical, hands-on type'; and even though making things was often motivated by physical need, it was also spiritually rewarding. Throughout his life, Prichard put his creativity to much practical use, and he gained further satisfaction from the knowledge that the things he fashioned – the pull-along toys he was to build for his children or the mosaic he created at St Michael's in Ruabon – would themselves become a source of delight. To young Gwilym, 'just making things' was more gratifying and worthwhile than producing art in a classroom, especially since the latter experience entailed working with decidedly inferior materials, including a 'brush that had hardly any bristle[s] because it was so worn out' after the many frustrated attempts to extract pigment from the 'hard cakes of watercolour' with which he and his fellow pupils had been so inadequately supplied.[8]

Not that signs of scholastic aptitude were wanting in Prichard. According to his school reports, the boy was 'very good at art'; indeed, he 'was top of the class'. Still, his art education was haphazard at best. The only encouragement and meaningful advice he received during those days came from a chemistry teacher, Mr Porter, who doubled as an art instructor. '[E]nthusiastic, communicative and interesting', Porter was 'the only teacher that inspired and influenced me', Prichard maintains. 'He praised me once on my observing that when oxygen was passed through water the bubbles as they ascended became smaller.' Aside from teaching young Gwilym how to make gunpowder, Porter also demonstrated to him how 'different metals produced different colours'. Neither the knowledge of explosives nor the longing for artistic expression translated into a clear path. Upon finishing his Ordinary Level examinations, Prichard was 'advised to leave school without anyone "advising"'. He 'hung about' until he was called to National Service. In 1948, after square bashing at West Kirby, he was posted to Yatesbury, Wiltshire, where he trained to be a radar mechanic. Training was cut short when he contracted scarlet fever; the severe case of rheumatic fever it brought on meant that Prichard spent much of 1949 in hospital in Swindon; here, in need of creatively dexterous occupation, he learned the art of embroidery. Returning home after completing his service, the youth was faced with the challenge of shaping a future for himself – and a life in art seemed a far from realistic prospect. Not that he was even contemplating such a career at the time. 'I did not set out to be an artist,' Prichard reminds us, 'it happened and I am grateful for being one.'[9]

'Despite the ageless beauty of its landscape', artist-craftsman Jonah Jones remarked, North Wales in those days could not boast 'any tradition in painting and sculpture such as exist[ed], for example, in Cornwall, at St Ives'; nor an 'atmosphere in which an artist [might] feel the support of fellow craftsmen around him'. Indeed, during the years immediately after the Second World War, Jones argued, it was 'inconceivable' that a young person growing up in that part of Britain

> *should embark on an art career. The few working artists there existed in more or less of a vacuum, making rare contact with each other, and even being forced, like Kyffin Williams, to seek a living in England.*

How 'astonishing', then, that 'one of the local village lads' in Llanystumdwy, where Jones had joined the engraver John Petts at the re-established Caseg Press, was 'showing a nascent talent' for painting, 'this most untraditional art form in Caernarvonshire'. In his amazement and admiration, Jones may have somewhat overstated his point; perhaps, the Welsh had 'traditionally held their light under a bushel', he considered years later, because there is so much evidence that 'belie[s] the legend that the Welsh have little visual sense'.[10] Prichard may have 'drifted into painting', as he himself once remarked, but he did so with the 'sometimes not-too-gentle pushes by established painters',[11] Charles Tunnicliffe and Kyffin Williams among them, both of whom lived and worked on nearby Anglesey. Jones, too, became a close friend. Prichard's greatest motivation to go in for the arts, however, was Claudia Williams, an aspiring painter two-and-a-half years his junior but already well on her way in the late 1940s. For however secluded or singular Prichard might have been, he was not the only young talent to stand out in or around Llanystumdwy. Jones, who met Williams during his days at the Caseg Press, was impressed to learn that, 'in this area where art could only struggle', the teenager – whose English parents had moved to Llangybi, a village some five miles from Llanystumdwy, shortly after the Second World War – had won first prize in a national newspaper painting competition, a prize that enabled her to attend Chelsea Art School.[12]

'Love and Art hit me at about the same time', Prichard declares, referring to a defining moment in his life when 'this girl on a grey horse' came riding 'down the road to the junction where [he] was daydreaming'. She stopped, looked down at him and he looked up at her. 'No smiles,' he recalls, 'just some contact on my part, which was shattering.' He went home and told his mother 'in vague terms about this girl' and was told that she was the daughter of a Mrs Frank Williams and that she was studying at some London art school.[13] The chance encounter – and the titbit about Williams' education – made a profound

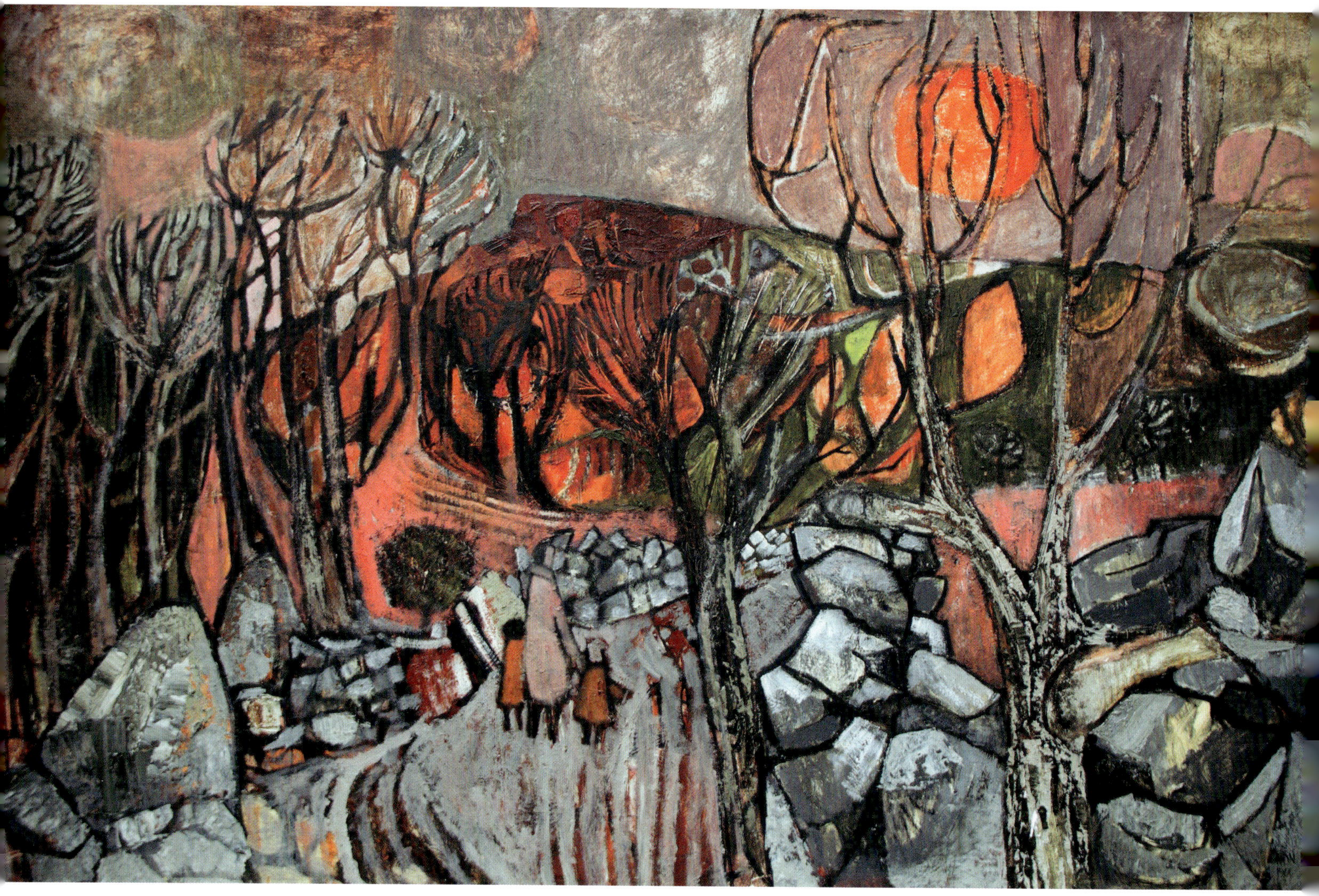

Fig. 2
Ceri, Claudia and Ben at Llwydiarth
1964 | oil on board | 122 x 184 cm
private collection, UK

impression on Prichard, who, to stimulate conversation and find common ground between them, mustered the courage to put together a portfolio of his early efforts – what he now deems 'pretty awful watercolours' – and show them to her. Williams, in turn, shared with him some of her life drawings. 'Can you do this at school?' he asked, incredulously. 'Yes, of course', she replied, upon hearing which he decided, in 1953, to enroll on a diploma course at Birmingham College of Art, not the least in order to be closer in spirit to Williams, whom he married the following year. 'Really,' Prichard insists, 'it was looking at Claudia's work and Claudia working with oil paint that made me think "so that's how it's done". Claudia's work was academic and my efforts were a bit messy and all over the place to start with.'[14] In turn, as Williams remembers, 'Gwilym did exciting lino prints' and 'encouraged [her] to be a bit more adventurous when applying paint'; her work was becoming 'a bit too Academic and needed freeing up'.[15]

'We were both dreamers,' Prichard comments on joining Williams in her bold venture into the arts, 'and at times our dreams have resulted in realities.'[16] Williams is Prichard's opposite in many ways; outgoing and impulsive, she provides the ideal counter-balance to his quiet and reserve, a contrast expressing itself in her joyous paintings of youthful family life and his communing with the wilds of an ancient land. 'I've always been interested in figures and the juxtaposition of bodies', Williams comments on the marked difference in the couple's choice of subjects, whereas 'landscape doesn't interest me one bit, although I appreciate living in a lovely landscape'.[17] The couple have learned to reconcile their life together with their individual careers as artists. At times of financial hardship, personal difficulties and illness, they could rely on their mutual support, which has sustained and strengthened both their bond and their art through the decades. As art historian Moira Vincentelli noted, it is the couple's 'shared life' that 'has brought strength to this remarkably complementary relationship'.[18] Yet as certain as Prichard was in the early 1950s about his future with Williams, there still remained doubts as to which direction his life in art should take, and neither art practice in general nor painting in particular were immediate or obvious choices. At Birmingham College of Art, Prichard 'did some painting', but the criticism he received was not always encouraging. In a life drawing class, he was told: 'You're painting a woman, not a pregnant cow with udders!' Afterwards, he would rarely attempt a portrait. Instead, he turned his attention to pottery and weaving, the 'colour and texture' of which he 'really enjoyed'. Drawing on the few kind and meaningful words he had received in his youth, the young man determined that he 'would be like [his] old chemistry master'; that he, too, would become a teacher.

In 1950, three years prior to his studies at Birmingham, Prichard had enrolled in an art education training course at Normal College, Bangor. In 1954, he was appointed crafts teacher at Llangefni County Secondary School on Anglesey, having

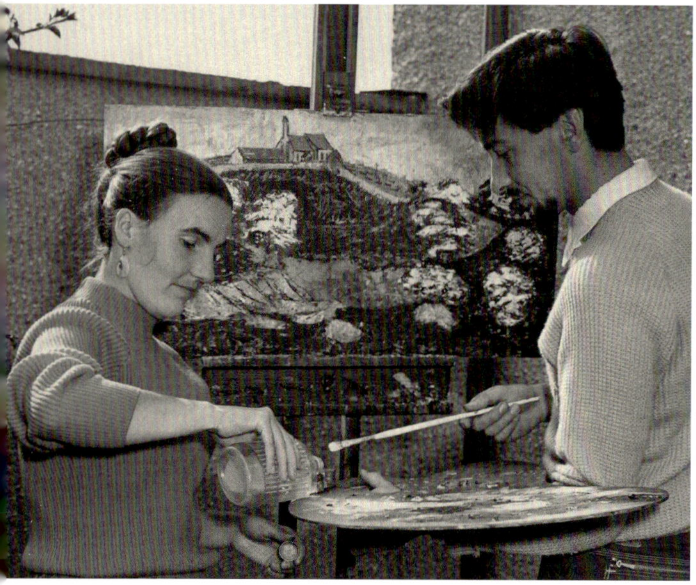

Fig. 3
Gwilym and Claudia Williams at Pencraig, Llangefni, 1958
photograph A.J. Lennie

previously rejected a post he was offered in Blackburn, Lancashire. His decision was not a matter of economics, of status or advancement. He simply 'wanted to live in the country'.[19]

After a period of living together in digs in Birmingham during Prichard's studies there, the couple's first 'real home' was a 'tiny flat' above a stationer's shop in the High Street of Llangefni. In 1954, when their first child, Ceri, was born, they were allocated a three-bedroom council house on a new estate on the edge of the town. There, Williams gave birth to a second child, Benjamin, in 1956, in anticipation of whose arrival the anxious father nearly burned down the school as he rushed home that evening from his ceramics class, keeping the kiln firing throughout the night. In August 1958, Prichard and Williams moved to Beaumaris on the southeast shore of Anglesey where the Irish Sea enters the tidal waters of the Menai Straits, a town that, 'as the name implies' – and as eighteenth-century Welsh naturalist and antiquary Thomas Pennant observed – is 'pleasantly seated on a low land at the water's edge'.[20] Here, their third child, Justin, was born in 1963; 16 months later, the couple adopted an infant girl, Clare. 'Time passed swiftly', Williams recalls. The young parents 'were so busy trying to paint or at least to draw' while family and work demanded their attention (*Ceri, Claudia and Ben at Llwydiarth*, 1964; fig. 2). Prichard shared in the 'inevitable daily chores', which entailed early mornings spent washing 'terry towelling nappies in the bath'. There were '[n]o disposable nappies in those days', Williams reminds us. While Williams found a ready subject in her children, Prichard, taking advantage of the family's camping holidays on Anglesey, made drawings of landscapes that he could work up into paintings.[21] The artist couple's domestic circumstances attracted the notice of newspapers in Wales and England, which ran headlines like 'After the Children Are Put to Bed…' and 'Happy Ending to 6 Months' "Hard Labour"'[22] (figs 3 & 4).

At Llangefni County Secondary School, Prichard taught crafts for 11 years, during which time he managed to create a viable market for his paintings and, with the encouragement and promotional efforts of Jonah Jones, became a regular contributor to group exhibitions in Porthmadog and Portmeirion. By the early 1960s, Prichard and Williams had 'built up a steady patronage'. Their work was 'known throughout the Principality', their careers an 'indication of the growth in Wales of appreciation of the visual arts'.[23] In November 1959, Prichard and Williams gained further prominence when their art was featured on the inaugural broadcast of the Welsh television programme *Cwmpas*, a series devoted to contemporary art, for which they were interviewed in Old Bank House, their Anglesey home, by the noted poet, translator and literary critic Dyfnallt Morgan. The interview was prefaced by the artist Ellis Gwyn Jones, who remarked that '[p]ainting in Wales is an art in embryo'. One reviewer of the programme, whose transmission suffered from technical difficulties, thought that Prichard's 'more impressionistic

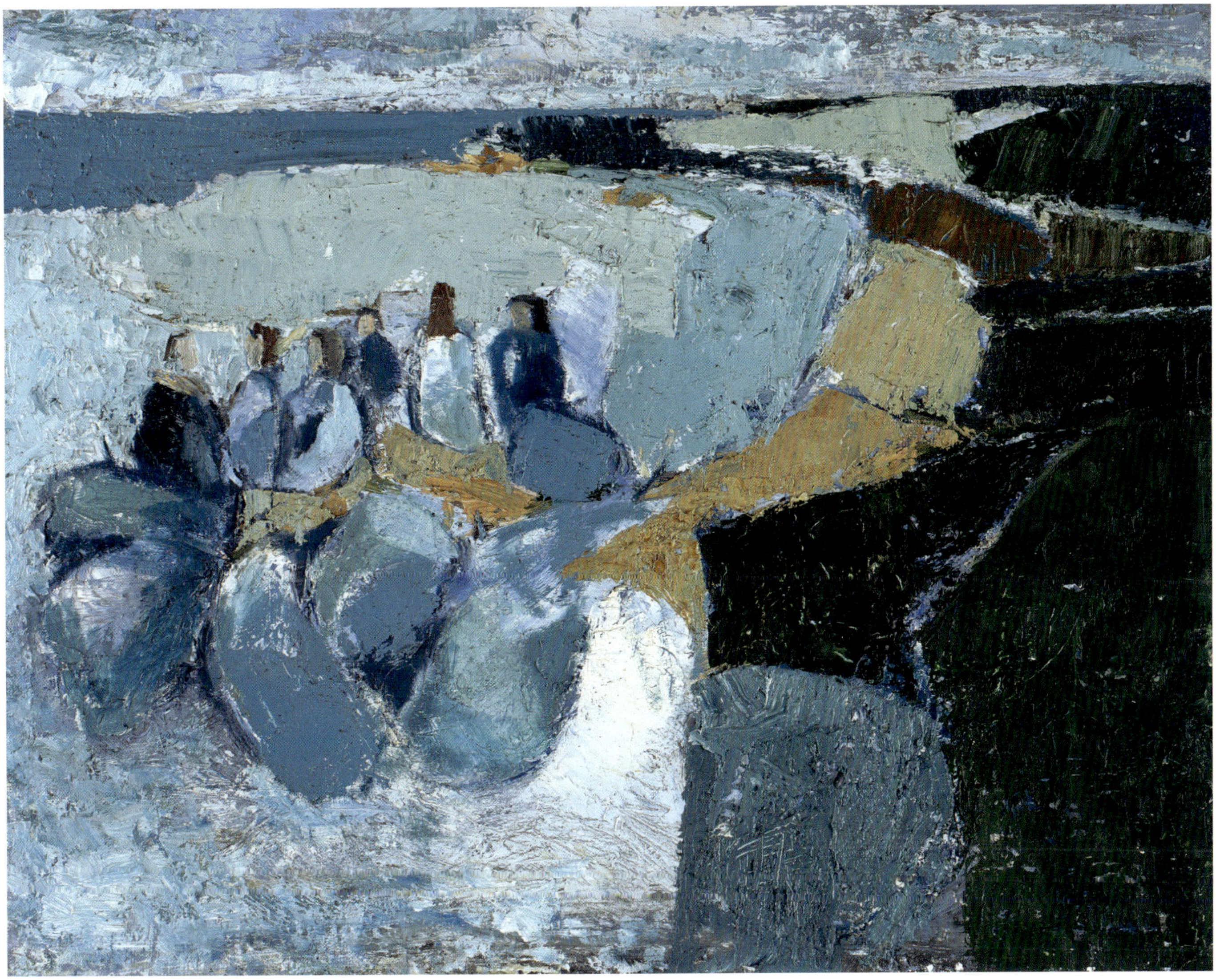

Fig. 4
Figures on a Beach
1958 | oil on board | 41 x 51 cm
the artist

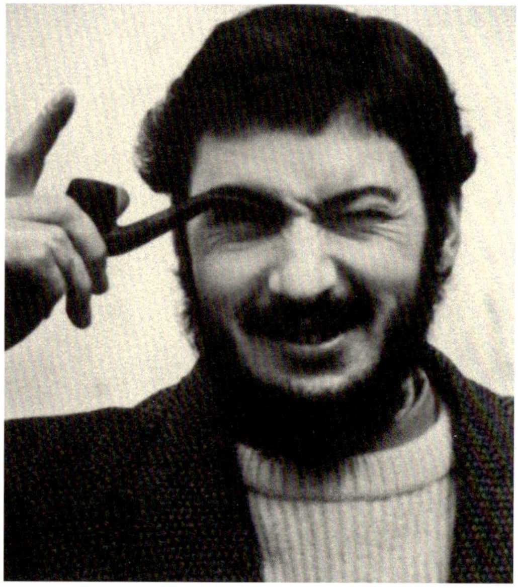

Fig. 5
Gwilym, 1965
photograph John Joyce

landscapes' did not translate as well to the black-and-white screen as Williams' figure compositions.[24] Whether or not the programme served to promote his art, Prichard that year sold 22 works from the Bangor Arts Festival Exhibition alone. Noted supporters and buyers of Prichard's early works include cleric and editor Iorwerth Jones, Cedric Morris, who bought *Penmon Priory* on behalf of Merthyr Education Authority, and Lord Snowdon, who purchased *Thorn Trees – Anglesey* for the Contemporary Art Society for Wales, which would acquire four more of Prichard's paintings. Another valued patron was artist Lady Mary Rennell of Rodd, whose own interpretation of a *Welsh Landscape* (1973) is in Tate's collection. During the 1960s and 1970s, Rennell bought and owned 'at least ten' of Prichard's paintings, opened one of his shows at the Howard Roberts Gallery in Cardiff and wrote the catalogue introduction to an exhibition of his works at the Heal's Gallery in London.[25]

Meanwhile, Prichard's older brother, Arthur, who had been an articled pupil in the County Surveyor's Office in Caernarfon and, as a chartered surveyor, became area engineer for Gwynedd County Council's Highways Department at Llangefni, felt encouraged to take up painting as well. Growing up, the two boys had often been rivals; and young Gwilym became particularly envious when Arthur began to impress relatives with his juvenile watercolours. '…and can you paint, Gwilym?', they enquired, and the boy became flustered, insecure about meeting the challenge of competing with his elder sibling, a challenge for which the indifferent art education at grammar school had so ill equipped him. When Prichard was able to answer the question conclusively, his brother started painting in oil, using materials borrowed from Prichard. Eventually, Arthur Pritchard (1927–93) established himself as an artist and went on to exhibit throughout Wales and in London. From the late 1950s onwards, the brothers frequently showed their paintings in group exhibitions in Cardiff and, in June 1974, were featured together on BBC Radio Wales programme 'Llathen o'r un Brethyn' ('Two of a Kind') to talk about their lives and art.[26]

Among the staff at Llangefni, no one was more pleased about Prichard's appointment than the school's art teacher, Ernest Zobole. Zobole, who had accepted the post on Anglesey straight after he left college in Cardiff and balked at 'this terrible slide into teaching', was relieved to find a kindred spirit in a 'starchy' environment that 'crackled with conformity' and struck him as being 'all wind and chapel'[27] (fig. 5). The two artists lived in council houses at either end of Llangefni, about two miles apart. Time permitting, they got together for the 'occasional pint at the Railway Inn'. Since neither of them owned a car, getting their paintings to exhibitions posed a challenge; but they arrived at a mutually beneficial arrangement with a senior colleague, the Welsh dramatist, novelist and translator Francis George Fisher, who at the time was head of the mathematics department. In the mid-1950s, Fisher was in the process of converting a local barn into a performance space, the Theatr Fach

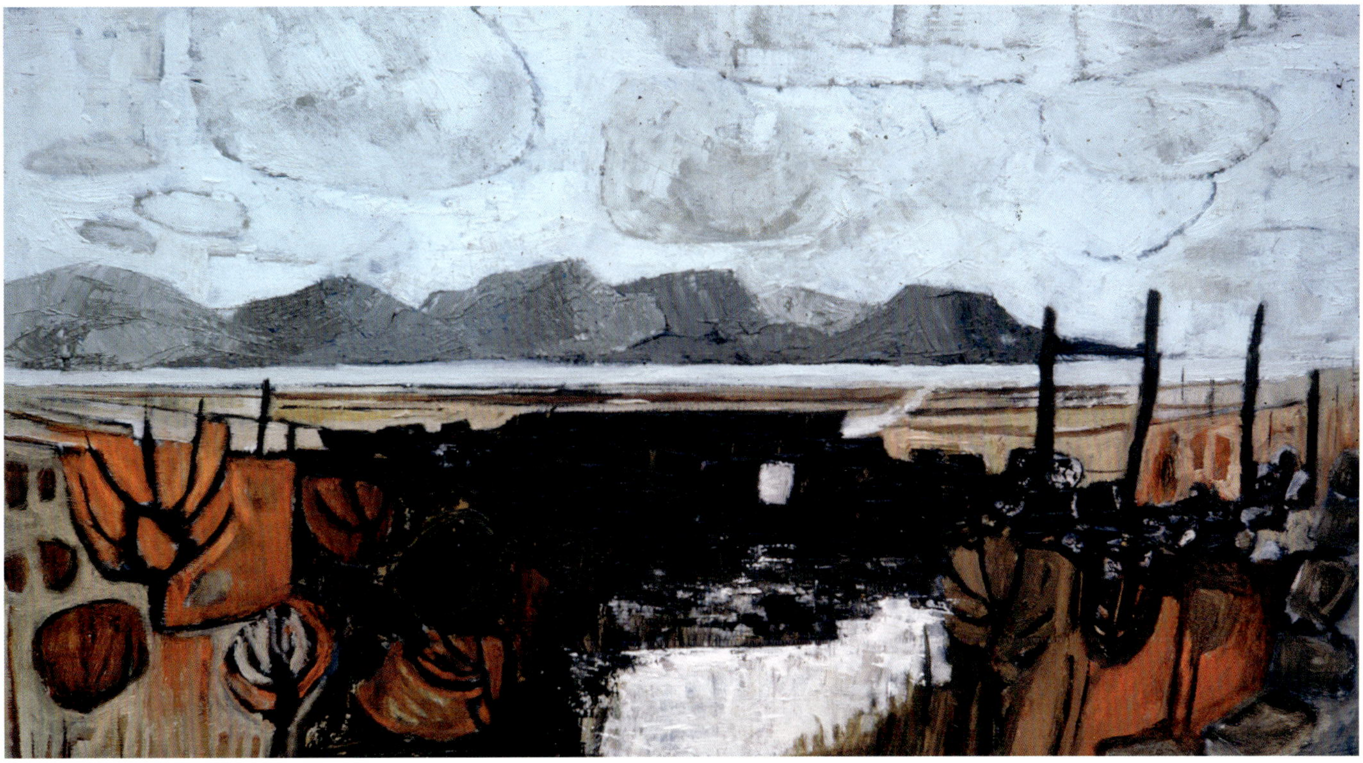

Fig. 6
Lleiniog
1963 | oil on board | 51 x 92 cm
private collection, UK

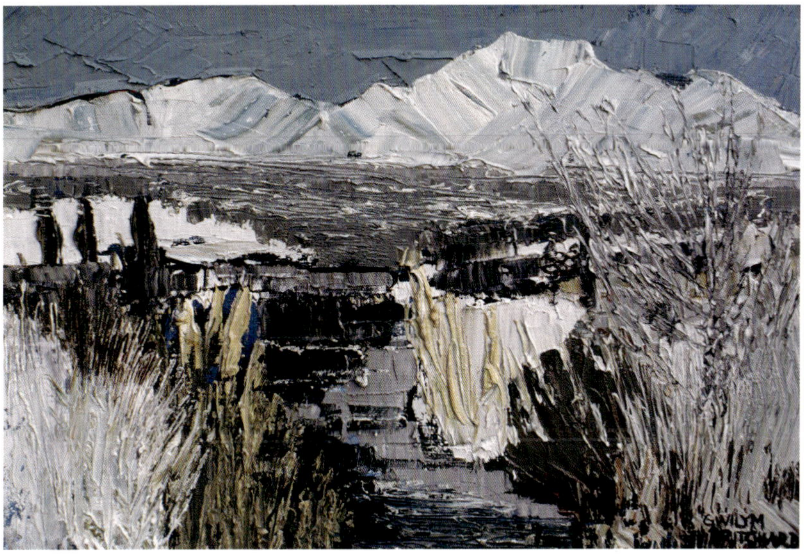

Fig. 7
Lleiniog
1973 | oil on board
private collection, UK

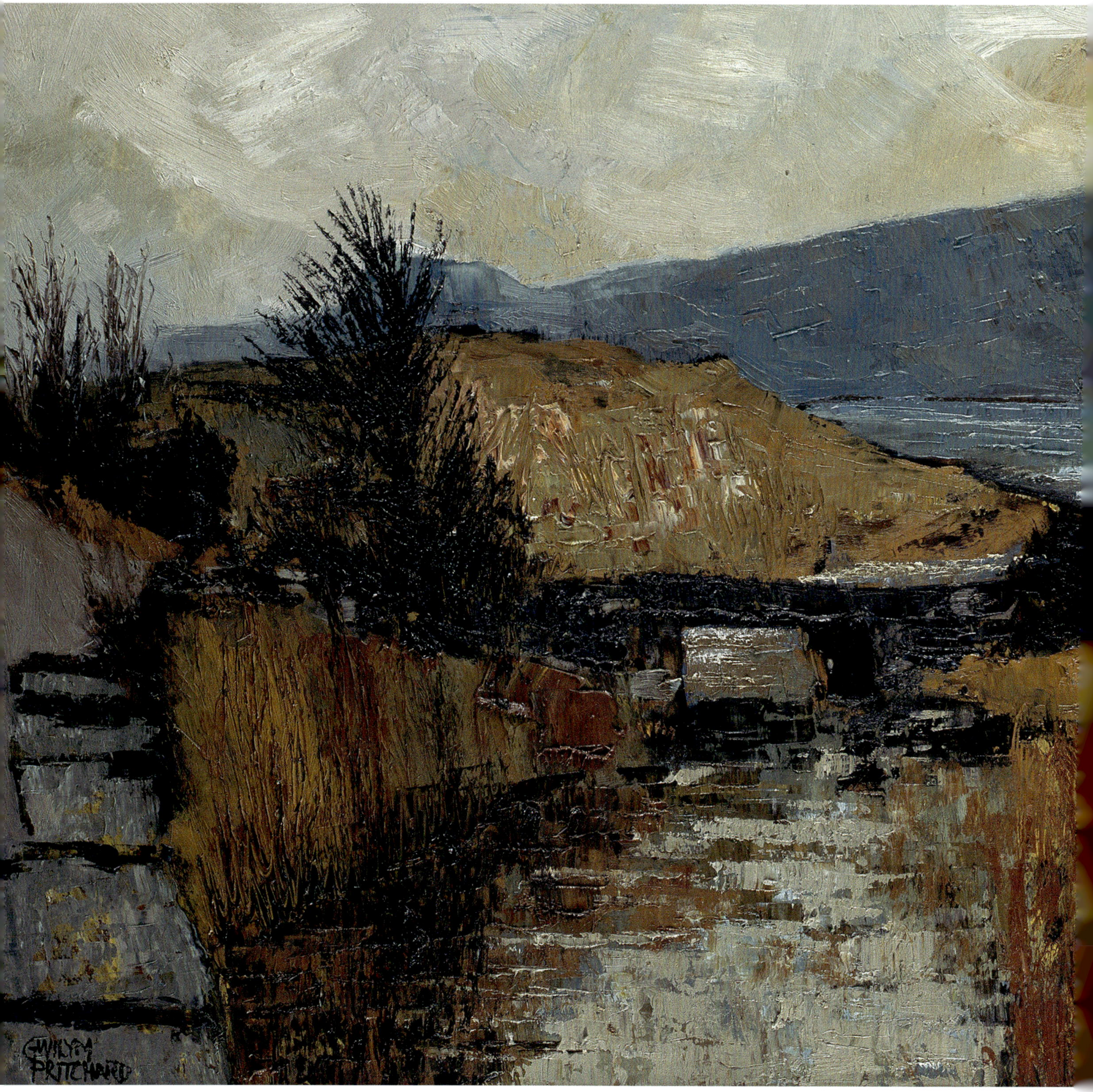

Fig. 8
Lleiniog, Anglesey
1972 | oil on board | 61 x 122 cm
National Library of Wales, Aberystwyth

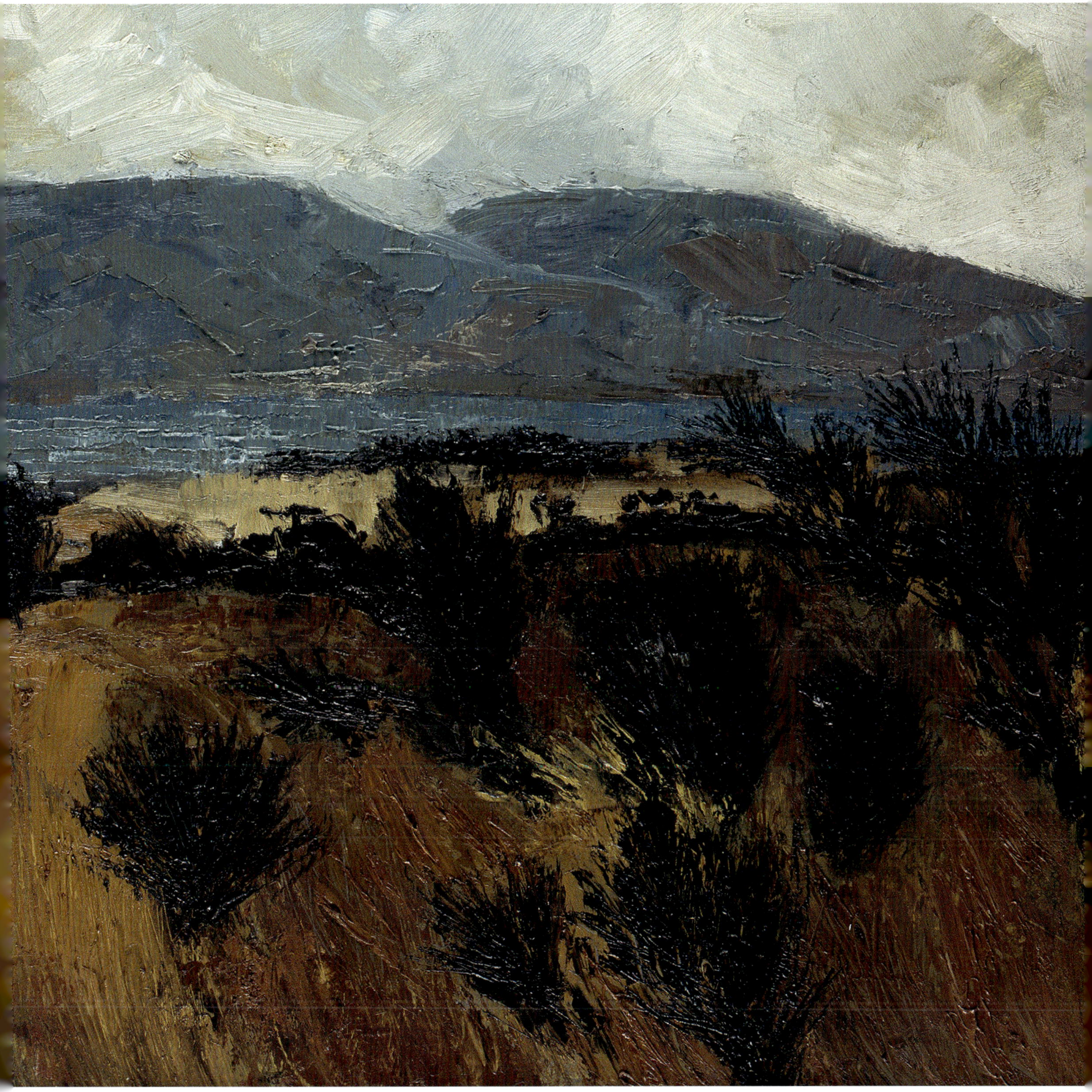

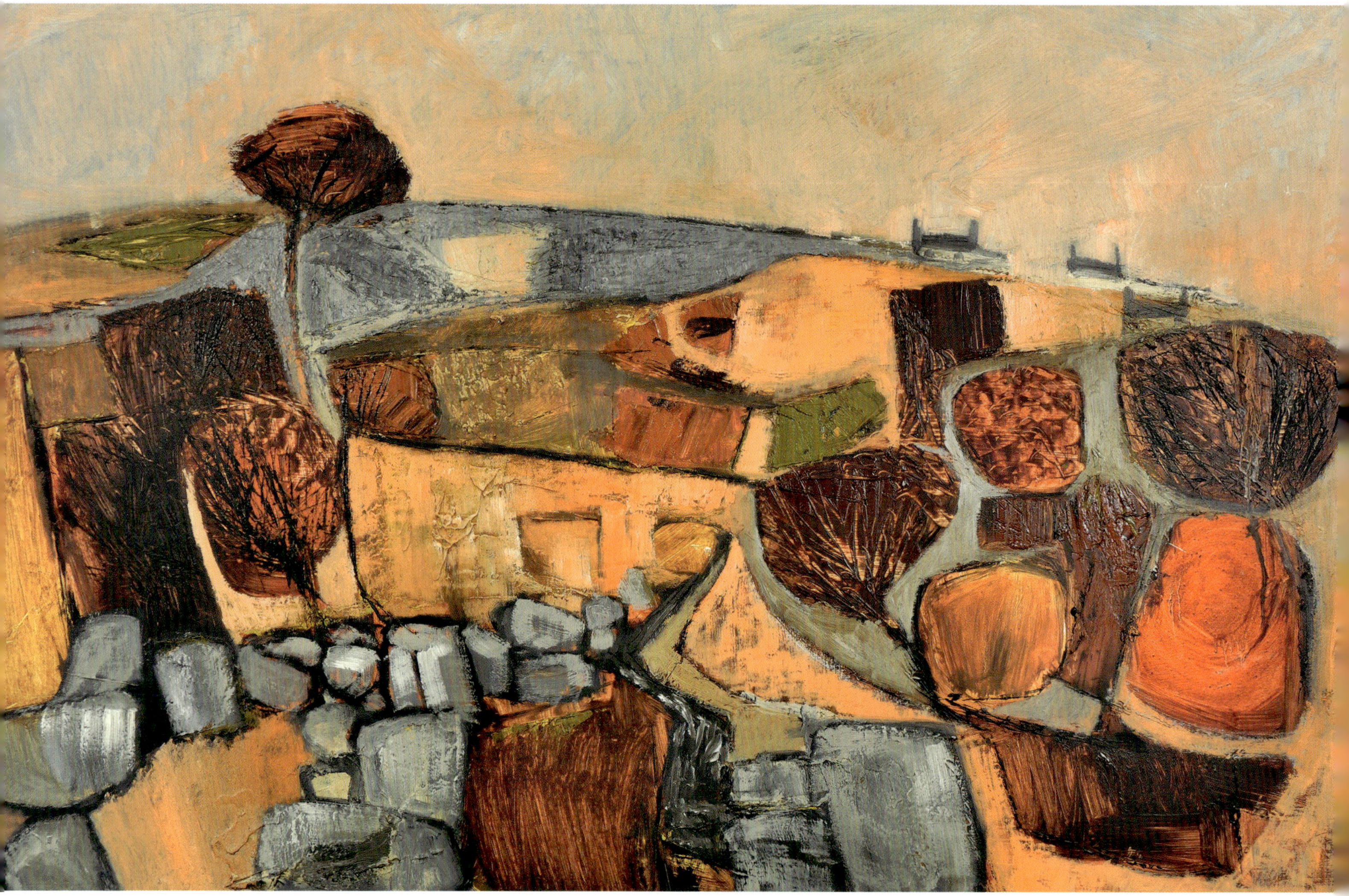

Fig. 9
Hydref, Sir Fôn
1961 | oil on board | 61 x 91.5 cm
Oriel Ynys Môn

in Pencraig, Llangefni. In return for making his vehicle available to them, Fisher could rely on Prichard and Zobole to design and paint sets for the theatre. This was a project well suited to the manual skills and ingenuity of Prichard, whose flair for stagecraft would find expression elsewhere in charades and puppetry and who himself would tread the boards in amateur theatricals. For the South Walian Zobole, though, neither the less than 'starchy' company nor the creative outlet were enough to divert him from what he perceived to be a culturally and topographically 'desolate' region; for him, the widely spoken Welsh language posed a barrier while the seemingly featureless landscape held no appeal. So, in 1957 – after a four-year absence during which he had produced little work – Zobole felt it 'necessary' to return to the Rhondda, the native soil that to him was as comforting as a 'warm bed'. Like Prichard, Zobole felt strengthened by his love of a place, without the 'personal connection' to which there would be a 'danger of changing with every influence and having no real content'. In his case, that place close to his heart was simply not Anglesey, an island the twelfth-century clergyman and chronicler Giraldus Cambrensis described as 'an arid and stony land, rough and unpleasant in its appearance' despite its being 'incomparably more fertile' than other parts of Wales[28] (figs 6–10).

Prichard, on the other hand, not only thrived in North Wales but found his work recognised beyond the region and indeed beyond Wales, albeit mainly in a Welsh context. In October 1958, he contributed to 'Paintings and Drawings by Welsh Artists', a group exhibition at the New Art Centre on Sloane Street, Belgravia. Encouraged by a favourable response, the Centre invited Prichard to stage a number of solo exhibitions that proved to be commercially successful, bearing out George Clausen's 1904 observation that landscape art appeals to the 'primitive instincts of cultivated people', of urbanites who look at it 'with a sentimental longing toward a more simple state'[29] – a wildness for which the west of Britain is often made to stand. In 1961 alone, Prichard sold 22 oils and one watercolour through the New Art Centre, sales that generated for him an income of £464 6s 8d (after commission) – more than half of his annual teacher's salary.[30] The successes in London continued. Surviving records show that at least 40 of Prichard's oil paintings sold at the New Art Centre between May 1966 and July 1968, by which time the gallery changed ownership and began to specialise in abstract and minimalist art. At the suggestion of the Centre, Prichard developed a similar relationship with the prestigious Mansard Gallery. Established in 1917 on the roof level of Heal's flagship Tottenham Court Road store, the gallery had long showcased new and established artists, from European modernists such as Pablo Picasso, Henri Matisse and Amedeo Modigliani to emerging British talents like Jacob Epstein, Mary Fedden and Terry Frost.[31] Between 1966 and 1974, Prichard staged six solo exhibitions at Heal's, followed by a joint show with Liz Sherburne, a Bristol-born landscape painter and former textile designer, in 1975 (figs 11 & 12).

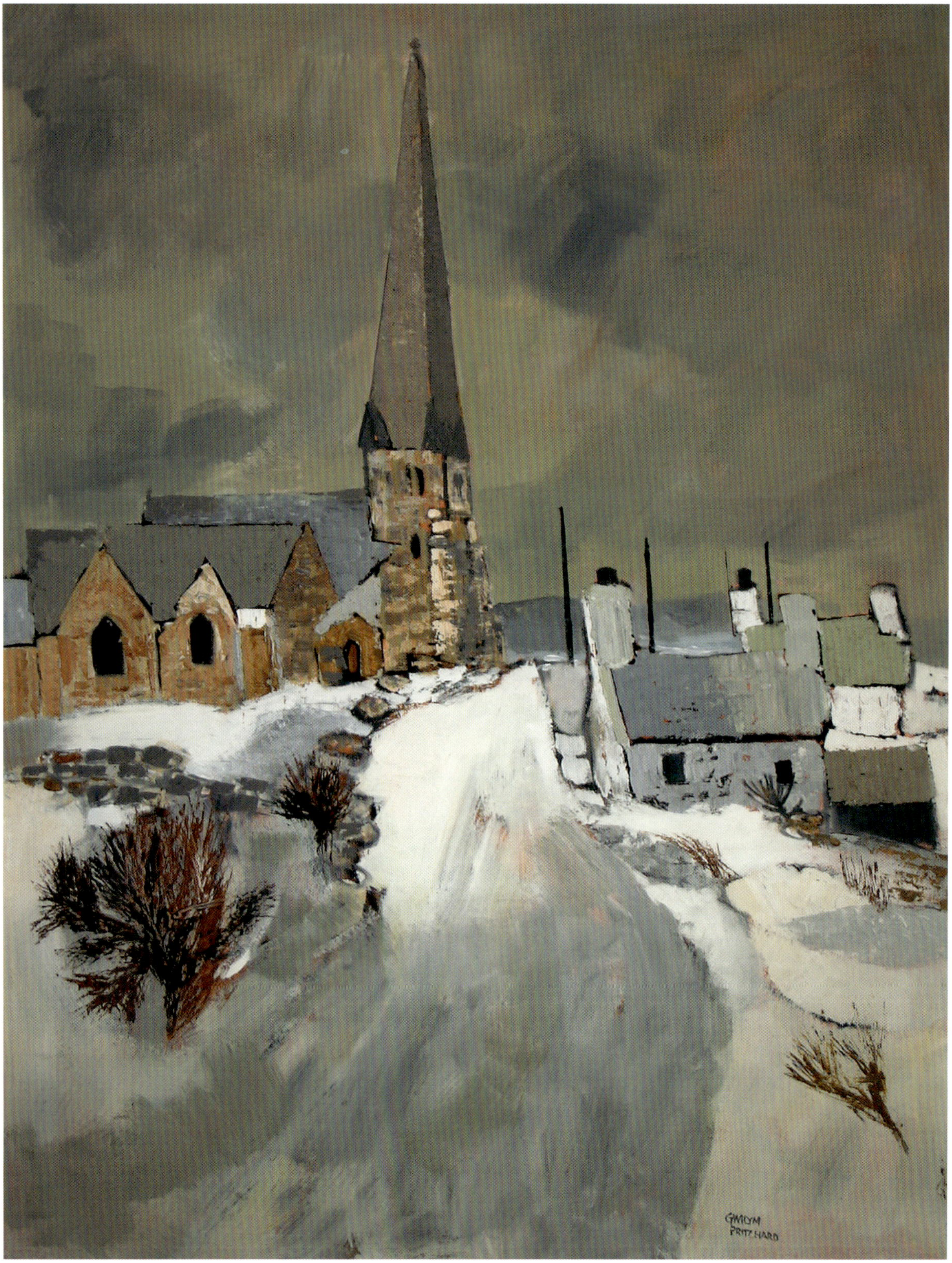

Fig. 10
Hydref, Sir Fôn
1968 | oil on board | 122 x 82 cm
private collection, UK

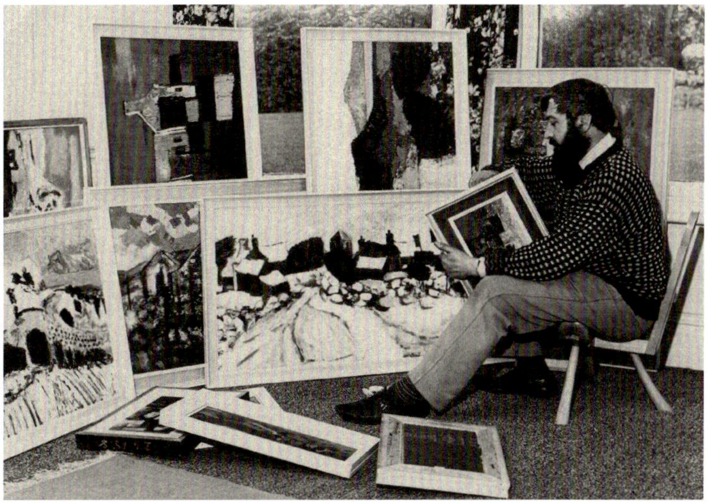

Fig. 11
Preparing for an exhibition, 1966
photograph Douglas Cowan

Exhibiting his landscape paintings beyond the Welsh border also made it possible for Prichard to attract new patrons. One of them was Michael Croft, 2nd Baron Croft, an art collector and supporter of Austrian and German émigré artists during the 1930s and 1940s, Oskar Kokoschka and Fred Uhlman among them; Prichard exhibited alongside Uhlman in the 1959 group exhibition 'Autumn Collection of Paintings' at the Howard Roberts Gallery. Croft became aware of Prichard through the exhibitions at the New Art Centre. On behalf of the Nuffield Foundation, he purchased a number of Prichard's paintings for the foundation's Pictures for Hospitals scheme. At one time, Croft owned some 20 works by Prichard, some of which, including one of the Malt House on the Croft Castle Estate at Leominster and of the Church of St John the Evangelist in Shobdon, Herefordshire, he commissioned. Croft became an important contact; he made recommendations on Prichard's behalf, opened his exhibition at Hereford City Art Gallery in 1976 and contributed the introduction for the catalogue accompanying Prichard's joint show with Claudia Williams at the Tegfryn Gallery on Anglesey in 1978.

Commenting on the success of Prichard's 1961 exhibition at the New Art Centre, Kyffin Williams remarked: 'So far Gwilym Pritchard has achieved much.' On the gallery walls of the New Art Centre, the public had seen

> *pictures of Penmon, Glanrafon and Llanddona: the old stone walls, light grey against the small green fields, chunky white cottages, rich weeds against grassy banks, the turn in the lane and always the feeling of the sea beyond. All these moulded by the palette knife were a hearkening proof that here was somebody who knew what he wanted to paint and wasn't afraid of showing he loved it.*[32]

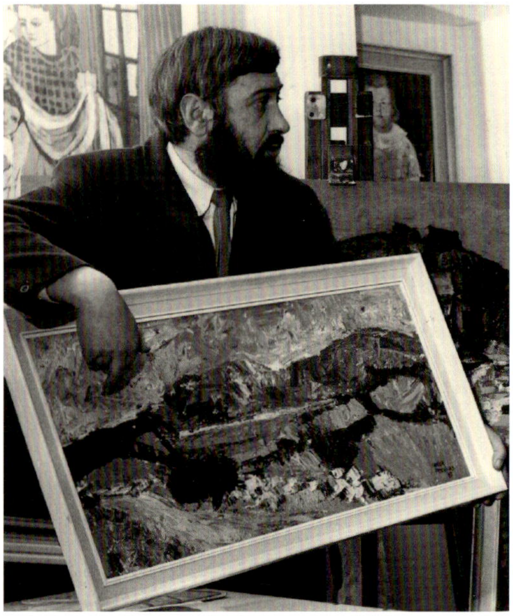

Fig. 12
Gwilym in 1967

What London gallery goers may not have gathered by looking at the Welsh landscapes is the distinction Kyffin Williams made by calling Prichard an artist who came to Anglesey from Caernarvonshire but who had, along the way, 'become a real Anglesey man'. These words of praise drive home that what many would label Welsh only few could appreciate as regional; that what had 'warmed the coldness of the London scene', as Kyffin Williams put it, were Anglesey subjects (fig. 8). More specifically still, they were of a single and singular corner of the island, 'centred on Penmon'. It was here, Jonah Jones remarked in 1961, that 'Gwilym range[d]', in a region

> *still imbued with the holiness of its priory and the attendant dovecot. Geologically it is extremely interesting, this corner, for Penmon limestone is a rare and hard old rock which shapes and colours the landscape and its dwellings. This is Gwilym's world of broken wall, bracken, ancient thorn, green elder and speckled meadow.*

'Although his searching eye finds subjects in all parts of Anglesey', Williams added a few years later, it was in the 'triangle formed by Pentraeth, Penmon and Beaumaris' that Prichard had 'really matured and found himself as an artist'.[33]

An advocate of Prichard's work as the 'pictures of a happy island, painted by a happy man', Kyffin Williams also became a 'great friend' and, as Prichard acknowledges, 'a strong influence at one time'.[34] He had known of Prichard through their mutual friend, Charles Tunnicliffe – 'an amusing character', Claudia Williams recalls – who lived at Malltraeth, some 18 miles from their home in Beaumaris. Kyffin Williams, who lived nearby in Llansadwrn, had one day come to Beaumaris to introduce himself: 'I'm Kyffin Williams,' he said to Prichard, 'I believe you are an artist.' Valued as a kindly, encouraging critic, and beloved by the couple's children, whom he delighted by playing charades at Christmas parties (draping himself in lace curtains to play Cleopatra to Prichard's Antony), he remained a family friend until his death in 2006. He was a vocal and influential advocate of Prichard's art and, in his foreword to a 1973 exhibition catalogue for one of Prichard's shows at Heal's, expressed himself convinced that 'many more' art enthusiasts would 'feel the benefit' of Prichard's 'Celtic exuberance'.[35] Celtic. That is an attribute often used by viewers and reviewers to describe Prichard's work. Indeed, Prichard has referred to himself on various occasions as an 'emotional Celt' possessing a 'romantic Celtic mind'.[36] How does this 'Celtic' character express itself, and to what extent did living and working in Wales – or in certain parts thereof – define or delimit Prichard's vision?

A 'CELTIC VISION'

However unlikely a career in fine arts might have been for a lad from Llanystumdwy, Prichard could not only rely on the encouragement and support from professional artists such as Kyffin Williams and Ernest Zobole; he could also benefit from post-war initiatives designed to change the cultural climate for artists in Wales. As John Petts put it in his comments on an open exhibition organised by the Arts Council's Welsh Committee in 1953, the aims of the Council were to

> *stimulate wider public interest in the work of contemporary artists in Wales; to help these artists by providing them with an opportunity to produce and exhibit large works and to find a market for them by encouraging industrial and public bodies to become patrons.*[37]

David Bell, who served as one of the panellists selecting the works for that exhibition, later declared the 'coming of state and public patronage and responsibility for the arts' to be 'one of the most important factors in the development of art', especially in Wales, 'where private patrons ha[d] been few and far between'.[38] Establishing his place in a developing art world, Prichard could enjoy – and did take advantage of – opportunities to participate in exhibitions of contemporary Welsh art mounted by the Arts Council, the Society for Education through Art and the National Museum of Wales, as well as the National Eisteddfod.

In 1955, when he first exhibited at the National Eisteddfod, held that year in Pwllheli, Prichard was runner-up for the Gold Medal for Fine Art, an award that had been introduced in 1951 to enhance the reputation of the Arts and Crafts Pavilion. Called upon to award the first prize, the panel of judges – painters Charles Tunnicliffe, William McAllister Turner and Kyffin Williams – were divided between Prichard's *Farm House*, Jonah Jones' *Bathers*, Brenda Chamberlain's *The Doves* and *Wrth a Ddaear* ('Gone to the Earth'), which was the work of D.C. Roberts, a teacher at a high school near Pwllheli. Unable to reach a verdict, the judges invited Royal Cambrian Academy and Liverpool School of Art president Henry Percy Huggill to adjudicate. Eventually, first prize went to Roberts, whose painting depicted hounds and hunters gathered around a fox-hole. Both the individual entries and the selection process, not least the artist-judges in charge of selecting, suggest that painters in 1950s Wales were expected and indeed encouraged to be painters of Wales at its presumably most representative – that is to say, traditional. According to Bell, the 'concern with environment', which was apparent in pictures that 'conveyed' a sense of 'love and compassion for humanity and a consciousness of the relations of men and women to nature, buildings, and everyday life in Wales', seemed to 'auger well for the future of a Welsh School of Painting'.[39] As Peter Lord has pointed out, this vision – and the conservative, nationalist attitudes it reflected or resonated with – did not remain uncontested, as it suggested that, defined thus, art produced in Wales was 'inward looking and consequently second-rate'

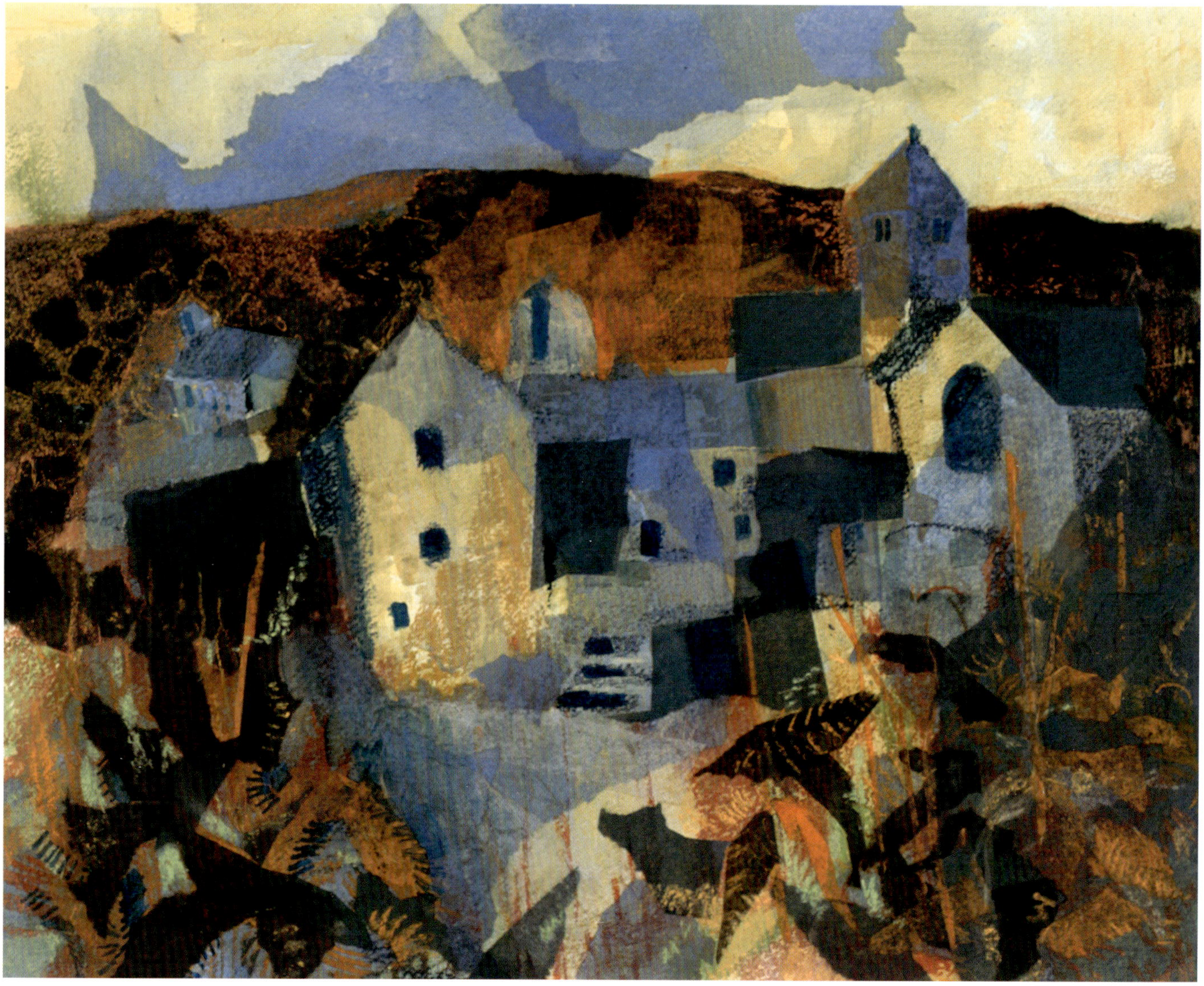

Fig. 13
Penmon Priory
1983 | collage and mixed media | 30 x 37.5 cm
private collection, UK

compared to the international, transnational art of modernists who advocated a 'denial of the particular cultural experience' and sought instead to achieve universality through the 'fundamental elements of visual language in a non-figurative manner or through the creation of highly personalized languages'. Yet while his art may have served 'to reinforce [a] sense of a Welsh art to which the cultural resonance of particular landscapes gave meaning',[40] Prichard did not set out to take on an ambassadorial role; and his work is not so much an overt, let alone programmatic, affirmation of national identity as it is an intimate response to his various surroundings, be it the *cynefin*, the place into which he was born, or the many places he lighted on throughout his life.

Beginning in the late 1950s, Prichard developed and maintained strong ties with commercial galleries in Wales, Cardiff in particular. Given his birthplace, the subject matter of his paintings and the venues in which they were shown and judged, it is not surprising that Prichard was, from the very outset of his long career, looked upon as a representative Welsh artist. It is in a Welsh context that he exhibited regularly at the Howard Roberts Gallery in Cardiff, where he contributed to themed shows such as 'Welsh Names in Painting' (1958), which included paintings by John Elwyn, Augustus John, David Jones, Wyndham Lewis, Ceri Richards and Claudia Williams, along with sculptures by Jonah Jones and Ivor Roberts-Jones, 'Contemporary Welsh Painting' (1958) and 'Wales through the Eye of the Artist' (1959). In 1957, Prichard exhibited three paintings at the Royal National Eisteddfod of Wales on Anglesey. The following year, at the 76th Summer Exhibition of the Royal Cambrian Academy, he was awarded the Saxon Barton Memorial Prize for his painting *Anglesey Landscape*, which was selected from over a hundred submissions from across Britain. With the aim of encouraging young artists to exhibit their work, the prize was awarded to the painting judged to be the best by an artist under 30 years of age who was in some way associated with Wales and who was not yet a member of a recognised academy or art society. The award – along with a cheque for 10 guineas – were presented by Dorothy Barton, widow of Dr Samuel Saxon Barton (1890–1957), a Liverpool surgeon with a practice in Llandudno.

In March 1959, Prichard was himself elected Associate Member of the Royal Cambrian Academy, of which he became a full member in 1963. In 1965, he co-founded the Gwynedd Artists Association, which drew on and consisted mostly of professional artists who had been members of the North Wales Group. The Association's first exhibition, held at Wrexham Public Library and Bangor Art Gallery, included paintings by Elfyn Jones, Donald McIntyre, John Scott, Claudia Williams and Kyffin Williams, as well as sculptures by Jonah Jones and ceramics by studio potter Eric Stockl. Prichard also continued to exhibit at the small but reputable Tegfryn Gallery on Anglesey, run by Gwyn and Harry Brown, which has since been taken over by

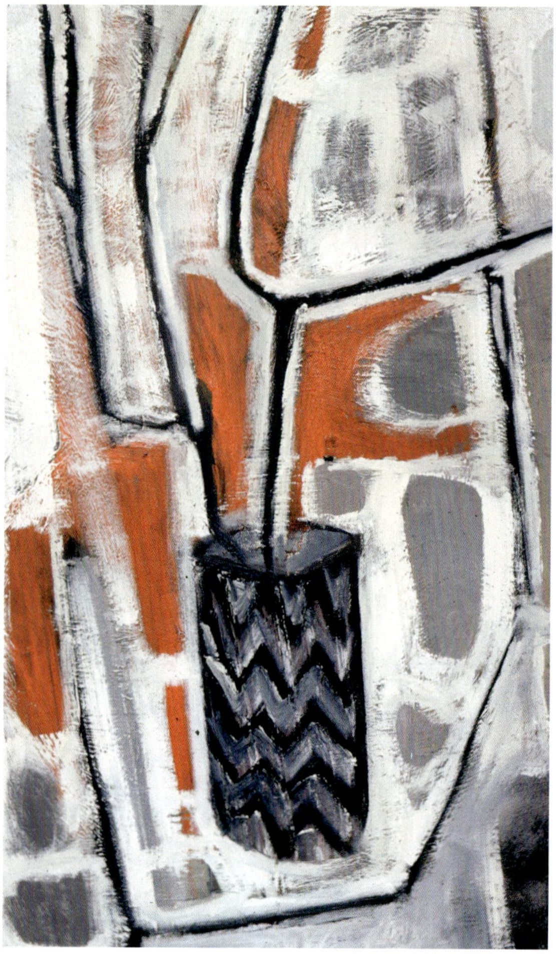

Fig. 14
Twig
1963 | oil on board | 61 x 35 cm
private collection, UK

Martin Tinney, who has been representing both Prichard and Claudia Williams since 1996. During the 1970s and early 1980s, Prichard also showed works at the Attic Gallery in Swansea and the Albany Gallery in Cardiff, in group exhibitions such as 'Looking at Wales' (1975) and 'Welsh Landscapes in Oils' (1982).

In addition to being shown in Art in Wales or Art from Wales contexts, Prichard's Anglesey landscapes were juxtaposed with responses to scenery elsewhere. In 1963, Prichard exhibited at the Howard Roberts Gallery with Manchester-born and Slade-trained artist Tom Cross, who had moved to Wales in 1959 upon his appointment as Assistant Director of the Welsh Arts Council. The joint show contrasted drawings exploring the effect of the intense Adriatic sunlight on the rocks and brick-work of Italian hill towns that Cross had visited the previous year with Prichard's paintings of the light and features peculiar to the Penmon area of Anglesey: bracken that is 'orange against the limestone, bleached and weatherbeaten elder', and 'tight, spiky thorn trees' in winter. In the catalogue for the exhibition, Prichard pointed out that his works, in their subject matter, fell 'roughly into four groups': at least two paintings featured the twelfth-century priory that lies at the heart of the site of an ancient monastery at Penmon, a subject to which Prichard returned in 1983 (*Penmon Priory*; fig. 13). Another group was of townscapes in winter, captured in paintings such as *Cluster of Buildings in Snow* (1963; fig. 15). A related subject was farm-houses and cottages, while yet another group consisted of still lifes such as *Twig* (1963; fig. 14), representative of the days on which Prichard was confined to the indoors; the depth of winter 'is the only time that I retire into the studio', Prichard explained; a time when 'Claudia paints our three boys and I my dried flowers'[41] (fig. 17).

Prichard had previously explored the region in his 1959 paintings *Penmon Priory* and *Penmon and Puffin Island* (fig. 18); and he would revisit it in 1965 for *Raincloud, Penmon* (fig. 19) – a view of Trwyn Du, the black-nosed lighthouse that marks the rocks amid the strong currents of the Strait between Anglesey and Ynys Seiriol (or Puffin Island). What is noticeable in *Penmon and Puffin Island* is its degree of stylisation, which is representative of his early, experimental period in exploring formal interpretations of his environment – approaches that are distinct from his later, more emotional responses to his subjects. Even when they tend 'towards abstraction', Prichard later insisted, 'the finished work must have its roots and foun-dation in reality and … must not be so far removed as to have lost the first inspiration'.[42] In and around Penmon, Prichard experienced 'the holy silence', the 'solidity of landscape and the insignificance of man'. It is a region he singled out as being 'rich in history and in colour', denoting an influence of time on place that Prichard explores chiefly through his observations of the effects of the seasons on the land: from the spring in which the blossoms of the hawthorn 'turn Anglesey into a mass of

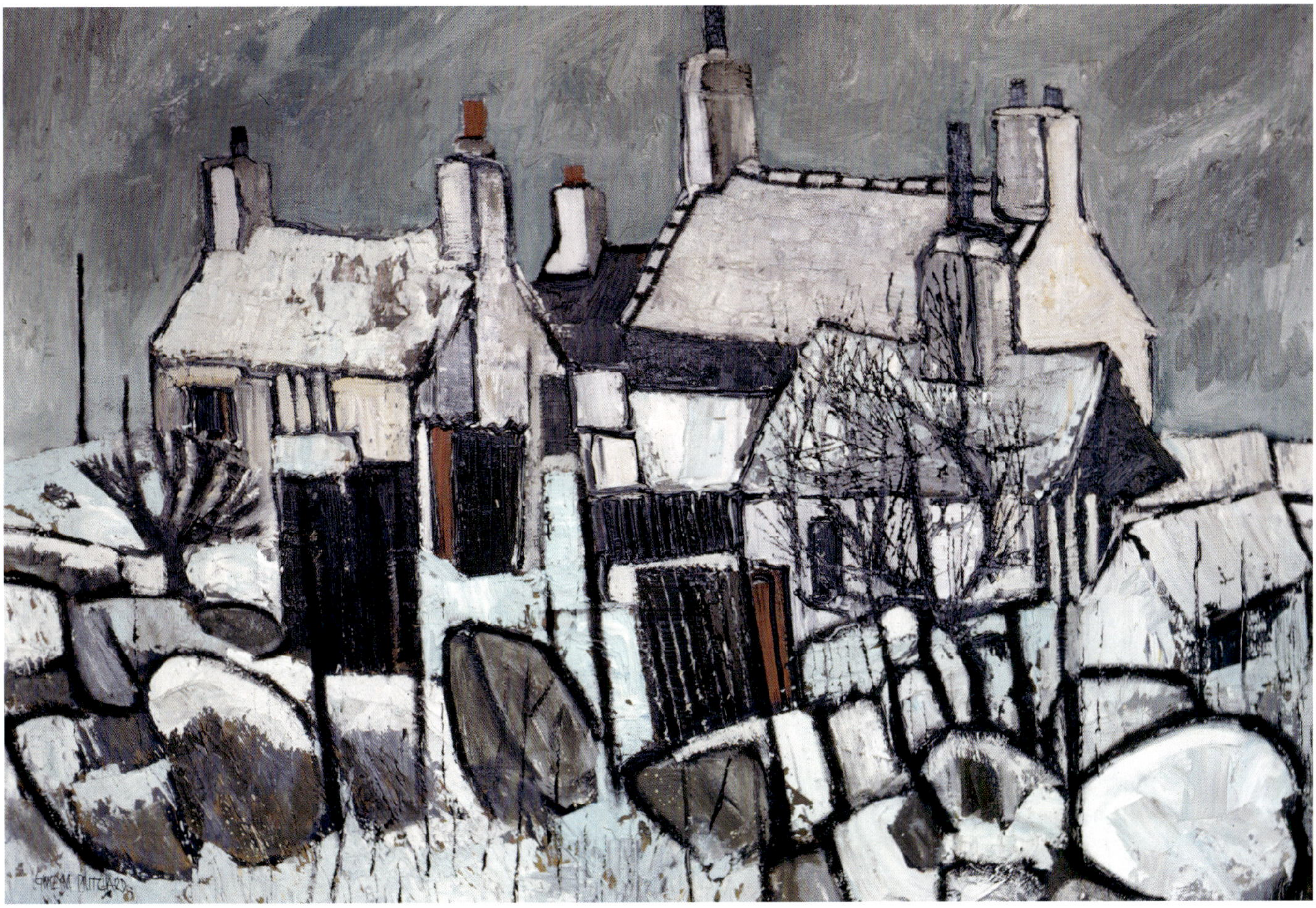

Fig. 15
Cluster of Buildings in Snow
1963 | oil on board | 60 x 91 cm
private collection, UK

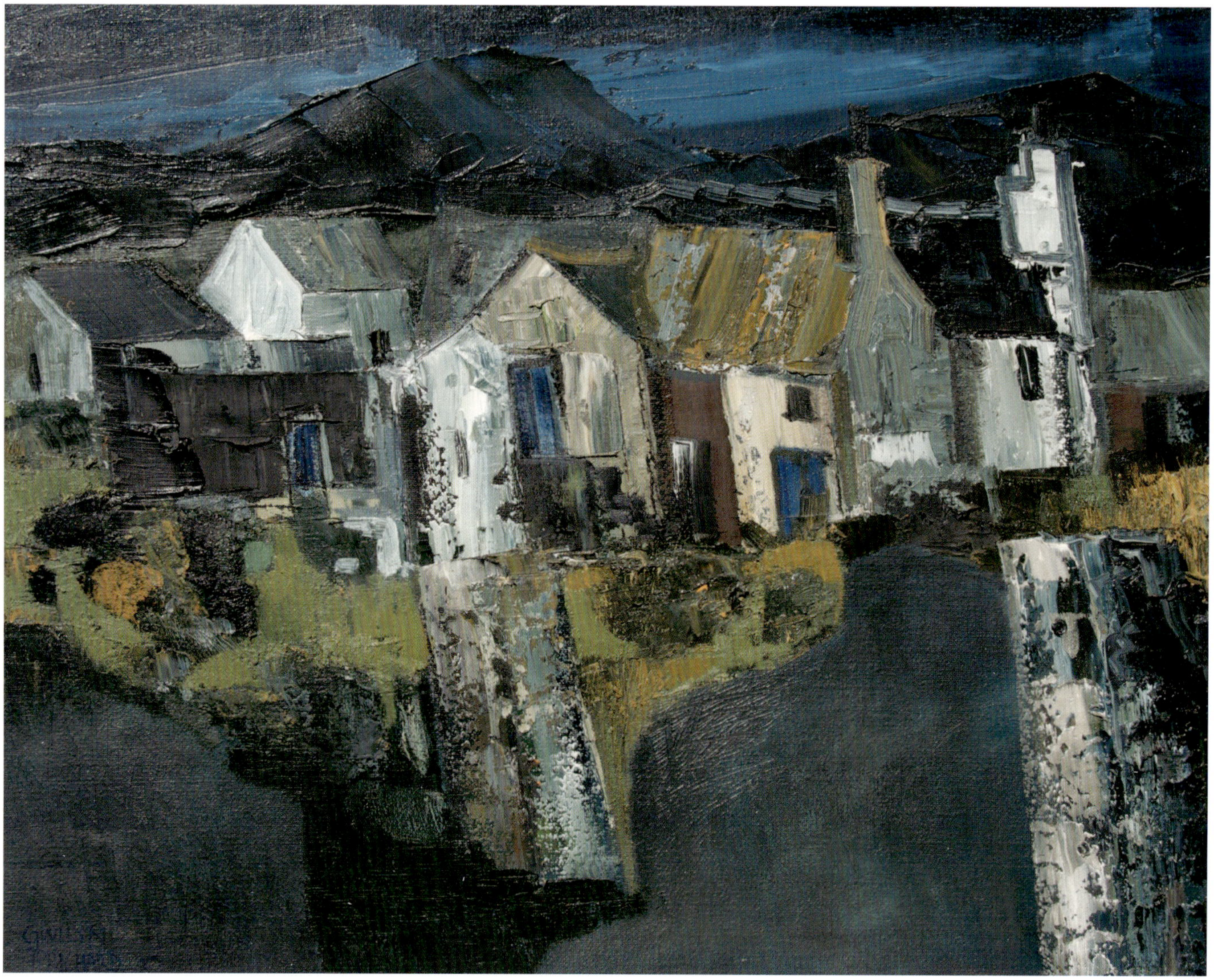

Fig. 16
Farm Buildings, Winter
1982 | oil on canvas | 60 x 73 cm
private collection, UK

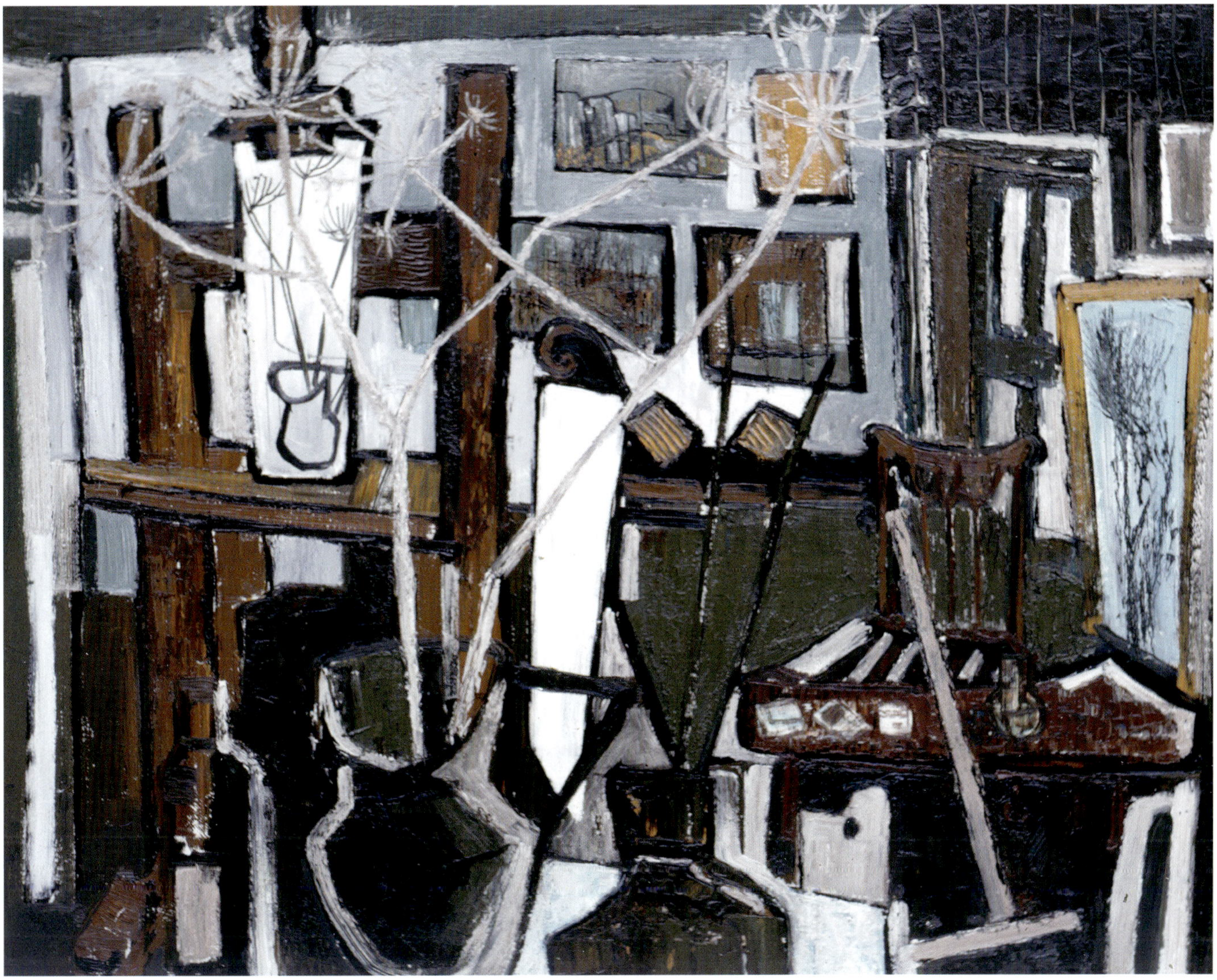

Fig. 17
In the Studio
1963 | oil on board | 61 x 76.5 cm
private collection, UK

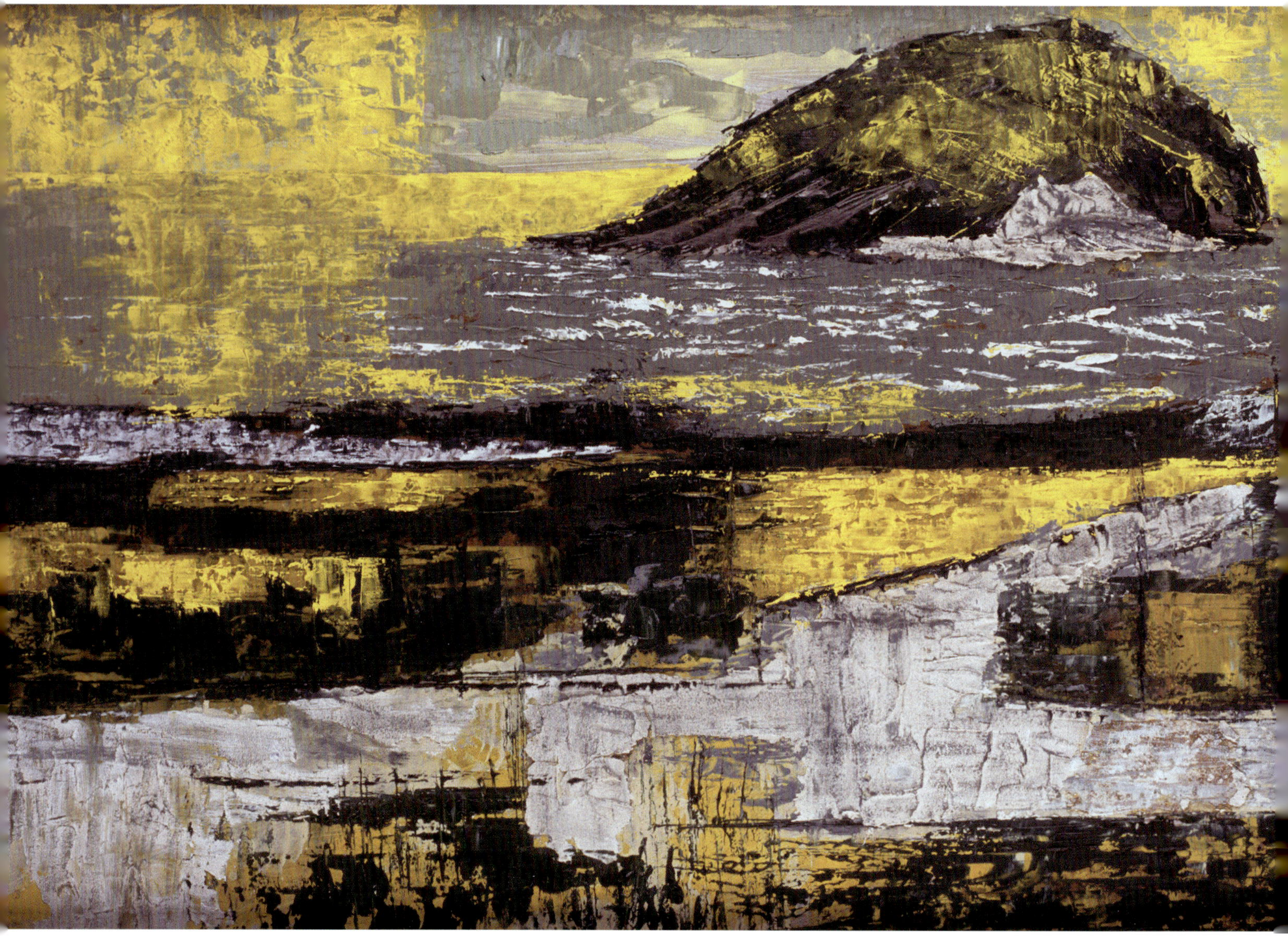

Fig. 18
Penmon and Puffin Island
1959 | oil on board | 46 x 122 cm
National Library of Wales, Aberystwyth

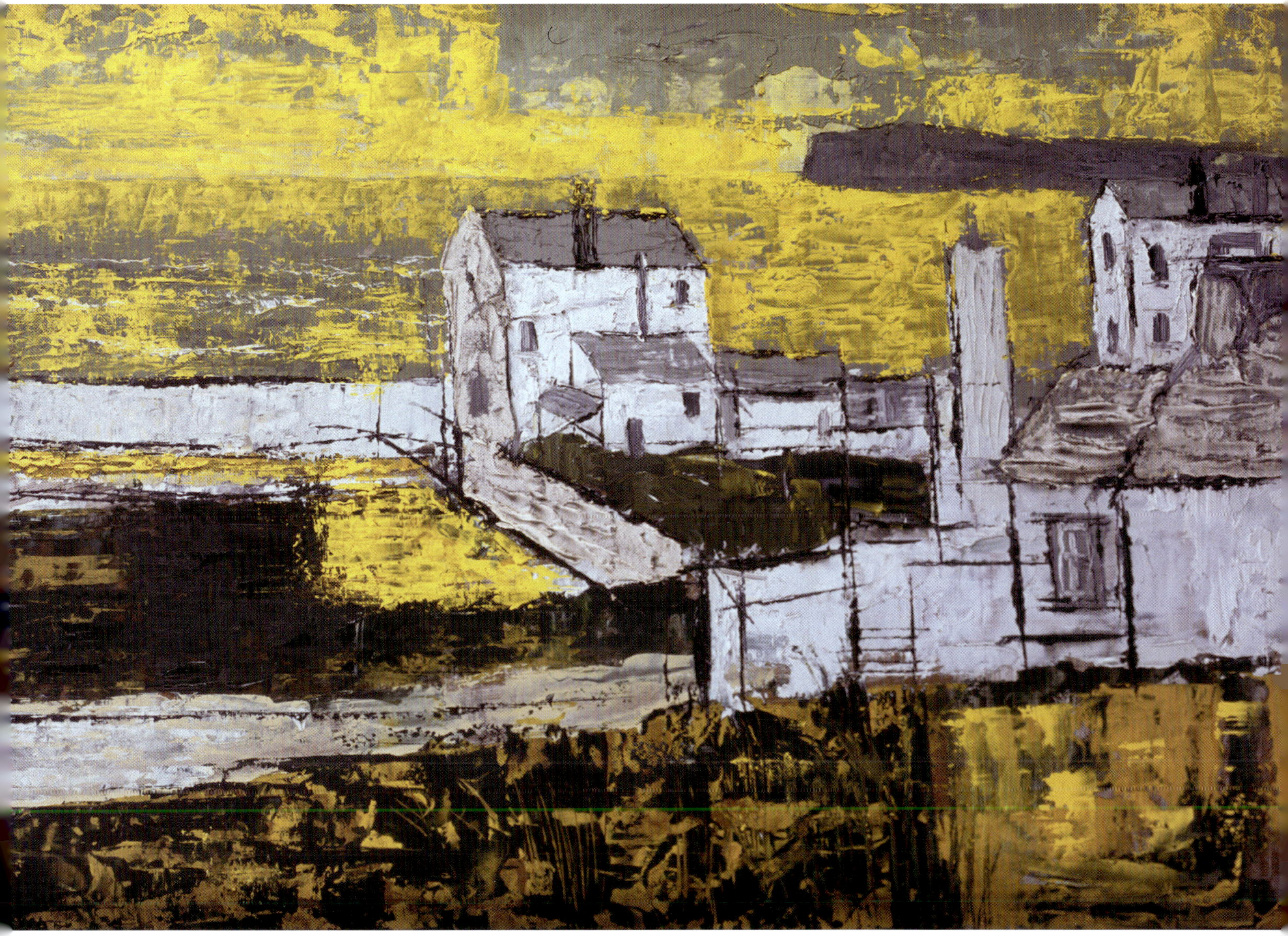

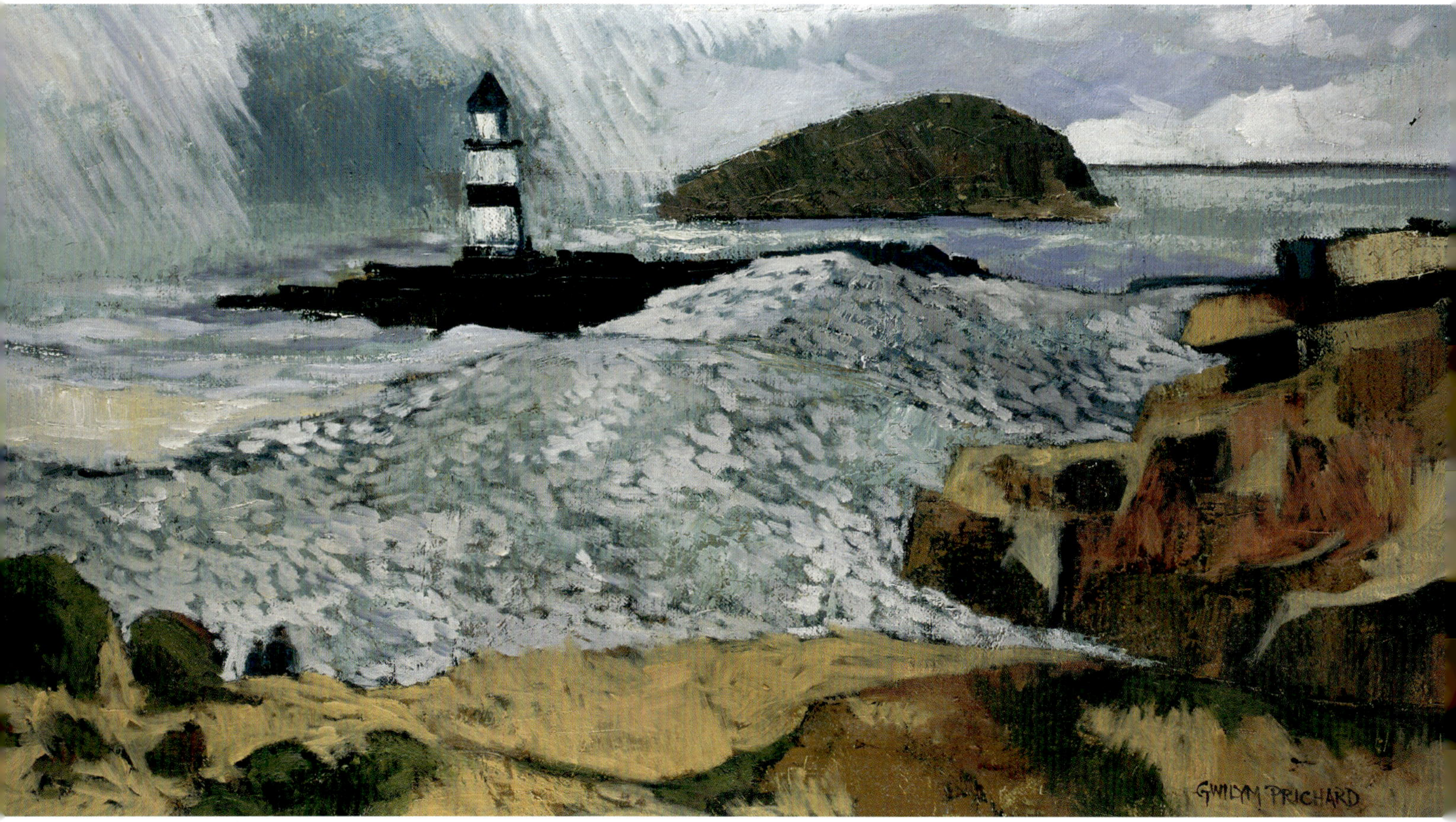

Fig. 19
Raincloud, Penmon
1965 | oil on canvas | 51 x 92 cm
private collection, UK

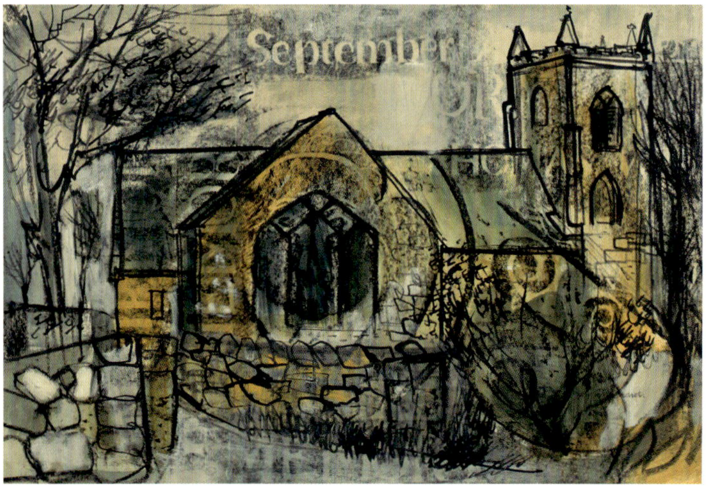

Fig. 20
Bryn Siencyn
1965 | watercolour and wax rubbing | 30 x 54 cm
private collection, UK

white primitive shapes and subtle tones' and the '[s]ummer of ripe corn' on Môn Mam Cymru (Anglesey, the 'Mother of Wales') to autumn and early winter – a 'productive period' for the artist – with its 'clear light, even on dull, cloudy days', a 'time when cold skies show up the warm colours of the land'. Prichard continued to paint the 'stark trees' and the cottages of Llangoed until, 'in late winter, the east wind ha[d] killed the colour, and brought with it cold, dull and dark skies'.[43]

The works in the 1963 Howard Roberts Gallery exhibition – and indeed most of Prichard's subsequent paintings – are at once a contemplation of the land and a communion with it. 'My paintings are straightforward statements of my reaction to my environment', Prichard declared; but he invited viewers to 'look again' and 'find mysterious undertones and passages of highly textured surfaces in these Celtic landscapes'.[44] What contributed to the mystery – and what many viewers have noticed since – is something Prichard acknowledges to be characteristic of his subjects: 'I hardly ever have people in my landscapes.' The lone figure in the scene he observes, sketches and then vacates is the artist himself. 'I want to be part of what I am painting', Prichard writes, and it is through his eyes, his sustained and persevering vision, that his affinity with the land is communicated.[45] Reviewing Prichard's work in 1965, artist Bryn Richards observed that he found it 'difficult to believe' that the land and the farmsteads in many of Prichard's pictures could be present sites of human habitation; 'they have an ancient, deserted air, like monuments to a dead civilisation, and they have that quality of having been fashioned by the geology of the country'.[46] Such reflections evoke the oft-quoted lines from 'Welsh Landscape', in which R.S. Thomas famously declared: 'You cannot live in the present / At least not in Wales'; rather, to 'live in Wales is to be conscious, / At dusk of the spilled blood / That went into the making of the wild sky.'

Echoes of these words – and words as echoes from a historical past – can be sensed in Prichard's 1965 solo exhibition at the Howard Roberts Gallery. It included a series of drawings of churches, which were made over rubbings of the inscriptions on tombstones such as those at Bryn Siencyn (fig. 20), an at once palpable and intangible link between the Wales of his forebears and the present experienced by the artist. Whereas Thomas argued that there is 'no present in Wales, / And no future', that there is 'only the past', Prichard, by engaging with the environment in which he lives and works, is never in danger of being lost among the 'sham ghosts' of what R.S. Thomas called an 'impotent people'.[47] Nor are his landscapes ahistorical, as many of them document culture's influence on nature. 'Generations have lived in and adapted the corner of Anglesey that I paint', Prichard pointed out; 'Farmhouses and cottages are sheltered by outcrops of limestone, stone walls surround small fields'[48] (figs 21 & 22). And even though '[p]eople seldom appear in [his] work', the 'effect of God and man' is 'ever present in the life that is lived in the fields, barns

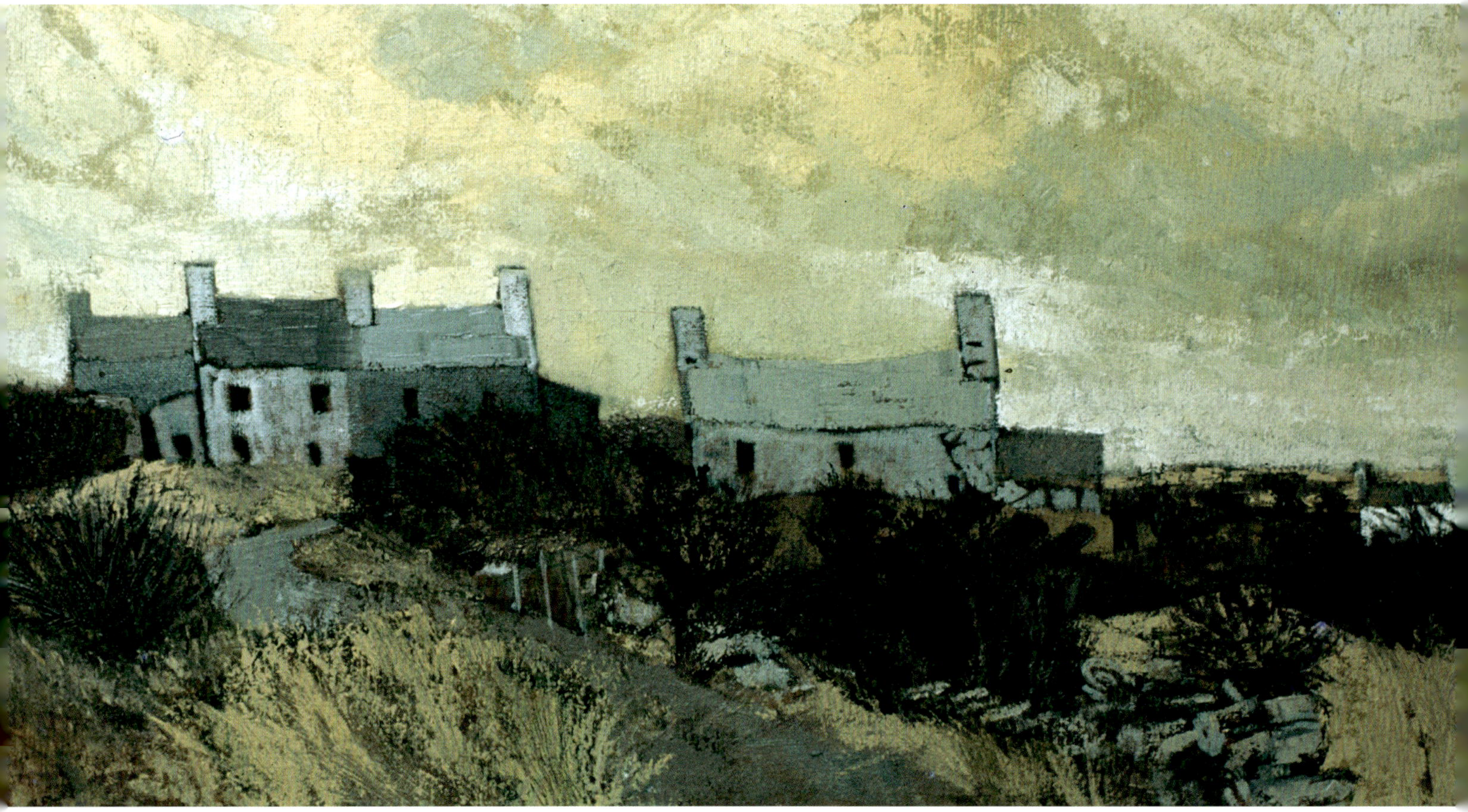

Fig. 21
Pentre Pella, Anglesey
1979 | oil on canvas | 51 x 92 cm
private collection, UK

and inviting farmhouses'.[49] Indeed, as he paints, Prichard imagines the 'life that is lived' inside those houses; and sometimes he 'speak[s] to' his paintings as they come into being on the canvas. 'I tell this to my pupils', he once said, 'have a conversation with your painting. The damn thing is a living thing, because it's growing in front of you.'[50]

What Eric Rowan once said about the tendency of 'native Welsh artists' certainly applies to Prichard, who tends to be 'individualistic' in his work, 'self-conscious about the use of words to describe [his] ideas', and loath to engage in 'any form of collective theorising'.[51] 'I am a Welsh painter because I am Welsh', Prichard remarks tersely. His paintings are neither an expression nor an extension of a nationalist agenda. In this, he rather resembles novelist Alun Richards, who declared:

> *As to whether I am Welsh or not, it is a highly self-conscious question which I have never felt the need to ask myself. I am. It is enough, and the rest is propaganda.*[52]

'I paint the land and farms, the sea and sky', Prichard insists, because they are 'the things that I know and love and have grown up with, and that shaped my life'. Prichard never attempted to represent Wales in its entirety; rather, he is an artist of regional expression whose landscapes are 'records of actual places, painted in a way that is intended to reflect [his] feelings towards and sympathy with the subjects'.[53] Like John Constable in Suffolk and Samuel Palmer in Shoreham, John Elwyn in Cardiganshire and George Chapman in the Rhondda Valley, Prichard returns to locations to which he feels personally connected. As Jonah Jones remarked:

> *There is always a strong accent in his work, such as the texture of a dry wall, or the pattern of a windblown*

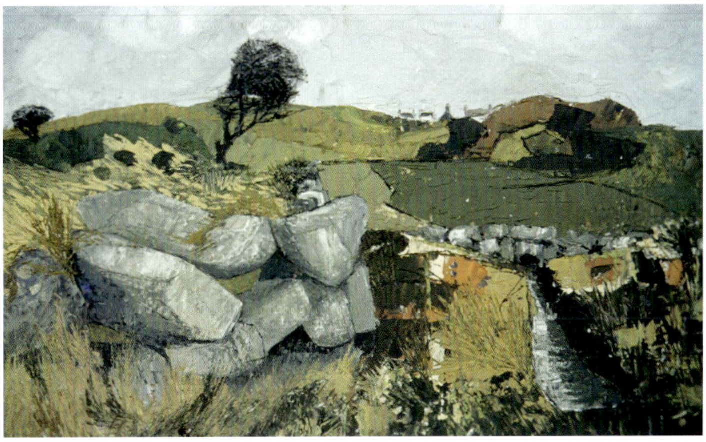

Fig. 22
Llanddona
1962 | oil on board | 61 x 92 cm
private collection, UK

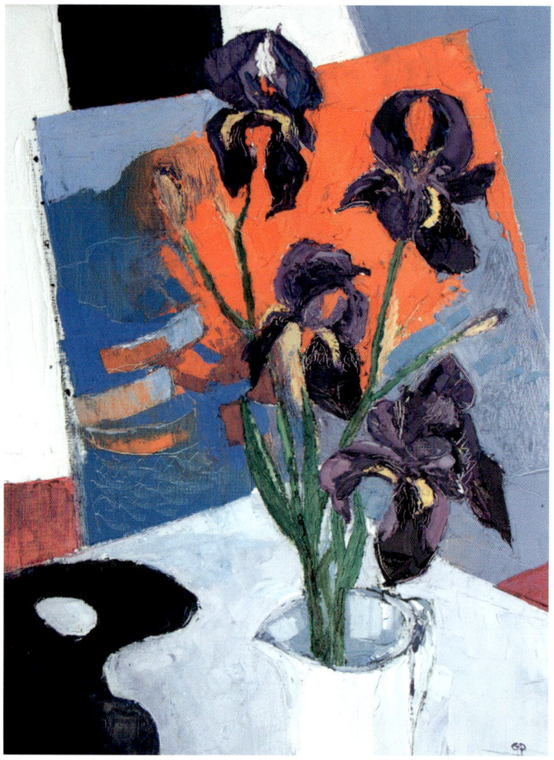

Fig. 23
Irises
1989 | oil on canvas | 73 x 54 cm
the artist

> *thorn. His landscapes are not so much portraits of place as notes in a context, directing our gaze to the world in an outcrop of rock or to the white face of a building in the idle distance.*[54]

Landscape, as the American philosopher Holmes Rolsten III defines it, 'is personal and cultural history made visible'. A 'section of the countryside that can be seen from some place', rather than a country in its entirety, it is a certain 'scope of nature, modified by culture … and in that sense landscape is local, located'.[55] Just what arrests Prichard's gaze is not always apparent to those who are drawn to the iconic or the picturesque sites that are, in Bell's words, 'the terminus of every charabanc'.[56] Having reached his 'chosen spot', Prichard 'start[s] looking, finding and recognizing shapes' rather than 'individual objects'. This helps him to avoid the 'dangers of selecting the picturesque'.[57] And while selection entails exclusion – modern architecture, wind farms and pylons 'have not moved me to paint them … yet!' he grants[58] – Prichard prefers to be 'concentrating on some unassuming scene' to arrive at paintings that Welsh scholar Bedwyr Lewis Jones has called 'lyrical poems in praise of dappled things'. The allusion to Gerard Manley Hopkins' 'Pied Beauty' is apt; for Prichard does indeed shun the ideal, the expected and the representative view. Instead, he looks for 'skies of couple-colour as a brinded cow'; for a '[l]andscape plotted and pieced—fold, fallow, and plough', for '[a]ll things counter, original, spare, strange'; 'Whatever is fickle, freckled (who knows how?)'.[59]

In this pursuit, Prichard is aided by a sound and reliable visual memory of 'places and objects' that makes it possible for him to 'find [his] way around the countryside having noticed a deformed windswept tree or a certain pattern on a stone wall – the colour of a house or shape'.[60] Once, painting *en plein air*, Prichard was approached by a traveller who, in an effort to direct his gaze toward the scenic and spectacular, informed him that he was 'painting the wrong view'.[61] 'Have a care', R.S. Thomas instructs us in 'The Small Window', one of Prichard's favourite poems. In Wales, one could 'grow rich / With looking'; but that 'wealth' was not to be gathered by those crowding a 'small window'[62] – and especially not in celebrated views that have already been framed for us by generations of artists before him. After all, as Clough Williams-Ellis suggests, the 'undoubtedly dramatic scenery' of Wales had been 'consistently over-written' in a 'frenzy of hyperbole' by those whose views on and of Wales were formed by the picturesque:

> *For the essential thing about the Welsh mountains, is, of course, that they are neither the Himalayas nor the Pyrenees, nor the Alps, even in miniature, but their own distinctive little selves with a perfection of detail and a finish and colour that is unique, and not to be matched even in Scotland nor yet in the English lakes…*[63]

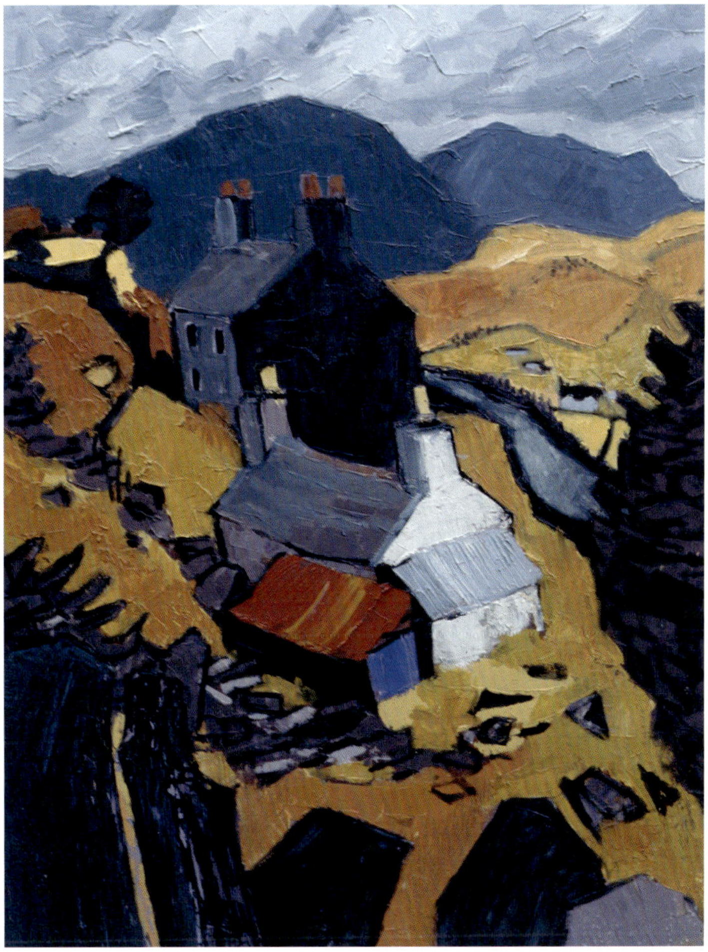

Fig. 24
Tanygrisiau
1989 | oil on canvas | 73 x 54 cm
private collection, UK

Rather than having the greatness of the scenery thrust upon him, Prichard is one of those 'modern artists' who, as Bell says of his contemporaries Sutherland and Piper, look 'less with a view to fitting [the scene] to some preconceived idea than to discover in it some … quality which may serve as a theme' for a painting. In this sense, Prichard is a romantic painter. As John Piper noted, romantic art

> *is the result of a vision that can see in these things something significant beyond ordinary significance: something that for a moment seems to contain the whole world; and, when the moment is past, carries over some comment on life or experience besides the comment on appearances.*[64]

Prichard may be said to echo the novelist and scholar Gwyn Jones, who held that 'the meaning of Wales' was not to be found in the 'famed vistas, the showplaces, the triadic Wonders of the Island of Britain'. Instead, it must be sought in 'some

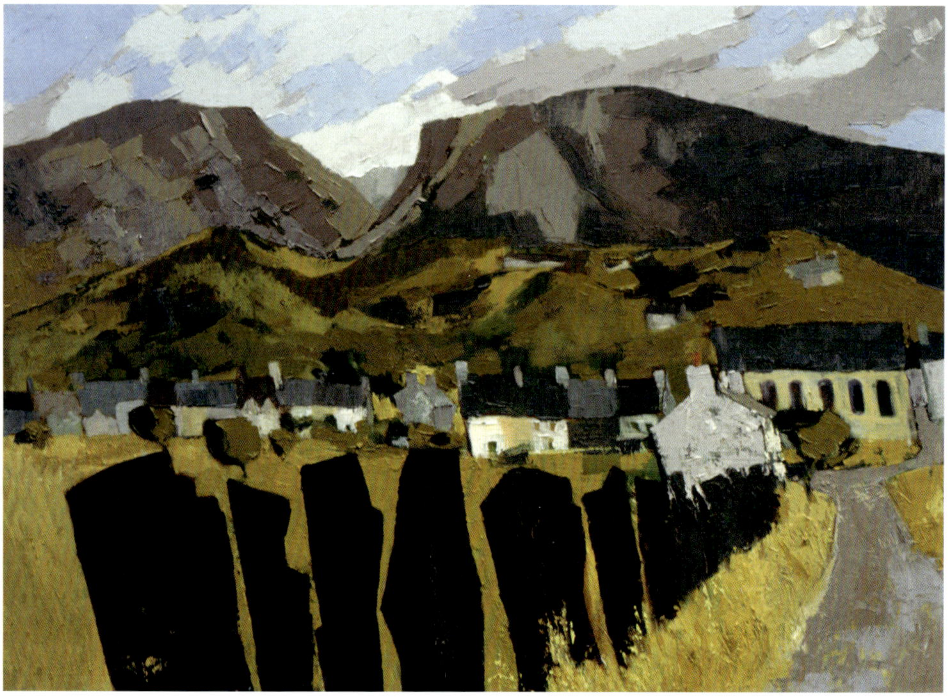

Fig. 25
Tanygrisiau
1988 | oil on canvas | 54 x 73 cm
private collection, UK

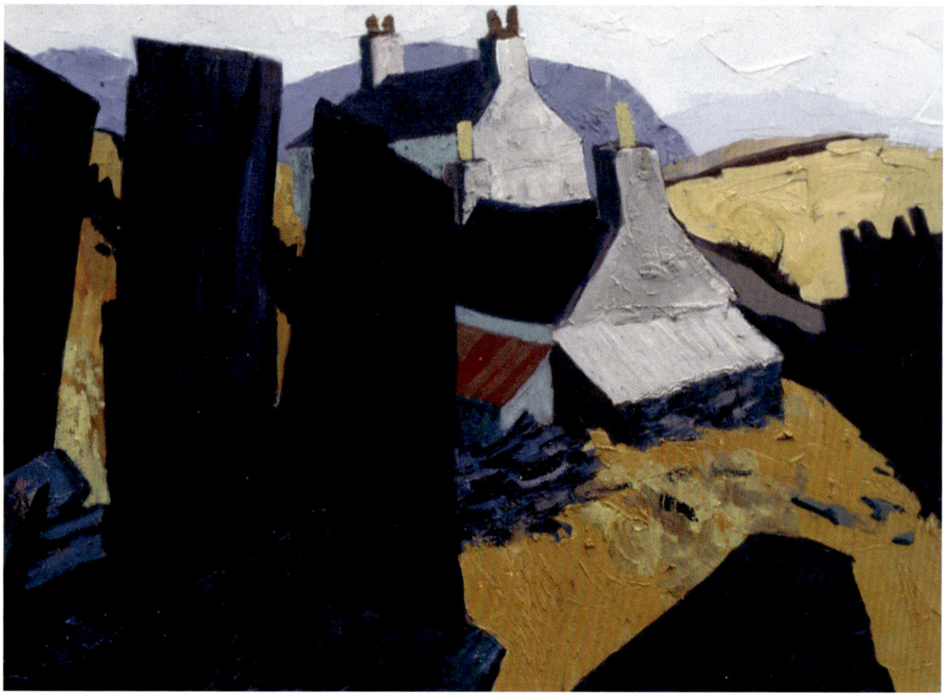

Fig. 26
Tanygrisiau
1989 | oil on canvas | 54 x 73 cm
private collection, UK

private place that can never engage a general admiration', be it 'some corner of a field, a pool under a rock, in a bare sheep-walk or a cottage folded in a gulley, in a hard road trodden by the feet of our fathers and their fathers before them'.[65] What Prichard arrives at, though, is not the 'meaning of Wales' but an intimate response to his surroundings and an expression of the experience of being outdoors, exposed to the elements.

In Wales and elsewhere, in the outdoors as well as in the studio, Prichard tends to train his eye on physical objects and sites that are immediately before or around him. As Kyffin Williams put it, Prichard 'really loves things. He loves the stone walls, the lichen, the cottages and small fields. They obviously mean something very strongly to him and he had to put them down'.[66] Apart from – or perhaps even more than – the material world, though, what Prichard truly loves is the act of looking by way of which he gleans the matter of his art. Some 'things', such as 'flowers and still lifes', however enjoyable, Prichard paints primarily as 'a discipline' designed to force him to 'look more carefully' at any given subject (fig. 23). Indeed, he had been observing carefully from the very start, his earliest 'artistic observation' having been a sketch of the flies in the family's kitchen executed when he was about three years of age. He spent hours sitting on the potty –

> *Enamelled cream with a blue trim – watching the house flies flying above my head and thinking how they managed not to crash into each other ... The fly path was a square with round corners, always in the centre of the room, although there wasn't a light bulb hanging there.*[67]

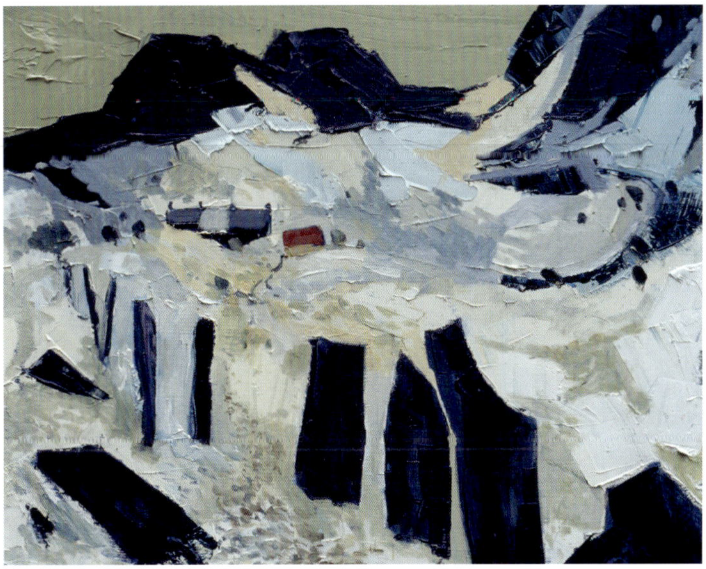

Fig. 27
Slate Fence and Snow, Y Moelwyn
1998 | oil on canvas | 50 x 65 cm
private collection, UK

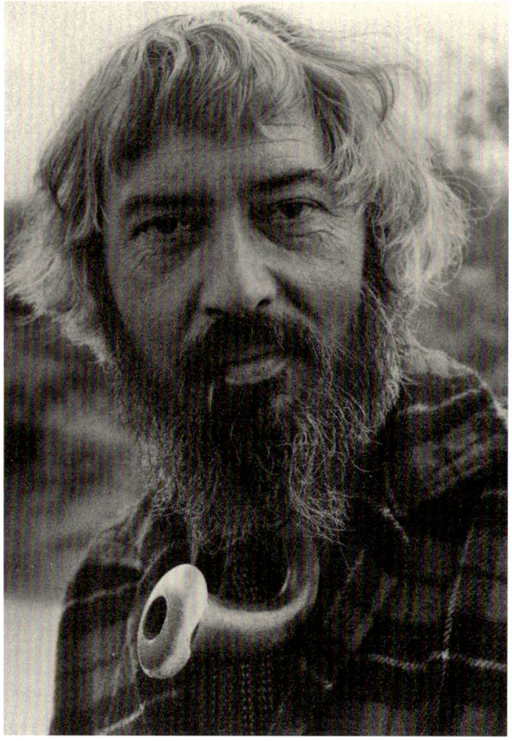

Fig. 28
Gwilym, 1974
photograph Howard Hughes

Like Graham Sutherland and John Piper, Prichard looks for the peculiar and the particular in the Welsh landscape; but, unlike them, he discovered something to look at nearby rather than feeling compelled to seek for it elsewhere.

'There is a deep sense of landscape that is in every Welsh man and woman', Jonah Jones asserted,

> *and Gwilym is a dyed-in-the-wool Eifionydd man whose childhood was spent within view of the Celtic Sea and the mountains of Eryri. The lanes, fields, farms and blue hills are his subjects and he treats them in uninhibited paint ... It is a boldness, a commitment, and a lifetime's gazing that comes forth from his paintings of his ancient inheritance.*[68]

Kyffin Williams professed himself 'baffled' by the 'yearly migration' of '[s]o many English artists [who] dash towards the Mediterranean as soon as the sun begins to shine in summer'; after all, he added, 'I am sure a painter can paint his own land better than anywhere else.'[69] The problematic reasoning of such a statement aside, the commitment to painting his environs has certainly enabled Prichard to focus and prolong his gaze and to deepen his study both of the land and of the act of contemplation. And although he has lived and painted elsewhere, in Brittany and Provence, has worked in England and Northern Ireland and has taken sketchbook and paints to Italy, Greece and Tunisia, Prichard has returned, time and again, to specific locations in Wales that, even six decades into his career as a painter, continue to engage him.

Apart from Anglesey and Pembrokeshire, it is Cadair Idris and the Moelwyn Mountains, Ffestiniog and the slate mining village of Tanygrisiau with its cottages beneath a tiered Snowdonian hillside that have intrigued him most (figs 24–27). However, as Kyffin Williams cautioned London gallery goers, we should not 'dismiss' Prichard as a 'provincial artist'. Doing so, Williams argued,

> *would be unwise and ignorant, for it has been proved in the past that an artist obsessed by a confined area of landscape or a monotonous theme has in turn triumphed over those who have sought the easier and more obvious paths to success.*[70]

Constancy and a commitment to the tried and true may well be equally 'obvious paths', but it is rather less obvious to keep looking for the unexpected, as Prichard does, and to find it among the sights with which one feels so thoroughly at home. And since he keeps exploring the characteristic without trying to arrive at the definitive, Prichard's paintings are less a definition of Wales than they are notes on the open-ended process of interpretation. The true reward of looking at familiar things, for artist and audience alike, is not validation but discovery.

Although he tends to return to what he feels to be closely familiar, Prichard does not strive for a reassuring sameness in order to confirm what he already knows; instead, he makes it his challenge to look again and to seek out the irregular that is to be reconciled with and worked into a formal composition: a configuration of rocks in a drystone wall, a bank of grass, a cluster of farm buildings. Exploring his translations of a certain view into a landscape, he once asked:

> *When I look at what I am going to paint, what do I see? What am I looking for when I am confronted with farm buildings? The unexpected ... rectangles of roofs, walls, doors, chimneys, the odd post whose duty has long been forgotten, all form the correct order and composition of the work of an unknown artist builder. As my eye travels around I am aware of various accents that break the harmony of rectangles. The roof with the broken 'spine', the chimneys that bisect the roofs, the stone that has rolled away from the wall. The wind-formed dark thorn trees. The ever present elm tree, whose roots are as old as antiquity, a talisman against witches. Here, as I stand and look, the shapes before me start to move into a pictorial composition.*[71]

In pursuit of the secrets to be mined from the commonplace, of what Ceri Richards referred to as the 'bones beneath the land',[72] Prichard delves into mysteries that remain unnoticed and recovers the charms that are unfelt by the less inquisitive or sentient, by the prosaic souls whose attitude toward their surroundings and the stories they might disclose is rather more matter-of-fact.

For this reason, Mary Rennell's phrase 'Celtic vision'[73] remains a convenient tag for Prichard's work, outlook and career, however much it may threaten to reduce their social, cultural and political dimensions to myth. 'What is this Celtic imagination, you may ask?', as Lord Croft addressed the opening-night audience of Prichard's 1976 exhibition at Hereford City Art Gallery. To his mind, it suggested a 'kind of mysticism' rooted in the 'capacity' not only to 'feel the spell of the past' that could be 'sensed in old buildings and in landscape', but also to 'find behind surface appearance a deeper sense of reality which relates the particular to the whole'.[74] Rather than the entirety of a region or the identity of a nation, that 'whole' may well be the unreachable sum total of an ongoing spiritual quest expressing itself in a need to relook, re-examine and relate. As Prichard discovered in the 1970s, an exposure to unfamiliar scenes does not always stimulate him, especially when he senses that his environment lacks certain qualities that are at once familiar and continually challenging: the ruggedness of a not quite cultivated terrain and the mutability of the temperamental sea.

Leaving Anglesey for Leicestershire in 1965 to teach at Ratcliffe College and for Herefordshire in 1973 to ensure a better education for his children proved a creatively stifling and dispiriting ex-

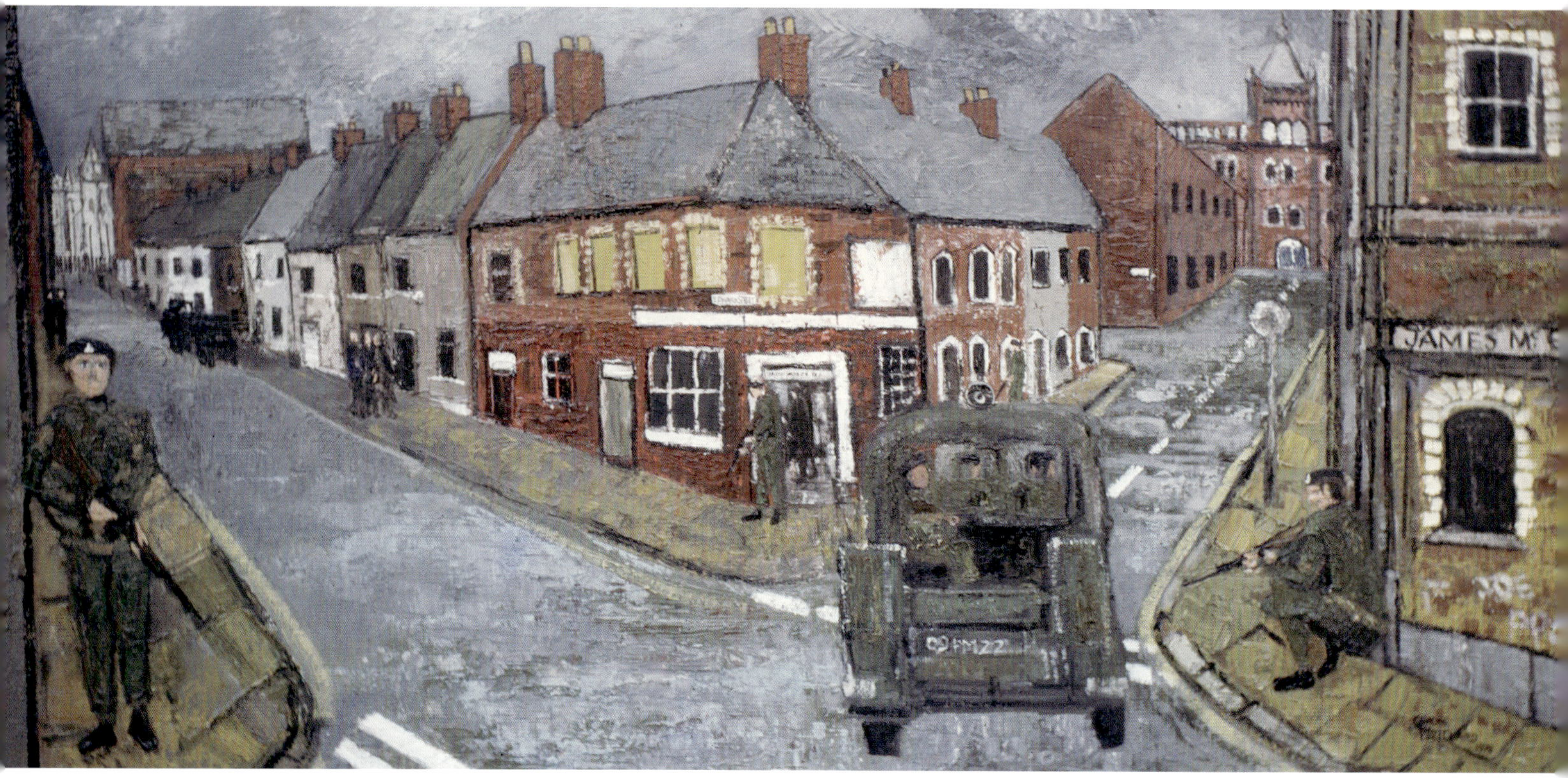

Fig. 29

Belfast, 25th Batallion

1975 | oil on canvas | 91.5 x 168 cm

Royal Artillery

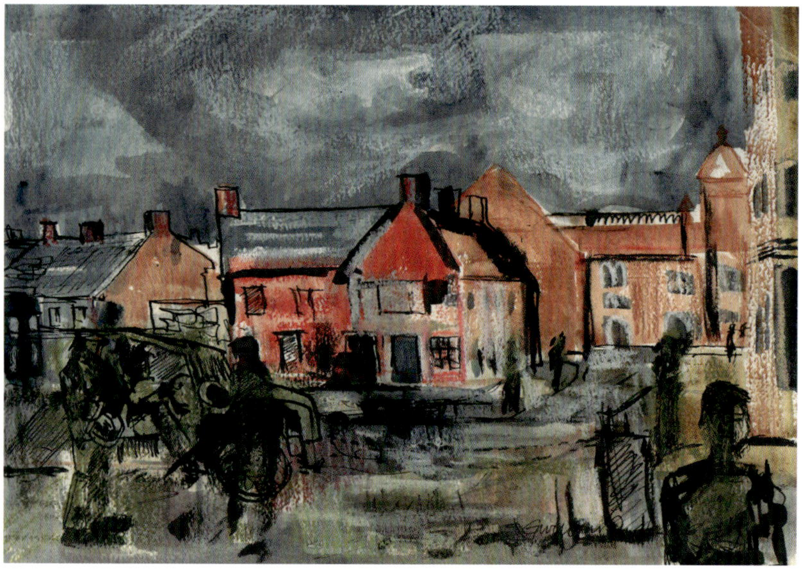

Fig. 30

Belfast

1974 | ink and wash on paper | 25 x 35 cm

the artist

perience. The post at Leicester having been such a consummate disappointment that he abandoned it within a year, Prichard returned to Wales to join the staff of Holyhead Comprehensive on Anglesey and subsequently became head of the art department at Friar's School, Bangor, a position he held from 1966 until 1973. The late 1960s and early 1970s marked a troubled period for Prichard; he had begun to drink heavily during his year at Leicester. This culminated in his hospitalisation in January 1973, up until which time Claudia Williams had not only kept the family together but also stood in for Prichard when he was unable to meet his teaching commitments. His recovery began with a referral to the Max Glatt detoxification unit in Southall, London. Prichard has been teetotal ever since; the only stimulants on which he relies as an artist are the sights before and the sounds around him.

After nearly two decades of living and working on Anglesey, the year in Leicester excepting, Prichard and Williams relocated to Weobley in Herefordshire. Here, the family moved into a medieval cottage that, reassuringly for Williams, who had converted to Catholicism in 1956, stood not far from one of the oldest Catholic churches in England. By this time, however, Williams' elderly mother was in need of care; and so that she could move in with the family, the couple bought a large if 'somewhat dilapidated' nineteenth-century vicarage in Norton Canon. As Prichard had relinquished his full-time teaching position in North Wales, the couple decided to open their studio and offer art lessons there. They became involved with the Norton Canon Art Group, a weekly meeting of amateur and professional painters who gathered to draw and paint the model, still life or landscape under Prichard's tuition.[75] And yet, despite the fact that he was recovering and generally in better health, Prichard, for the first time in his career, struggled to respond artistically to his environs (fig. 28). Many of the extant canvases of this period suggest Prichard to be ill at ease with his subjects. At Weobley, he 'spent some time just walking around', keenly aware that he 'had to start re-looking at things'. He had always been 're-looking', but here in Herefordshire, he found little to arrest his gaze and provoke him to pick up his paintbrushes; neither the land nor the light suited his temperament. Even after years of searching, as he wrote in 1978, he still could not 'really be moved to paint the area, apart from the occasional snow scene'.[76]

One such canvas is *Weobley, Herefordshire* (1974; fig. 31), in which Prichard explores not only the formal qualities of the view before him – the slatted fence against the white plain of snow and the mirroring of these verticals in the elongated church tower – but also the abstract qualities of the surfaces. 'If you go into a painting and select a small area,' he later explained, 'it can still be beautiful. Maybe it's completely abstract, but it's beautiful in itself.'[77] In this case, the landscape needed to become more abstract as the topography of Herefordshire held so little concrete interest for Prichard. 'Landscapes accept the way I translate them', Prichard once remarked, 'they don't object to the way I move things around' in the act of composing. Such artistic liberties, however, are not always an expression of freedom; and the move to Herefordshire proved limiting precisely because it confronted him with scenery that refused to move him. The cultivated, cultured land – the 'garden of England where most of the land has been landscaped under the influence of Capability Brown' – provided him with fewer challenges to reign in or else compositionally wrestle with – an unruliness that to him is a 'delight' not unlike the 'Disorder' of which poet Robert Herrick speaks: 'A careless shoe-string, in whose tie / I see a wild civility: / Do more bewitch me, than when art / Is too precise in every part.'[78]

In 1974, Lieutenant Colonel Roger Colvin Chamberlain, a portrait of whose children Claudia Williams had recently painted, commissioned Prichard to visit Northern Ireland and produce two large canvases to mark completion of the Royal Artillery's tour of duty in Belfast. Eager to get away from Herefordshire, Prichard spent a fortnight in Belfast, escorted by two armed soldiers, to gather preparatory material. There, he filled a sketchbook with watercolours and Indian ink drawings of the area around the Shankill Road (*Belfast*, 1974; fig. 30), the primarily loyalist working-class area of west Belfast. The graffiti-strewn residential streets, the omnipresence of the British military, the predominantly blood red buildings, the leaden winter skies – convey both the hostility of the scene and the anxiety experienced by the artist (*Belfast*, 1975; fig. 29).

An engagement with and a contemplation of the land during those troubled days required frequent painting expeditions to Wales, either to the north, where both Prichard and Williams continued to exhibit with the Royal Cambrian Academy in Conwy, or to the countryside around St Davids in Pembrokeshire, the coastline of which Prichard 'discovered' for himself at that time.[79] At half terms, the couple packed books and art materials and headed west for return visits that reinvigorated and re-affirmed Prichard's commitment to landscape art. 'I have always lived near water,' he pointed out by way of explanation, 'but I have yet to exploit its full possibilities for painting.'[80] The inability to paint in Weobley had thoroughly confounded Prichard, who had never before felt any need to seek far and wide for sources of inspiration:

> *Why travel a hundred and fifty miles to paint when I should be able to paint on my own doorstep? A very difficult question to answer. I miss the sea and the ever-changing pattern of the tides; the ruggedness of the land, the lime-stone walls, the windswept stunted trees – especially the thorn trees; the quality of light that is reflected from the sea (which even on dull days gives a pear-like light) and the sound of my own Celtic language. That is why I return to Wales to paint.*[81]

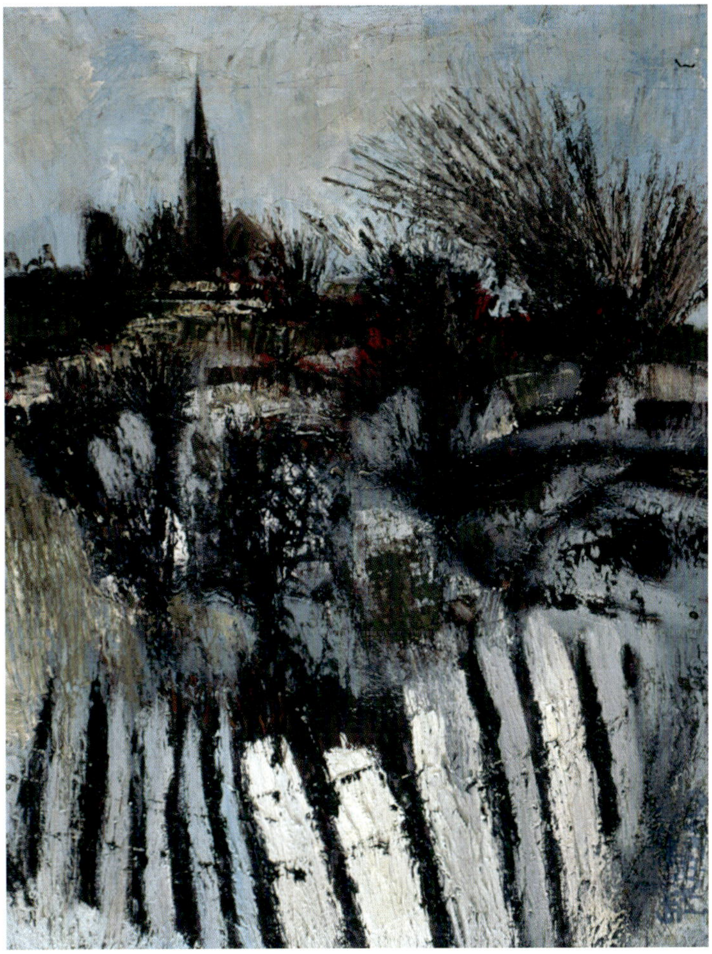

Fig. 31
Weobley, Herefordshire
1974 | oil on canvas | 41 x 31 cm
the artist

A more permanent arrangement seemed to be the solution, but the subsequent move from Herefordshire to Wales brought with it more problems than it helped to solve, so that Prichard wound up answering that 'very difficult' question at a remove far greater than a mere 'one hundred and fifty miles'.

'NOTHING IS REPEATED'

Although it is 'occasionally going mad in a riot of colour', as Kyffin Williams put it, Wales is primarily a 'land of ochres and umbers'. These are colours, he added, that Prichard 'likes to work with'; '[a]reas of warmth' that 'are bound by pink grey walls' and a 'sky' that 'has a richness and liveliness to go with the land'.[82] Indeed, they are colours to which Prichard was drawn not only in Wales but that also attracted him elsewhere. 'We marvelled at the shades of the earth and rock after rain', the couple recorded in a travel diary written in Greece in late 1984 and early 1985. Away from Wales, though, Prichard's palette began to broaden – 'lamp-black, Payne[']s grey, rich blackish brown, darkest blue grey, terracotta, pink, yellow ochre, burnt sienna' – as he was

> *trying to catch the shifting tones of the landscape and the quality of the light – the intense blues, subtle mauves and rich greys of the sea, the perfect diaphanous blue and pink of evening, the delicate shades of the fauna, the intensity of the oranges against the snow – so different from the colours of the landscape back home in Wales.*[83]

The 1984 journey to Greece was no carefully mapped-out jaunt; it was certainly no holiday in the sun. As Claudia Williams put it, their departure – in early December, no less – marked the 'start of a seventeen-year absence from Wales', that was to 'push our painting in new directions and change our outlook on life'.[84]

After leaving Herefordshire, the couple had relocated to North Wales, but had found – and quickly changed – homes that proved disagreeable to either or both of them as they had adverse effects on their physical health and their spiritual well-being. They had first moved into a 'rather unsuitable bijou cottage' on a 'one in four hill' at Llanddona on Anglesey. According to Williams, the 'only thing to recommend' it was the 'beguiling view of Red Wharf Bay' (fig. 33). Both artists found extramural work teaching at Bangor University; in addition, Prichard took on occasional teaching at St Gerard's Catholic School in Bangor and Plas Tan y Bwlch, the Environmental Studies Centre at Snowdonia National Park. Now middle-aged and living 'in another cramped cottage', they were 'wondering' whether they had 'done the right thing' in moving back to that remote region of North Wales, especially since Williams was suffering from depression. It was a 'hard period of adjustment', Williams recalls, as their children had left home and 'were finding their way in the student world'.[85]

Subsequently, the couple moved into a remote, eighteenth-century, stone-built farmstead near Rhostryfan in the Gwyrfai Valley, some four miles south of Caernarfon (fig. 32). It seems doubtful whether any general practitioner 'would have recommended' the spot, Williams comments on their experience at Gwredog Isaf, even though their friend 'Kyffin seemed to think it was agreeable' and Prichard, who 'fell in love with it', made it the subject of several paintings (*Gwredog Isaf and Washing Line*, 1980; *Gwredog Isaf*, 1983; figs 34 & 37).

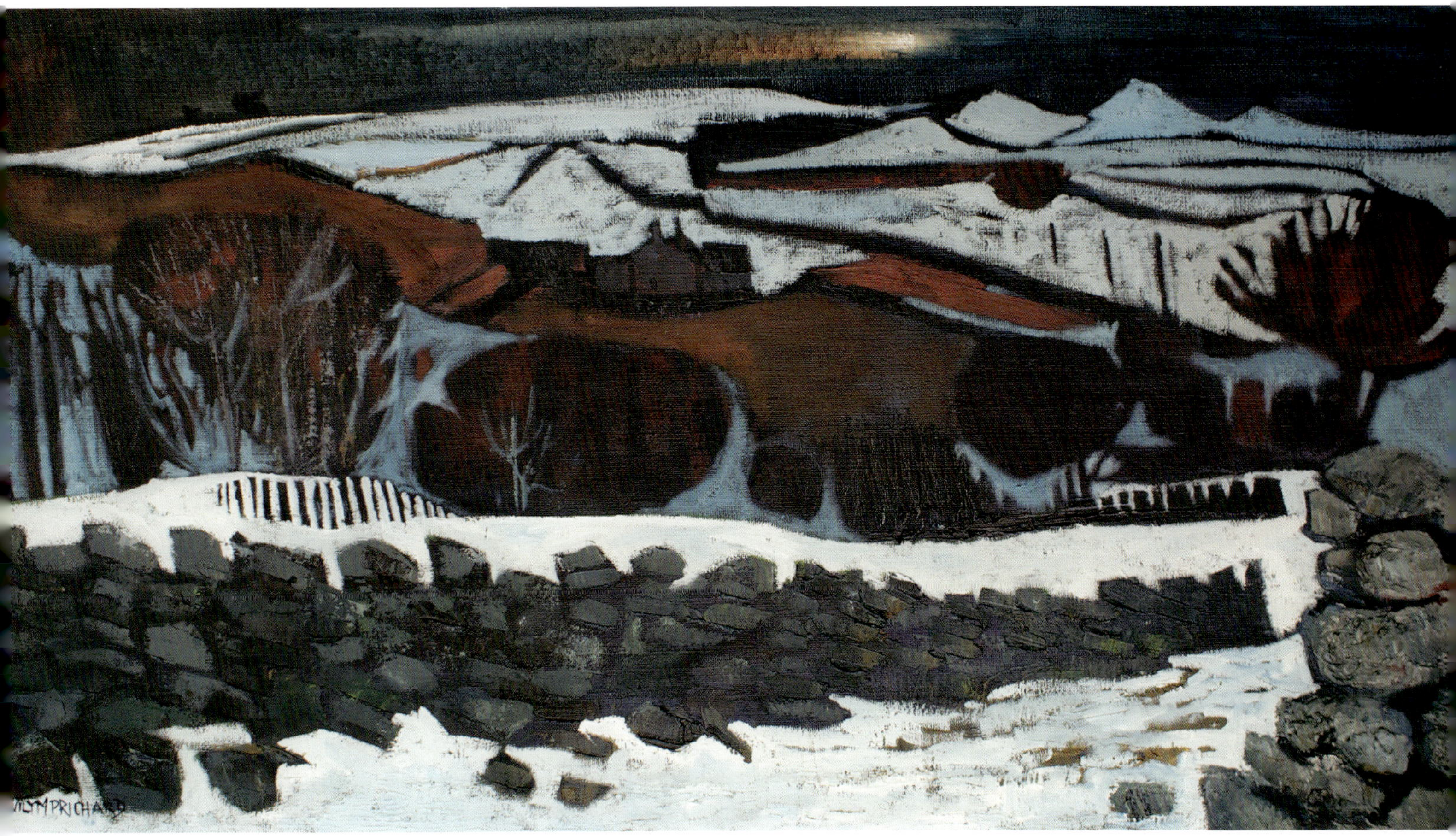

Fig. 32
Above Rhostryfan
1982 | oil on canvas | 51 x 92 cm
private collection, UK

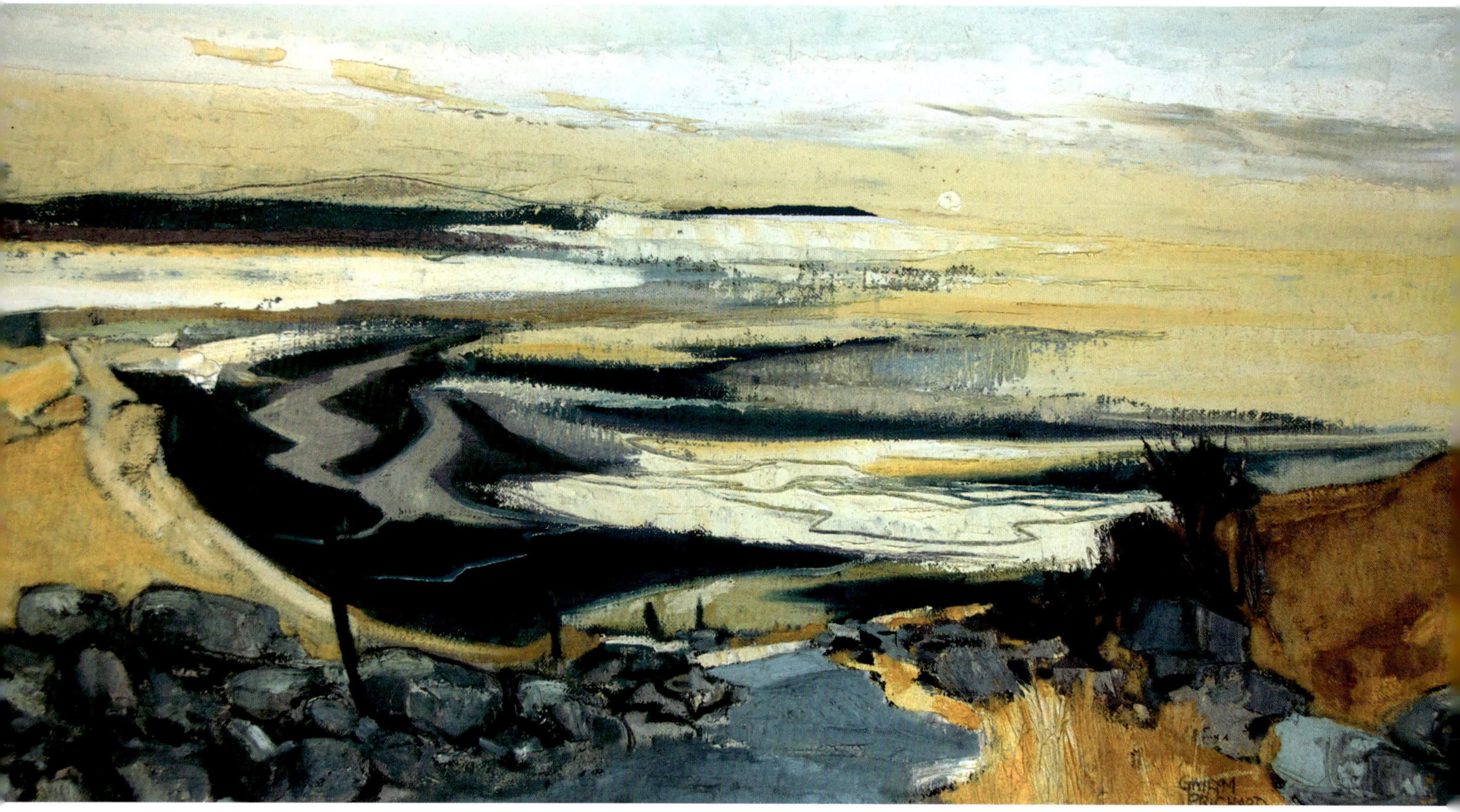

Fig. 33
Red Wharf Bay
1970 | oil on canvas | 52 x 92 cm
the artist

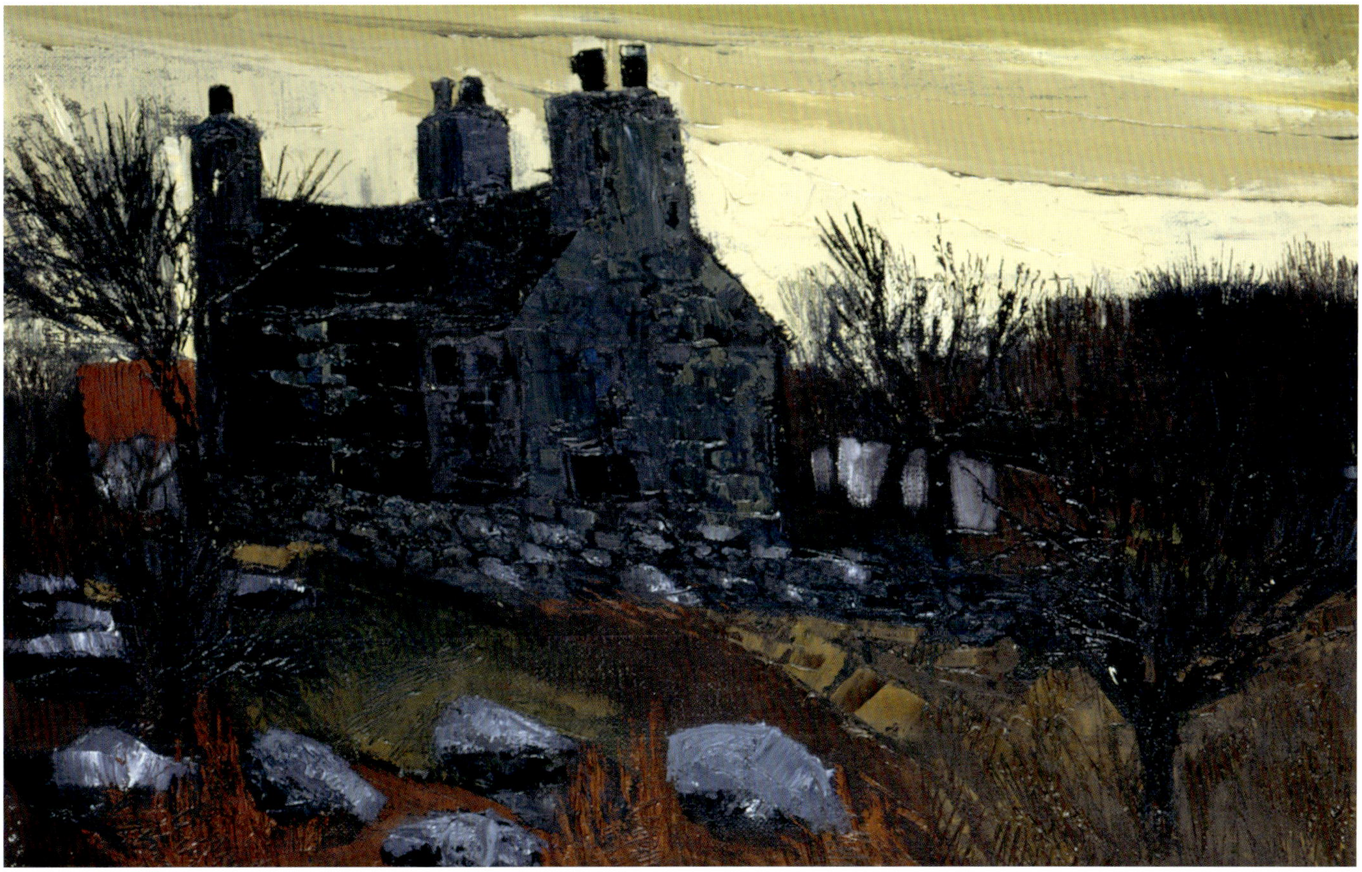

Fig. 34
Gwredog Isaf and Washing Line
1980 | oil on canvas | 52 x 77 cm
National Library of Wales, Aberystwyth

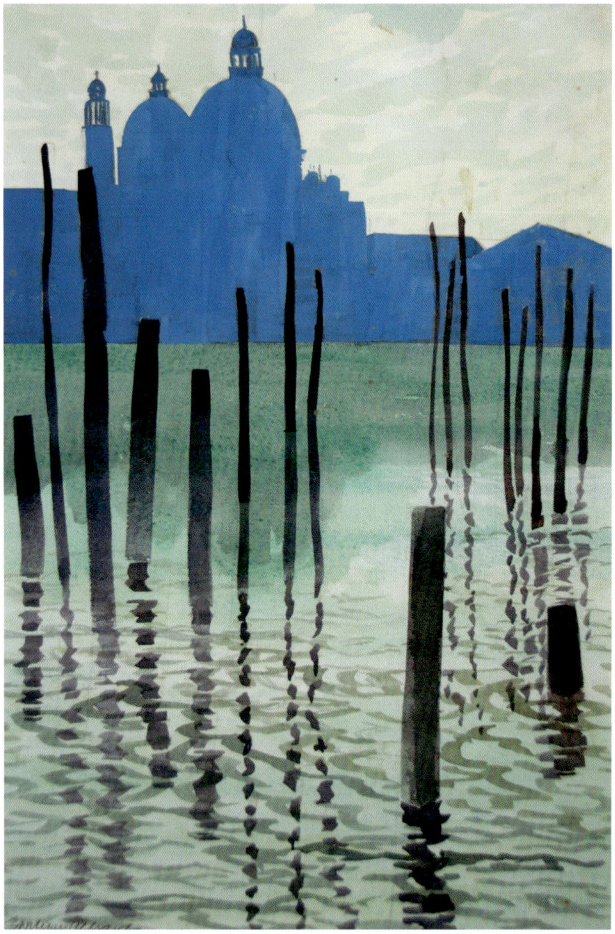

Fig. 35
Dawn, Venice
1984 | watercolour on paper | 52 x 34 cm
the artist

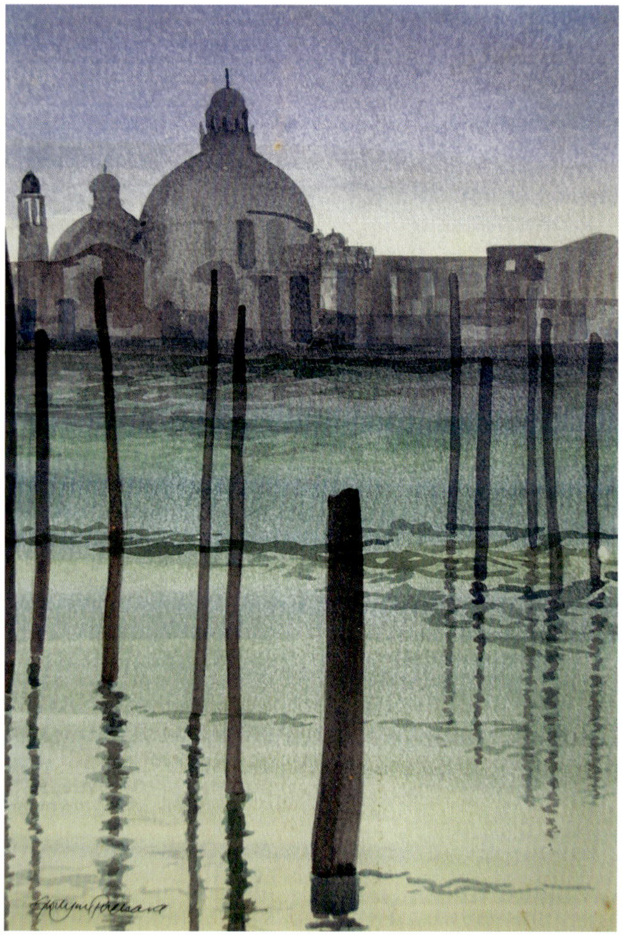

Fig. 36
Dusk, Venice
1984 | watercolour on paper | 51 x 34 cm
the artist

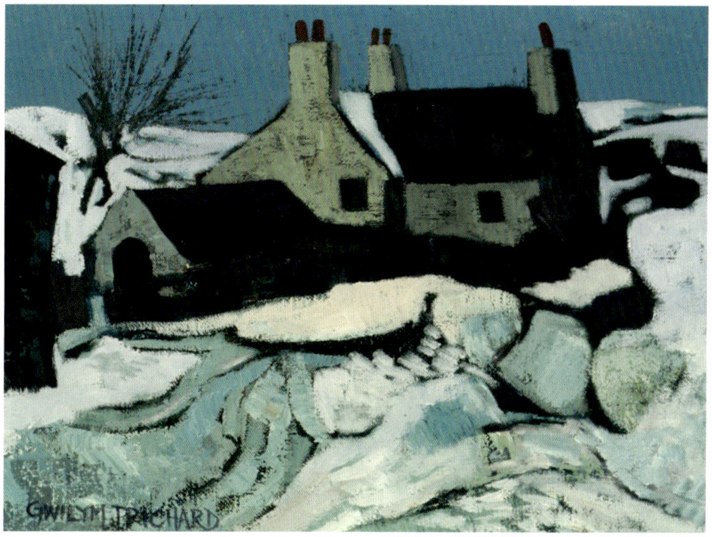

Fig. 37
Gwredog Isaf
1983 | oil on canvas
private collection, UK

Shrouded in mist for several months of the year, it made for an 'atmospheric place'; but, apart from being 'dramatic', it was also damp. The climate was beginning to take its toll on Williams, whose 'arthritic hands were feeling increasingly painful during the long winters'.[86] It was the couple's eldest son, artist Ceri Pritchard, who proffered a radical remedy by suggesting that they head toward the Greek islands, which neither of them had ever set foot on before. Friends of their son had offered free accommodation on Skiathos to anyone willing to look after their dog over the winter. The offer sounded so tempting that the couple, having found homes for their own pets, decided to sell their house and studio, the stability of which they exchanged for a peripatetic, uncertain existence. In the process of sorting out what among their worldly possessions to put in storage and what to consign to the scrapheap, Prichard destroyed a great many of his canvases.

Fitted out with little more than their clothes and an old school atlas to guide them – their camping equipment and painting materials piled high in their none too reliable estate car – the couple set out on an adventure that calls to mind the efforts of H.G. Wells' midlife doldrums, suffering Mr Polly to wriggle himself out of a 'Beastly Silly Wheeze of a hole!' – except that Prichard and Williams extricated themselves jointly, and did so by crossing bridges without feeling a need for burning them as well. On their wintry journey south, through Germany and Austria, they decided to change their route and call at Venice, where they delighted in 'the amazing façade' of 'glimmering' St Marks, 'catching the dazzle and sparkle' of the December sun reflected on the clear and 'palest blue green water of the sea'.[87] One morning, returning from her prayers at San Sylvestro,

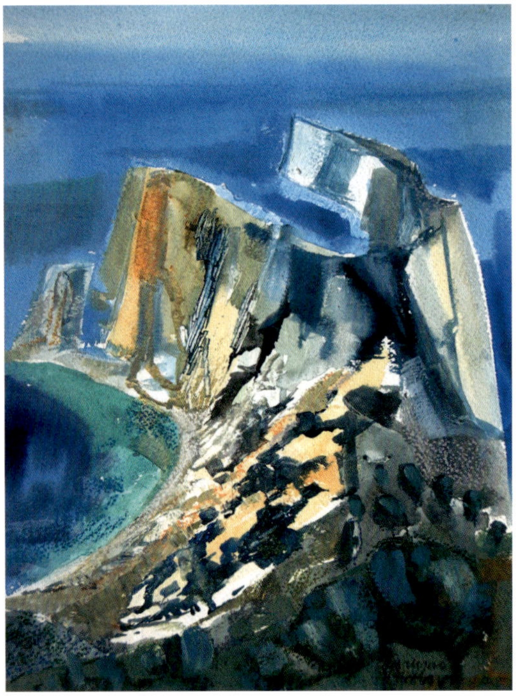

Fig. 38
Skiathos Headland
1985 | watercolour and chalk on paper
36 x 27 cm
the artist

Williams stepped out 'into the by now bright sunshine' and 'found Gwilym in the middle of a watercolour at the canal side' (figs 35 & 36). Travelling on to Ravenna, they marvelled at the Bzyantine splendour of the 'fabulous and sparkling' illuminated mosaics, before crossing the Adriatic Sea at Brindisi on the ferry to Igoumenitsa on mainland Greece. From there, they headed for Volos and, after a 'hair raising nine-hour journey' – Prichard's vision impaired by heavy snowfall and Williams nauseous from the diesel fumes of the ferry – they eventually arrived on the island of Skiathos, their home for the winter.[88]

That home brought back to mind all the misery of living in their bijou cottage on Anglesey; apart from the splendid view of the sea, their immediate surroundings were bleak and, as Williams noted in one of the couple's travel journals, there was 'certainly no art shop' as they had been led to expect.[89] Still, Prichard responded enthusiastically to the rough terrain of pine forests pierced by rocky outcrops, remote settlements surrounded by farmland, and a coastline of sandy beaches, coves and peninsulas (fig. 38). Above the whitewashed houses and red, pantiled roofs of Skiathos town, jade green olive trees cast cobalt shadows onto the ochre terraced groves against a backdrop of deep ultramarine waters (fig. 39). While the cold and changeable climate, as Williams noted, was 'not quite' what the couple had 'visualized',[90] the days of warm sunshine, blue skies and the intense Aegean light nonetheless provided a marked and welcome contrast to the gloom of a wet Snowdonian winter. In response to this light, Prichard's palette was transformed from one dominated by umber, sombre greys, black and steely blue to one of chalky pinks, powder blues and dusty greens.

On Christmas Day, he painted several watercolours of Skiathos town; on Boxing Day – 'another beautiful morning, the sea pale azure' – he set out to paint the dark, wedge-shaped islands.[91] When he was not working on a composition, many of which he mounted for sale locally, Prichard, after attending to daily chores and the couple's ageing vehicle, explored the island in search of further subjects. In his annotated sketchbooks, he made a record of what caught his eye – the bark of a pine tree, a spring blossom, a rock formation – and commented on weather conditions, colours and light. Among the detritus of civilisation, he combed beaches for rare shells and collected driftwood for fires; he watched fishermen mend their nets and took note of the hunters who were 'potting anything with or without feathers'. Prichard was intrigued as well by the indigenous architecture of Skiathos and the way in which inhabitants had dug themselves into the land or precariously perched themselves on the rock-strewn cliffs. 'It's amazing', he noted in his sketchbook, 'that a village can become part of the landscape'[92] (fig. 40). From Skiathos, he set out on long walks to Kastro, site of the island's medieval capital, high on a steep promontory above the sea. After several days of painting outdoors, he completed a 'large' composition of Kastro's ruined fortifications.[93] The

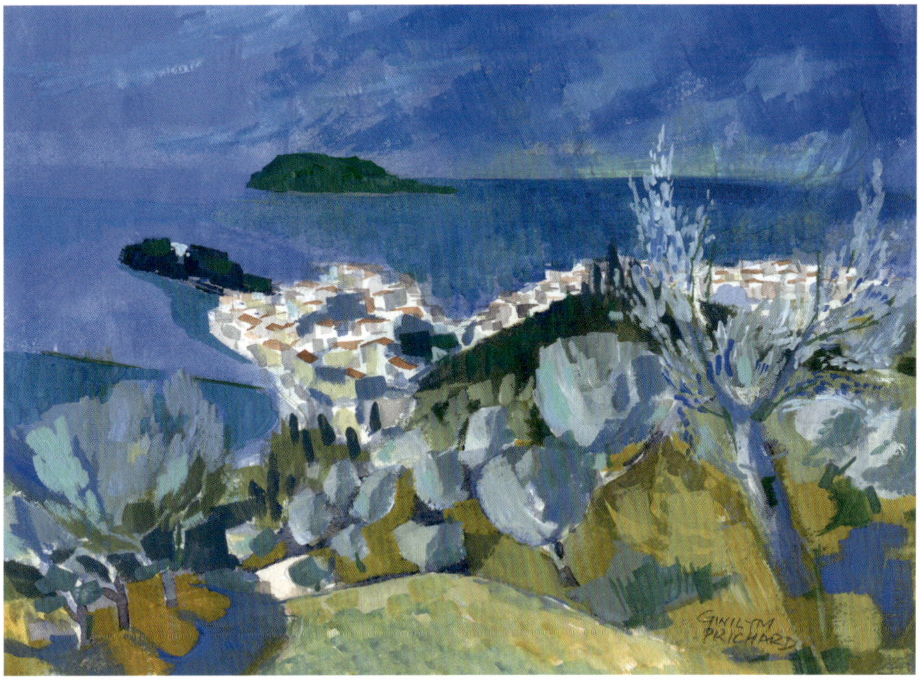

Fig. 39
Skiathos Town
1985 | watercolour on paper | 25 x 32 cm
the artist

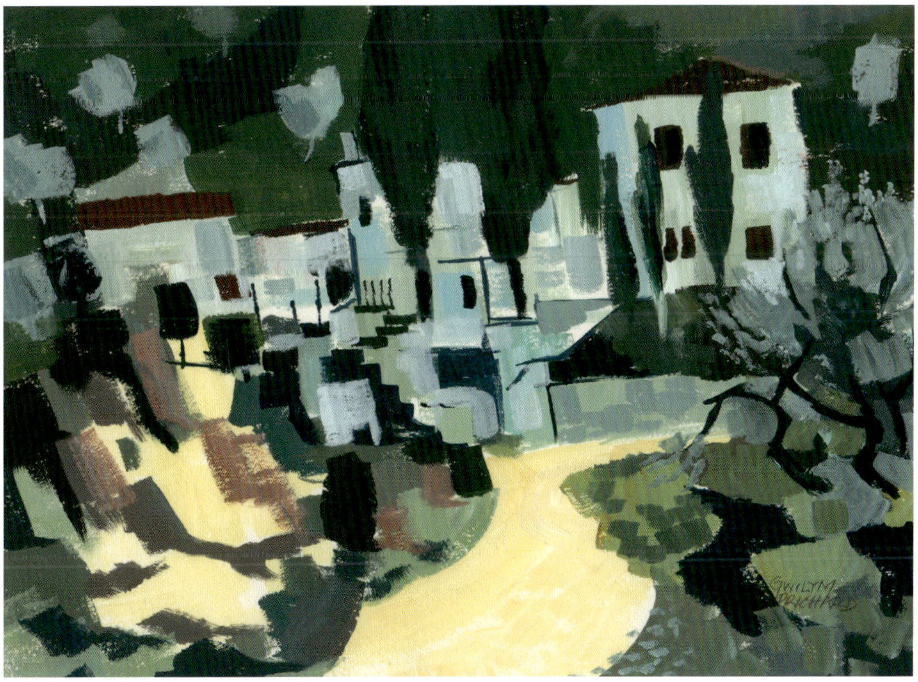

Fig. 40
Skiathos
1985 | gouache on paper | 25 x 32 cm
the artist

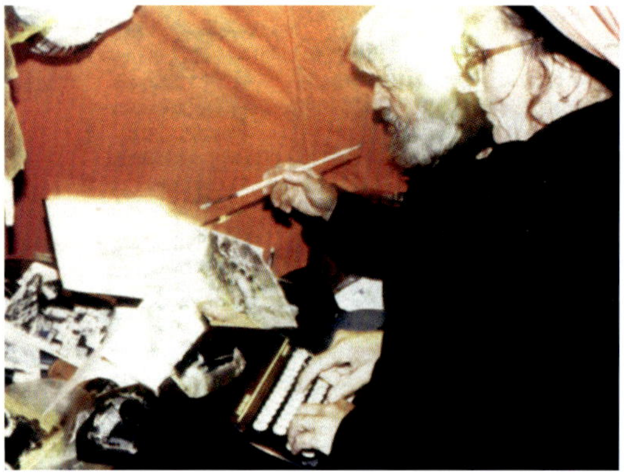

Fig. 41
Gwilym painting and Claudia Williams writing her travel journal in a tent on Santorini, 1985

vigorous layering of watercolour and chalks, along with the distressed, richly textured acrylics, bears a physical resemblance to the weathered rocks themselves.

'How extraordinary!', Williams wrote shortly after their arrival on Skiathos. 'Totally different lives to the one we are used to.'[94] In the months between 'the most bizarre Christmas time [they] ever had' and Mardi Gras, in the celebration of which they joined,[95] Prichard and Williams not only made the acquaintance of a number of writers and artists but also received commissions from local businesses and fellow expatriates alike. The time they spent travelling and living in Europe, Prichard remarked, had 'certainly changed [his] outlook' on humanity as well as on art, and it drove home the wisdom of 'just living for the day'.[96] In March 1985, their dog-sitting duties fulfilled, the couple were ready to move on; the proceeds from the sale of a few works executed during their stay on Skiathos allowed them to visit galleries and museums in Athens and, after a three-day stopover there, to take an overnight ferry to Santorini, whose original name, Kallístē, declares it to be 'the most beautiful' island in the South Aegean Sea. Indeed, Santorini's 'dramatic' volcanic landscape and the contrasts afforded by steep cliffs and gentle slopes, were, as Williams put it, 'really right' for Prichard.[97] Pitching their small, second-hand tent at an abandoned campsite, they lay awake listening to the howling wind and the waves crashing onto the black volcanic sands. Here, the couple endured gales, thunderstorms and heavy downpours, during which they learned that their shelter was 'not water-proof'. If the rain prevented them from sketching and painting outdoors, they worked 'from the car' so as not to lose a day's work. 'So far the tent is still standing,' Prichard recorded with good humour in the couple's travel diary, 'but only just!'[98] (fig. 41).

Despite the at times inclement and changeable weather, conditions for which life on Anglesey had prepared them, they 'spent a most productive two weeks' on Santorini, during which, as Williams recalls, Prichard 'complet[ed] some exciting gouaches'.[99] He painted townscapes of Thira (fig. 42), the erstwhile capital of Santorini, drew the windmills and terraced vineyards at Perissa and visited excavations of the Minoan site at Akrotiri. At Oia, he made studies of the hillside settlements against the backdrop of the caldera. In loose acrylics, he painted the densely clustered whitewashed stone houses within a maze of narrow streets clinging on to the steep cliffs that form the inner perimeter of the island (fig. 43). Further subjects for him were the 'red rocks' and the 'green and grey lichen', as well as 'light grey trees (fig or nut)' and the 'dark red volcanic earth', which he wanted to paint, 'but didn't' because he determined that they 'need[ed] to be' part of a larger, 'complete' composition.[100] Here as elsewhere, it was, for the most part, not the picture-postcard vistas that provoked his artistic response; whether or not a view was 'pretty', he insisted, had little to do with whether it presented 'something [he] could use in paint'.[101]

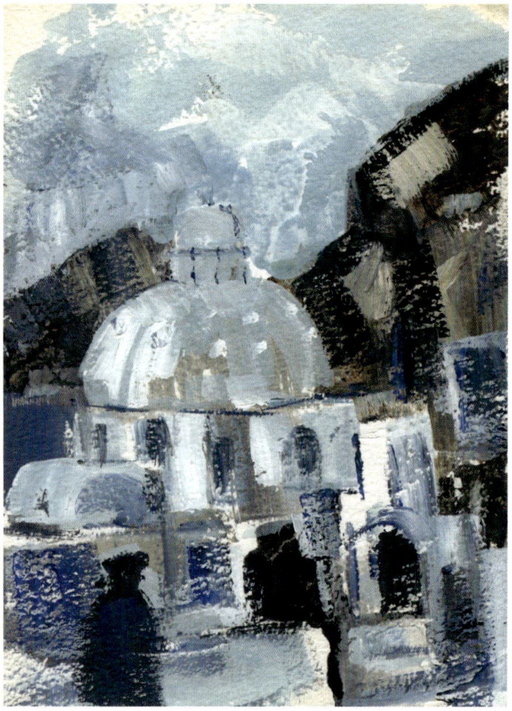

Fig. 42
Thira, Santorini
1985 | acrylic on paper | 32 x 25 cm
the artist

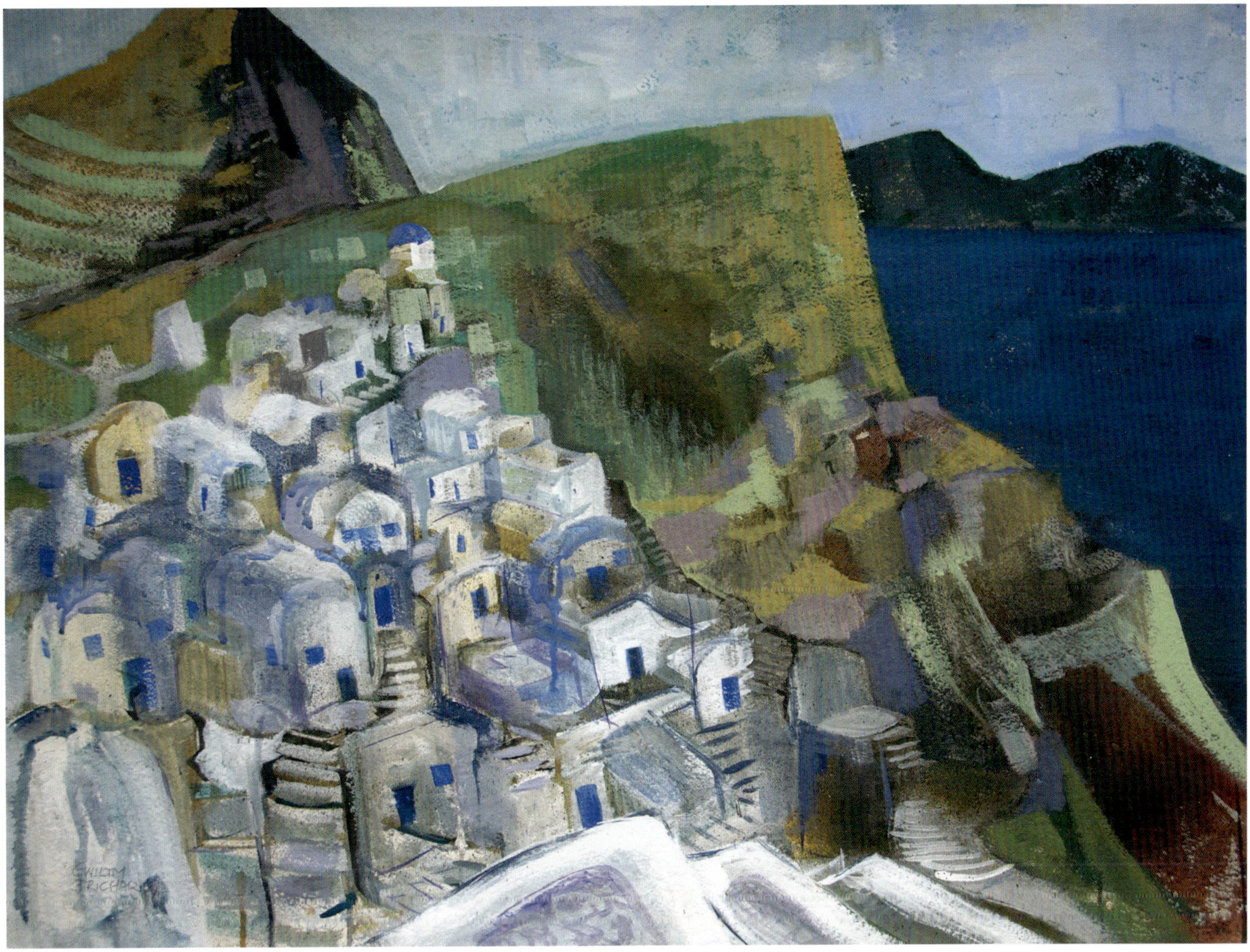

Fig. 43
Oia, Santorini
1985 | acrylic on paper | 76 x 57 cm
the artist

In late March, having been fined for exceeding their stay in Greece, the couple set out on a journey through Italy and southern France. As they had no home to return to, they camped en route to paint for days at a time. Driving toward Barjols, a town whose name Williams associated with a fondly remembered schoolteacher who had lived there during the 1960s, the couple were pursued and stopped by a motorist who, catching sight of their Cymru bumper sticker, identified them as compatriots, invited them to lunch and provided them with temporary lodgings. The appeal of Provence was so great that Prichard and Williams remained there for a year, during which time they rented an old farmhouse a few miles from Barjols in Brue-Auriac (figs 44–46). Heading north again, they found themselves in Vannes at the Golfe du Morbihan, a natural harbour on the southern coast of Brittany. Here, the couple bought a small

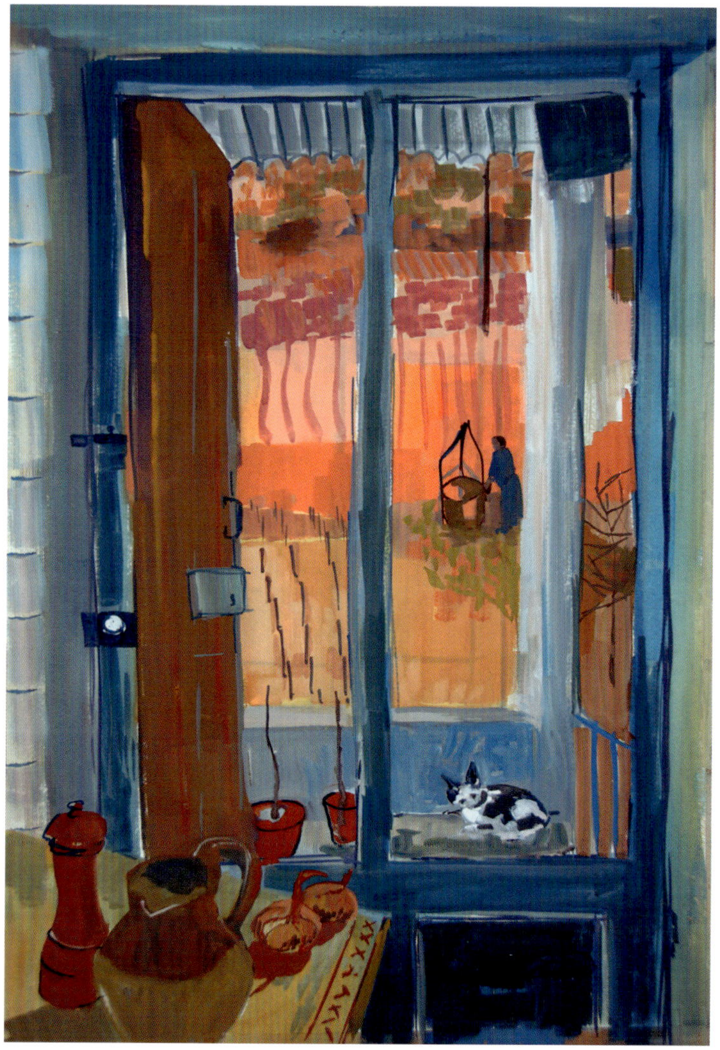

Fig. 44
View from Kitchen Window, Brue-Auriac
1986 | gouache on paper | 55 x 36 cm
the artist

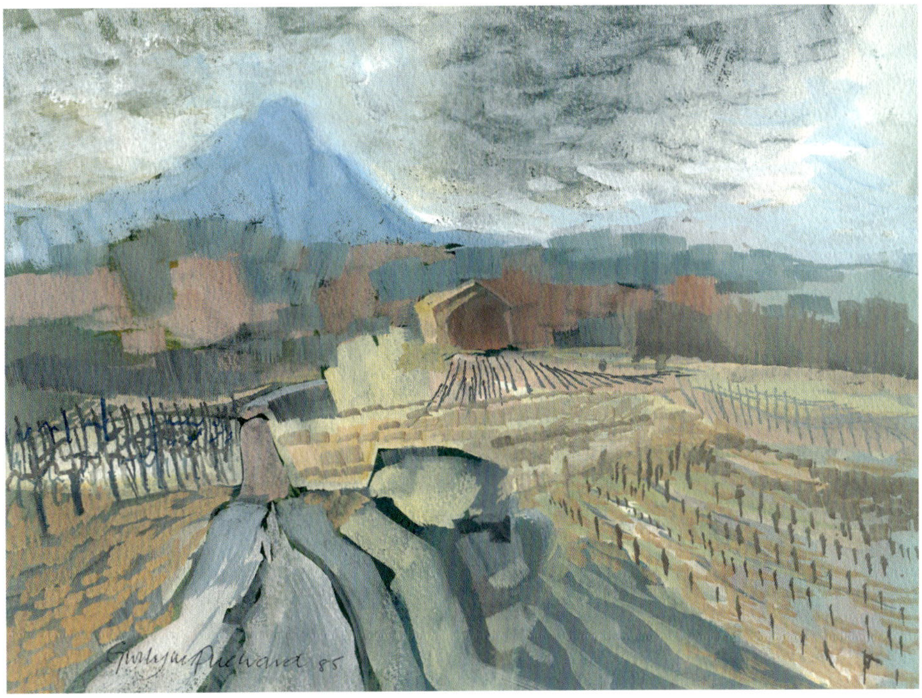

Fig. 45

Brue Auriac, Provence

1985 | gouache on paper | 27 x 35 cm

the artist

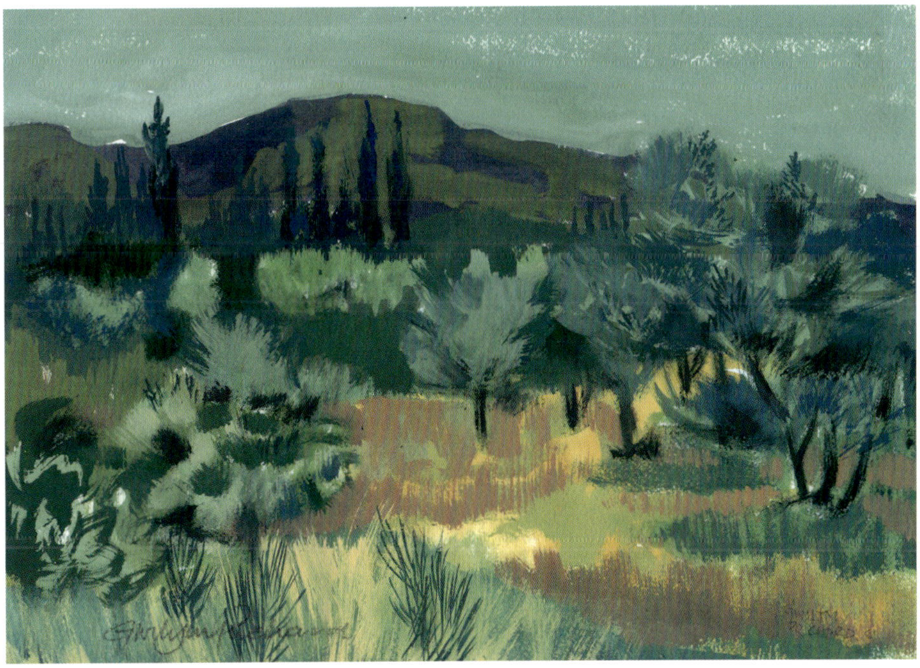

Fig. 46

Provence

1985 | gouache on paper | 27 x 35 cm

the artist

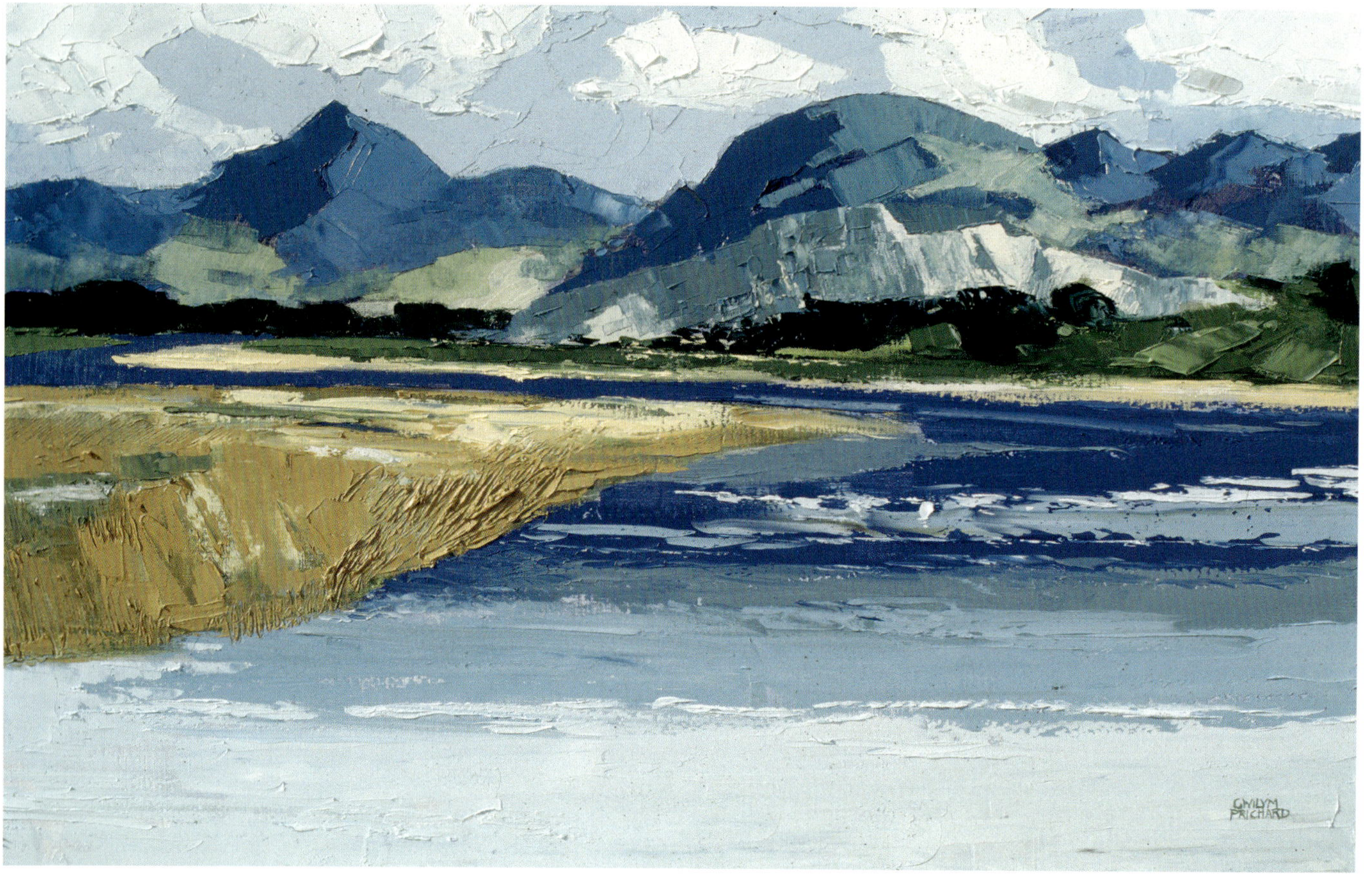

Fig. 47
Moelwyns
1998 | oil on canvas | 60 x 92 cm
the artist

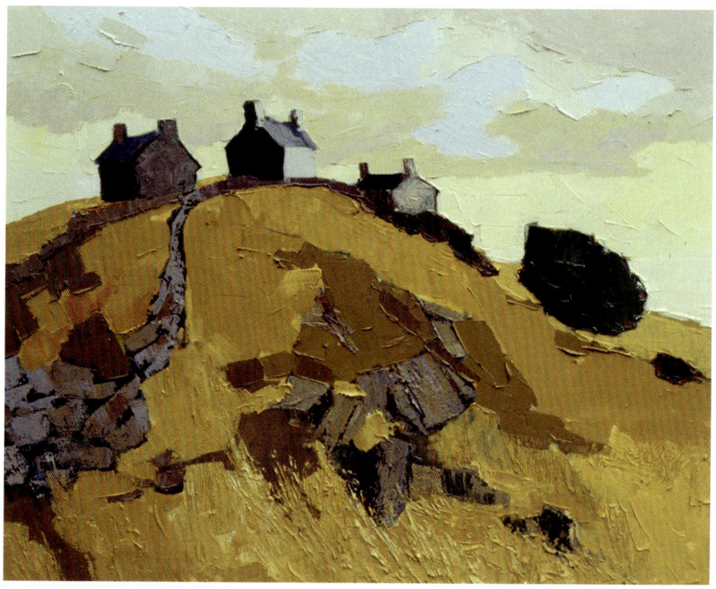

Fig. 48
Cwm Rheidiol
1988 | oil on canvas | 38 x 55 cm
private collection, UK

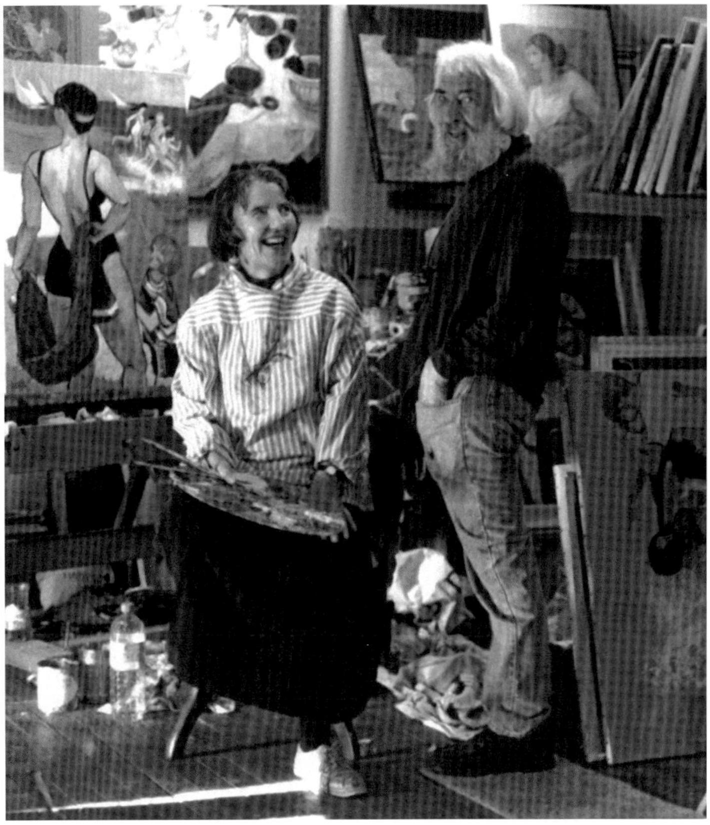

Fig. 49
Gwilym and Claudia Williams
in their Rochefort studio, January 1999
photograph Robert Meyrick

house near the sea where they lived and worked for four years, after which, in 1991, they discovered for themselves the Breton village of Rochefort-en-Terre, a *petit cité de caractère* overlooking the Gueuzon valley. According to Prichard, they both 'completely lost [their] hearts to the place'[102] – the medieval cobbled streets, the half-timbered buildings and the view of the sixteenth-century gothic church from their new home, a former bakery whose grain store they converted into adjoining studios (fig. 49).

Rochefort has a long association with the arts. In 1907, it became home to the French-born American painter Alfred Klots, who built himself a château amid the remains of Rochefort's medieval fortifications. In 1989, Isabel Klots of Baltimore, Maryland – widow of Alfred's son, the painter Trafford Klots – established a programme and set up scholarships to enable American artists to visit and work in Rochefort. 'She was a very warm and sociable person', Williams recalls, and the couple were frequently invited up to the château to 'meet painters from the Maryland Institute who spent several weeks [there] to paint the Breton countryside'.[103] The relaxed pace of life in France suited Prichard's temperament. 'It's just a different

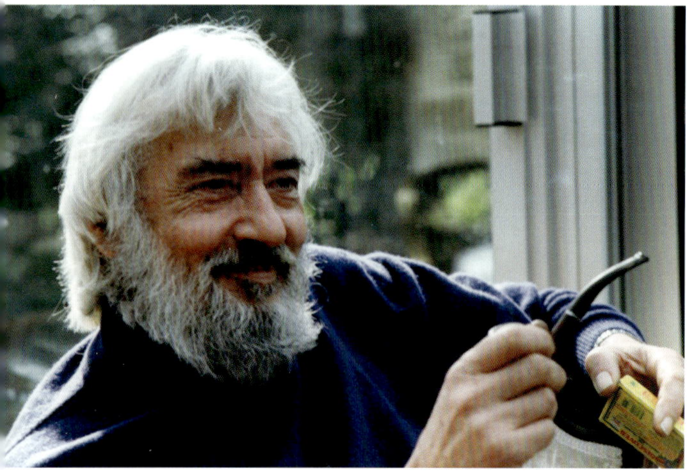

Fig. 50
Gwilym, July 1992
photograph Contessa Cecilia de Montaglion

pattern of life really', he observed at the time. 'There is more time here. I'm getting far more things done in a day somehow than I could in Wales'. The French, he also noted, seemed

> *more interested in painting. The postman will come in and say have you got any new paintings that I can look at. Or the person in the* boulangerie *will ask how's the work going.*[104]

Since Prichard had long been appreciated in Wales because of the 'love' he expressed for the land, Kyffin Williams reasoned, his equally exuberant interpretations of Brittany 'should receive the same response' from his 'Celtic cousins across the water'.[105] Instead, the response on the continent was rather more enthusiastic and immediate.

Before long, Prichard and Williams had established professional contacts throughout France and were exhibiting their latest works at galleries such as the Espace Gauguin in Pont-Aven, the Galerie Saphir in Dinard and the Galerie Moyen-Avenard in Nantes, where they showed their paintings alongside sculptures by Ceri Pritchard. The move to France had opened new and wider markets for both artists. In addition to continued group and solo shows in Wales – one of them, 'Paintings and Pottery', with their second son Ben Pritchard – they now exhibited in Paris and Amsterdam, where galleries and institutions expressed a keen interest in their work, which, as reviewers noticed, was at once so recognisably regional and so '[c]uriously' inflected. The 'firm, strong, vigorous and geometric structures' that demonstrated Prichard's 'love of the mineral world' and gave 'power and foundation to his landscapes' struck one French art critic as 'very Cézanne-like'. And yet, while in some ways Prichard seemed 'more Breton than the Bretons', the artist's 'love for this Brittany of ours' also appeared to be 'reinforced, exalted, enriched and magnified by the love' he 'still retains' for 'harsh, severe and honest' Wales.[106]

Indeed, during the couple's decade in Rochefort, Prichard returned to Wales at regular intervals to paint in Snowdonia National Park and to teach there at Plas Tan y Bwlch (fig. 50). The studies he made along the Precipice Walk, looking down towards the Mawddach Estuary and across to Cadair Idris, served as *aides-mémoires* for some of the compositions in oil that he produced of Welsh subjects while living in France (figs 47–48 & 51). 'Once you start painting Wales,' he realised, 'you're physically in Wales. You can even feel the wind and the rain.'[107] No lesser aids to Prichard's memory were the environs of Rochefort themselves; the domestic architecture, the granite outcrops, the oak trees and bracken on the hillside, and the slate mines nearby all brought to mind some of the places he had visited and painted in North Wales, particularly of the Welsh market town of Dolgellau. Prichard found it 'easy' to live and work in Brittany, he told an interviewer during his time there, 'because it is … very much like Wales'.[108] Meanwhile,

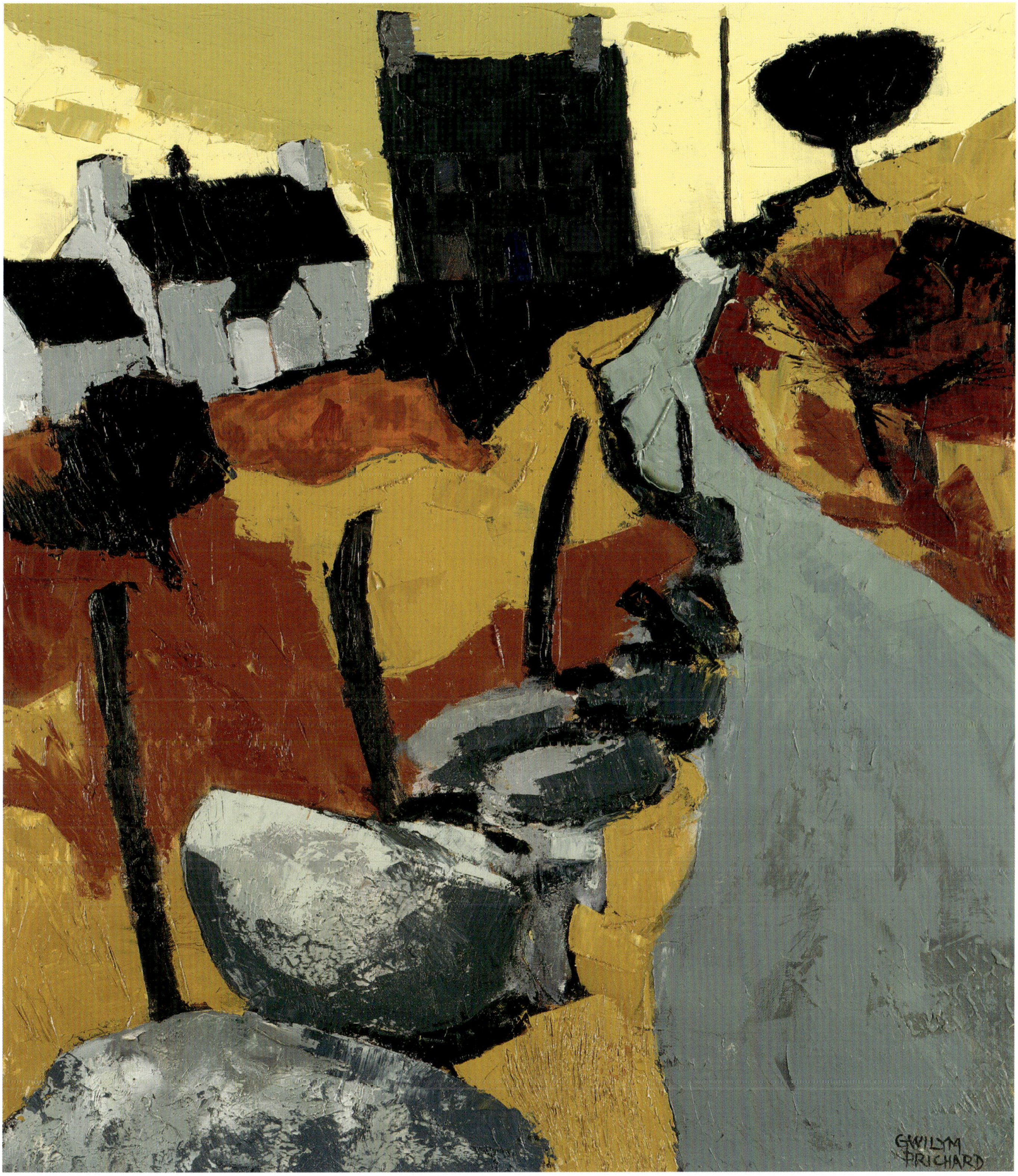

Fig. 51
Cwm Pennant
1998 | oil on canvas | 55 x 46 cm
private collection, France

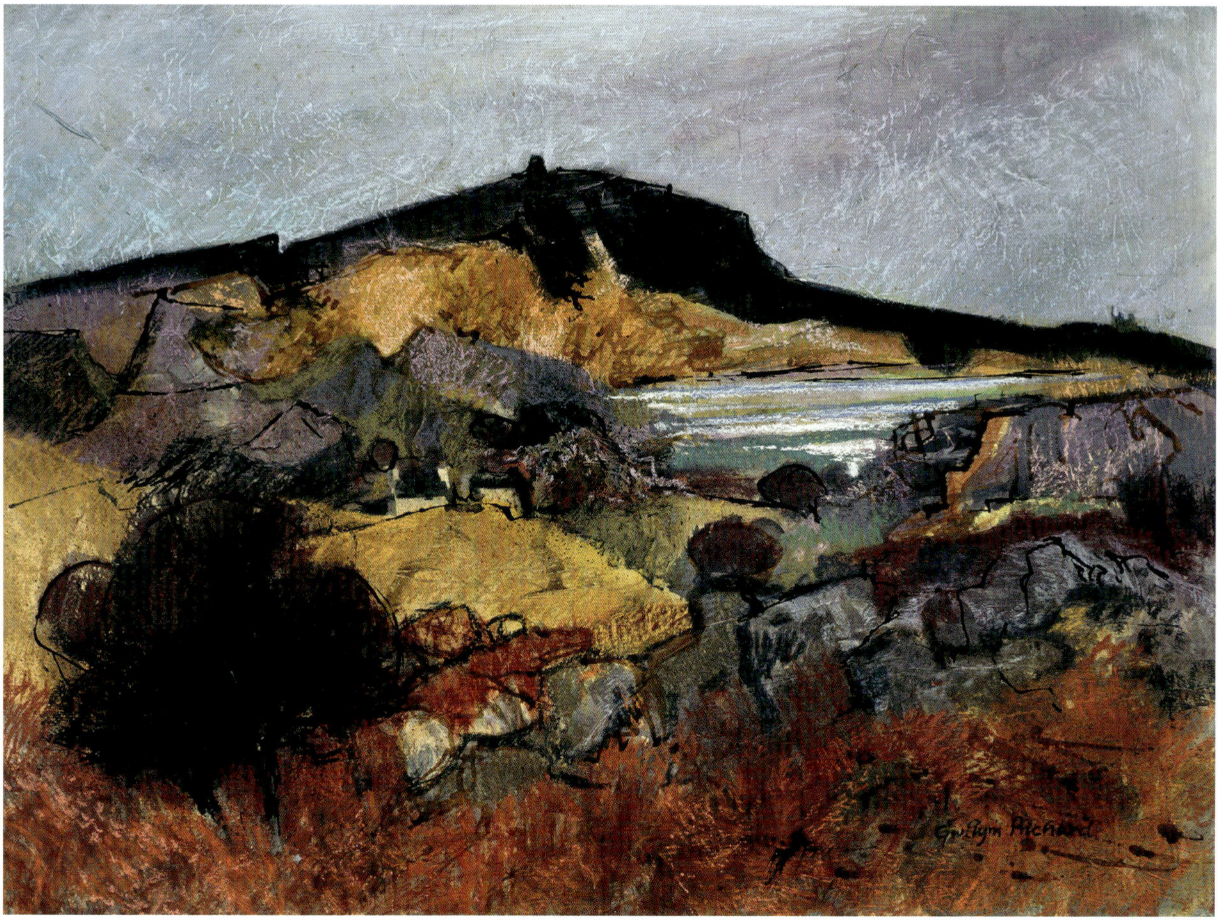

Fig. 52
Parys Mountain, Anglesey
1996 | oil on canvas | 46 x 65 cm
private collection, UK

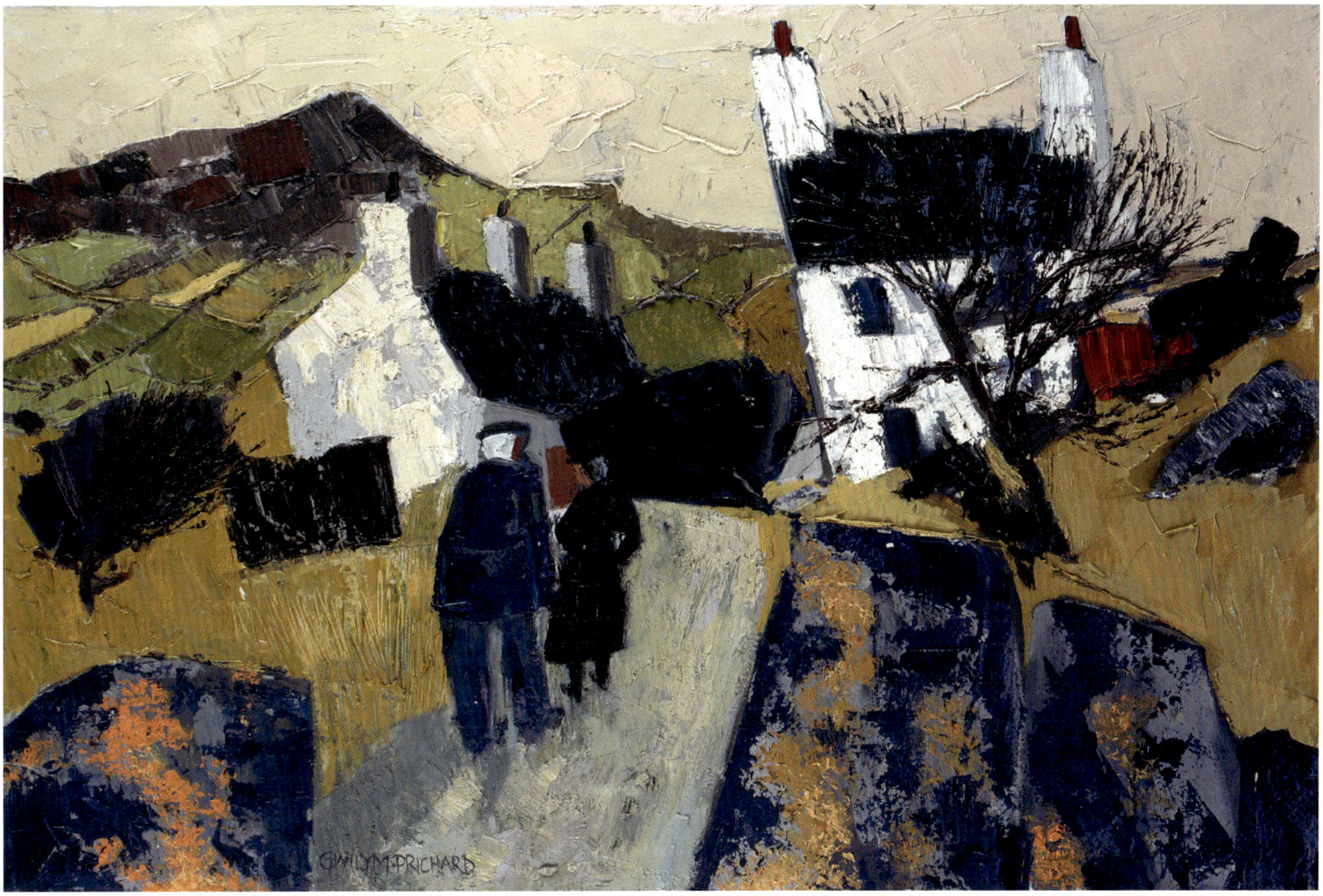

Fig. 53
Yn ôl o'r Capel
1966 | oil on canvas | 51 x 76 cm
private collection, UK

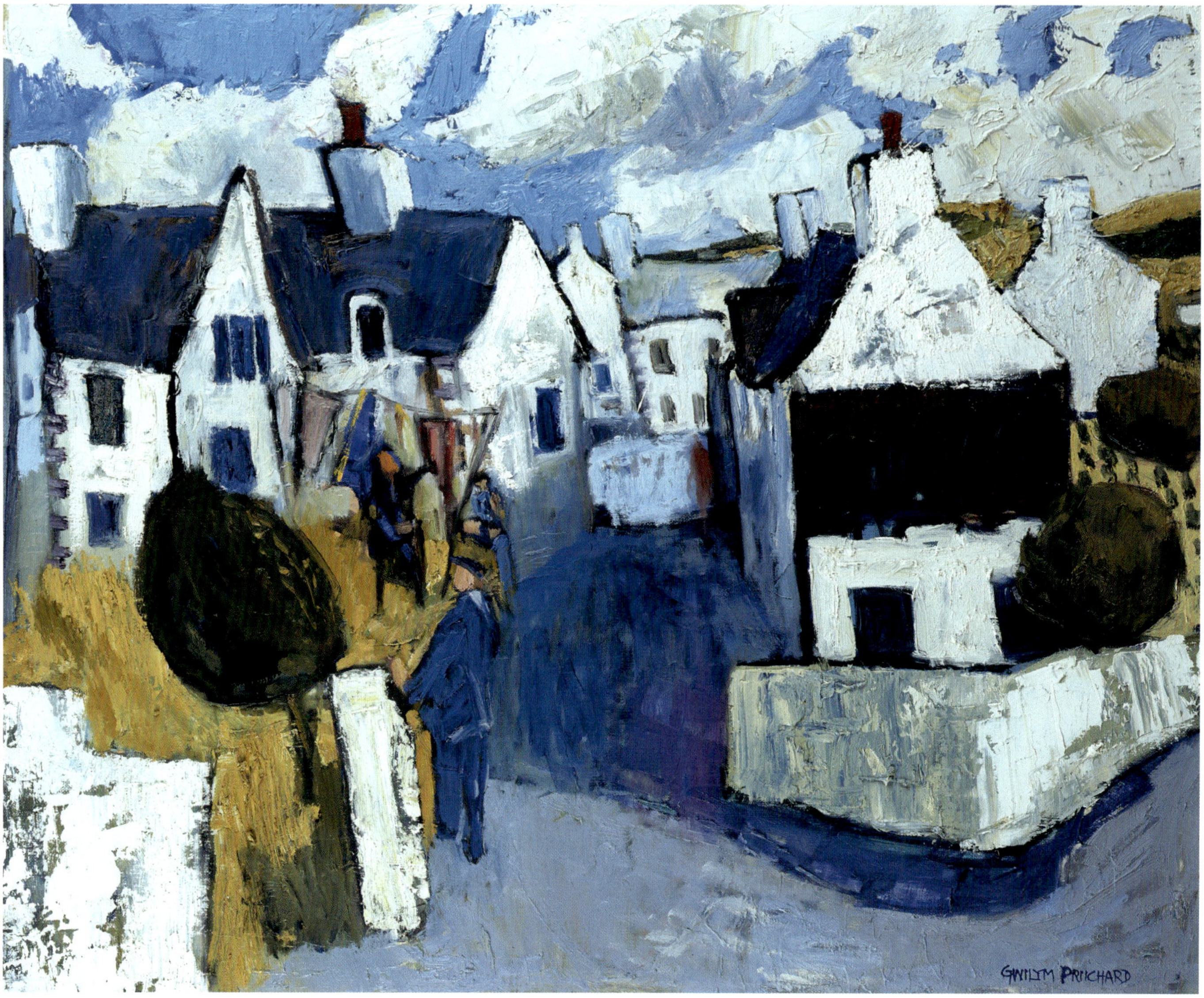

Fig. 54
Sunday Morning, Lesconil
1993 | oil on canvas | 60 x 73 cm
private collection, UK

Prichard's Welsh landscapes from that period betoken an artist whose eye has become accustomed to the light of the Brittany coastline. Just as Richard Wilson, who returned from Italy to bathe Cadair Idris in the warm light of the Roman Campagna, or Augustus John, who approached the Arenig Mountains in the remembered glory of the Provençal sun, Prichard now painted scenes such as *Parys Mountain* (1996; fig. 52), *Cwm Pennant Valley* (1998; fig. 51) and *Penmaenpool* (2000; fig. 55) in increasingly unmodulated planes of vibrant colours. 'And all the landscape under survey, / At tranquil turns, by nature's rule,' Gerard Manley Hopkins wrote on location in 1876, 'Rides repeated topsyturvy, / In frank, in fairy Penmaen Pool.'[109] Not restricted to 'nature's rule', or to a way of looking and painting that may have been second nature to him, it is Prichard who turns topsy-turvy our perception of the Welsh landscape and what it should look like when it is 'under survey' of his

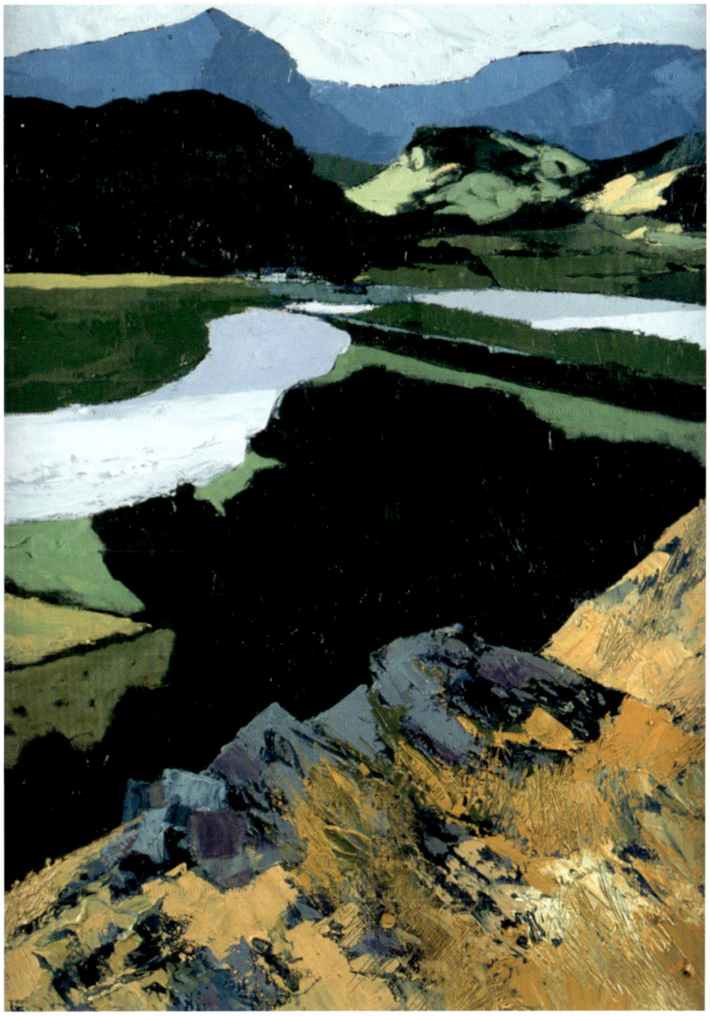

Fig. 55
Penmaenpool
2000 | oil on canvas | 73 x 54 cm
private collection, UK

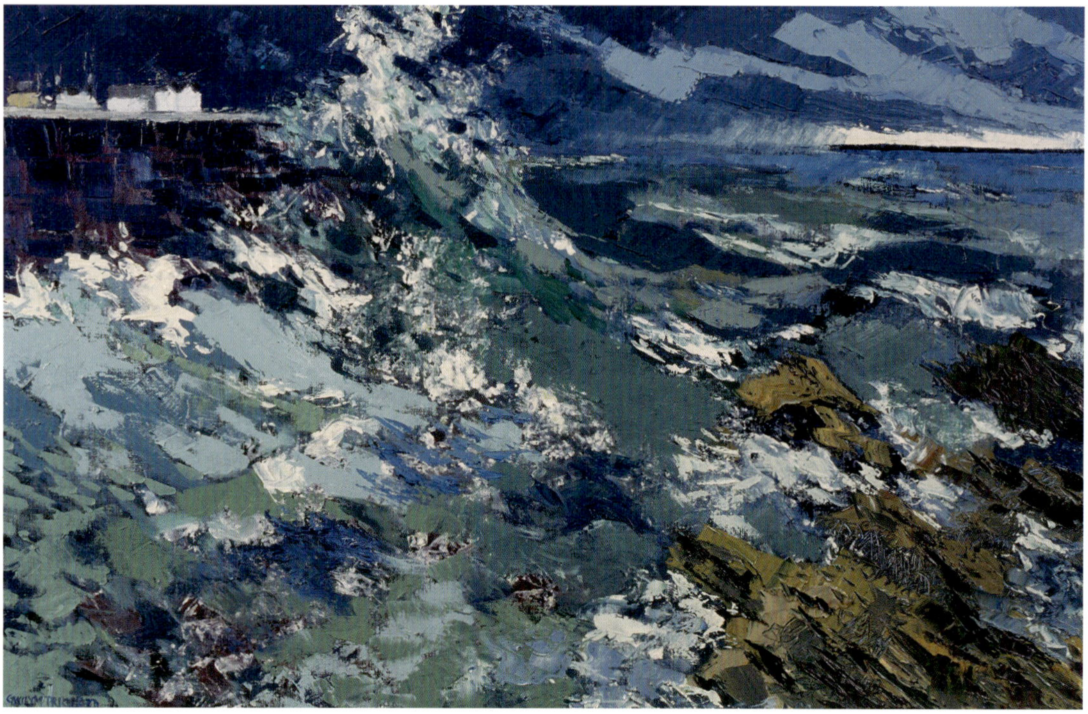

Fig. 56
Storm at Lesconil
1998 | oil on canvas | 50 x 65 cm
private collection, France

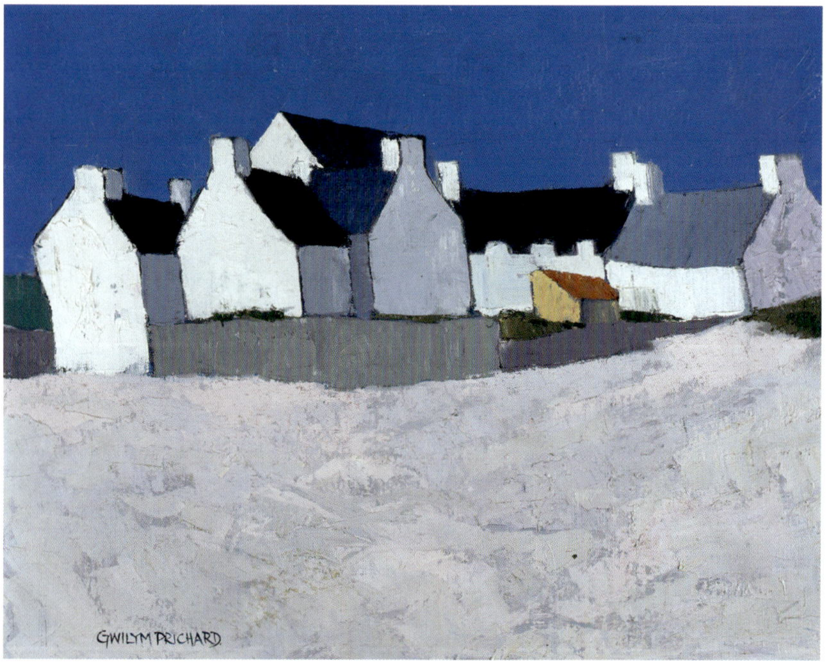

Fig. 57
Lesconil, Brittany
1989 | oil on canvas | 46 x 55 cm
private collection, France

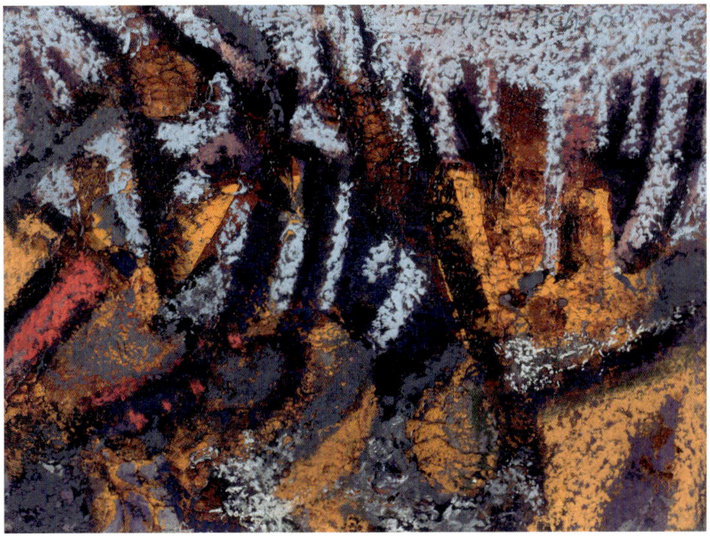

Fig. 58
Carcass I
1996 | mixed media on paper | 14 x 19 cm
the artist

searching eye. Once again, a return to the familiar for yet another look constituted a creative renewal, transfiguration rather than *déjà vu* (fig. 61).

During their time in Rochefort, Prichard and Williams went on expeditions throughout Brittany (fig. 60). Along the coast, Prichard painted the small fishing port of Lesconil, the jagged rock formations at Finistère, or 'land's end' (figs 54 & 56 57), beyond which they explored the island community of Belle Ile (fig. 59). In the seaside village of Camaret, he painted derelict fishing boats, the remains of whose structural frameworks he explored in near-abstract compositions such as *Carcass I* (1996; fig. 58). The lifeless form suggested in a title referring both to a disused hull and the body of a dead animal is not the site of nostalgia, of longing or mourning; rather, it is a sight transformed and inspirited in the act of abstraction. What Prichard brought to Brittany from his native land, a French reviewer observed, was a 'new way of looking';[110] imported or inspired, it invigorated artist and viewers alike. The cultural exchange apparent in his canvases was reinforced when, in 1992, Prichard and Williams co-founded the Rochefort School of Creative Arts. Students, some of whom had known the artist couple during their years in Vannes, travelled as far as 60 miles to attend classes in life drawing, watercolour and sculpture. Three years later, they were each awarded the Silver Medal by the Academy of Arts, Sciences and Letters in Paris. Often seen or claimed as a representative of – or an ambassador for – Wales, Prichard, although he was made an Honorary Fellow at Bangor Universityin 2003, has yet to receive any comparable honours in Wales; to this date, his works are not represented in the collection of the National Museum and Gallery of Wales.

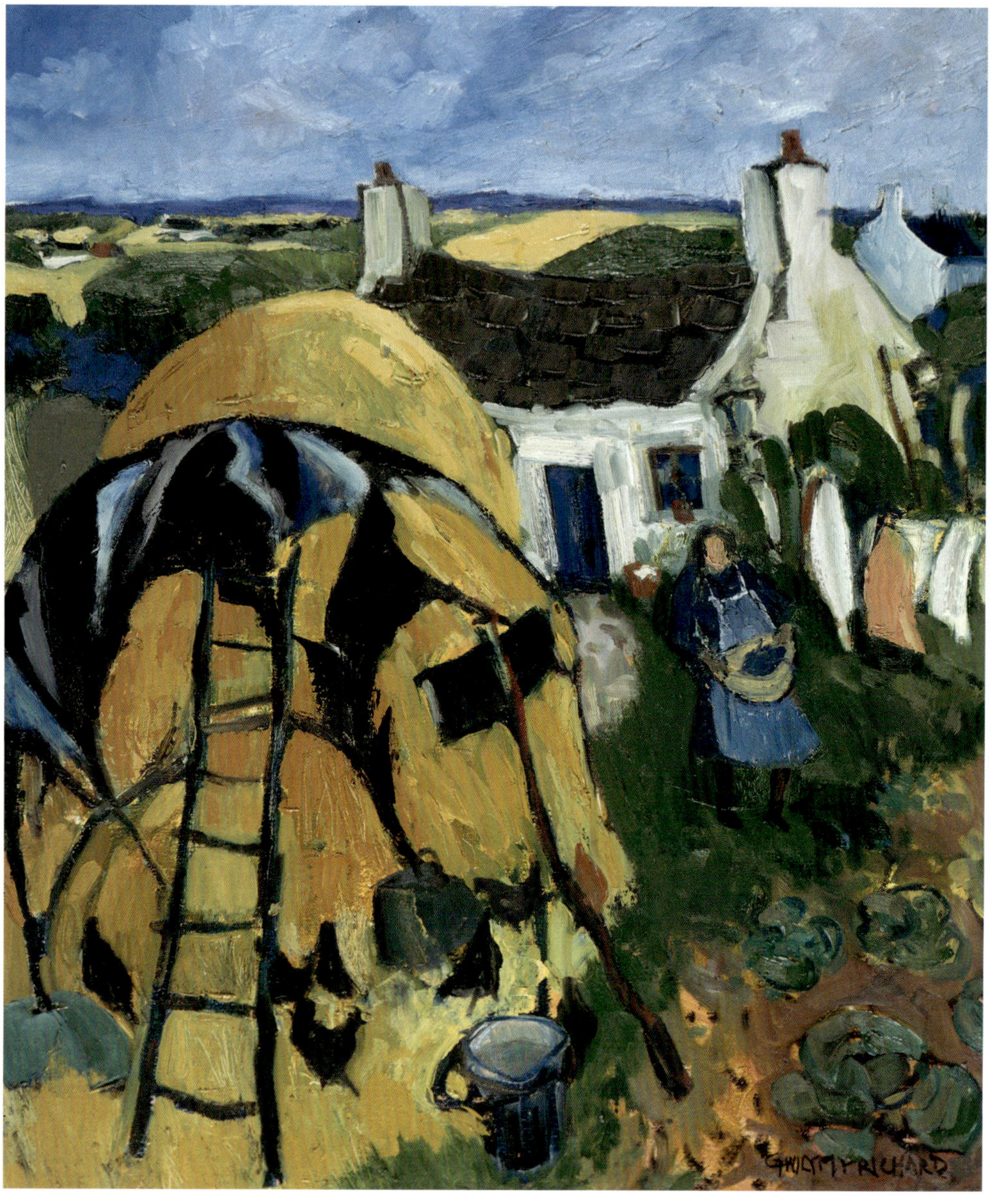

Fig. 59

Washing Day, Belle Ile

oil on canvas | 55 x 38 cm

private collection, France

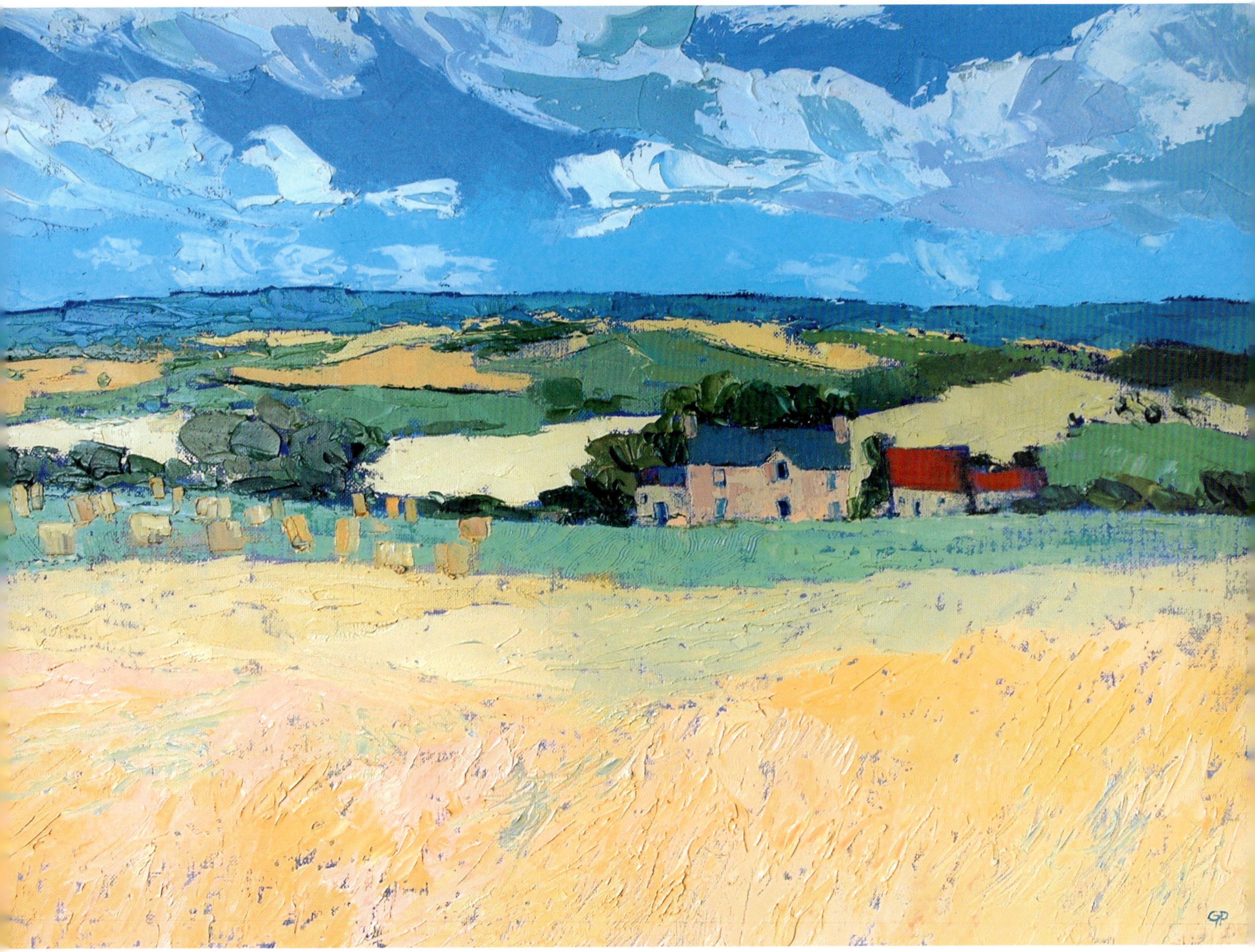

Fig. 60
Summer, Brittany
2004 | oil on canvas | 54 x 73 cm
private collection, UK

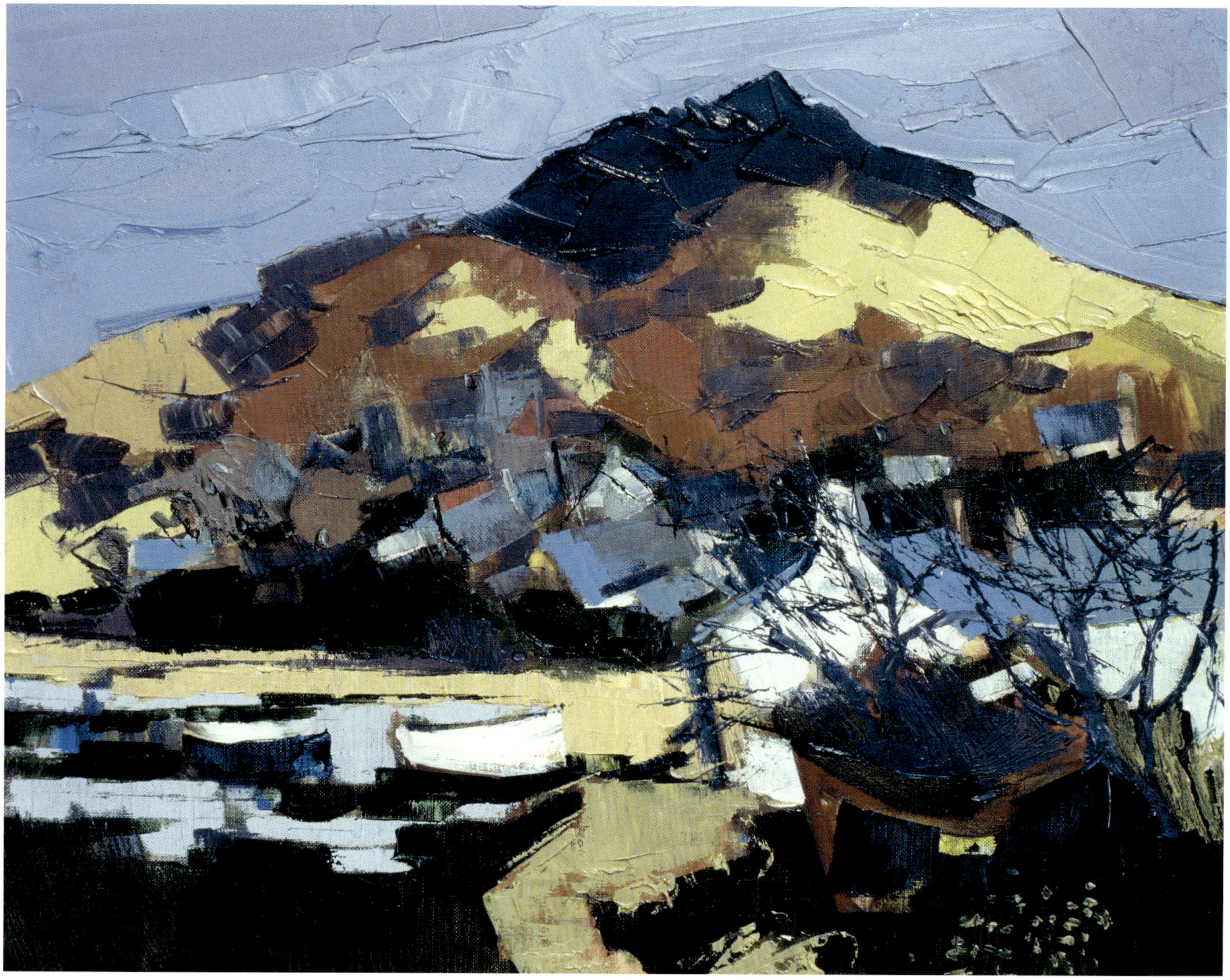

Fig. 61
Y Parrog with Garn Llidi
1997 | oil on canvas | 50 x 65 cm
private collection, UK

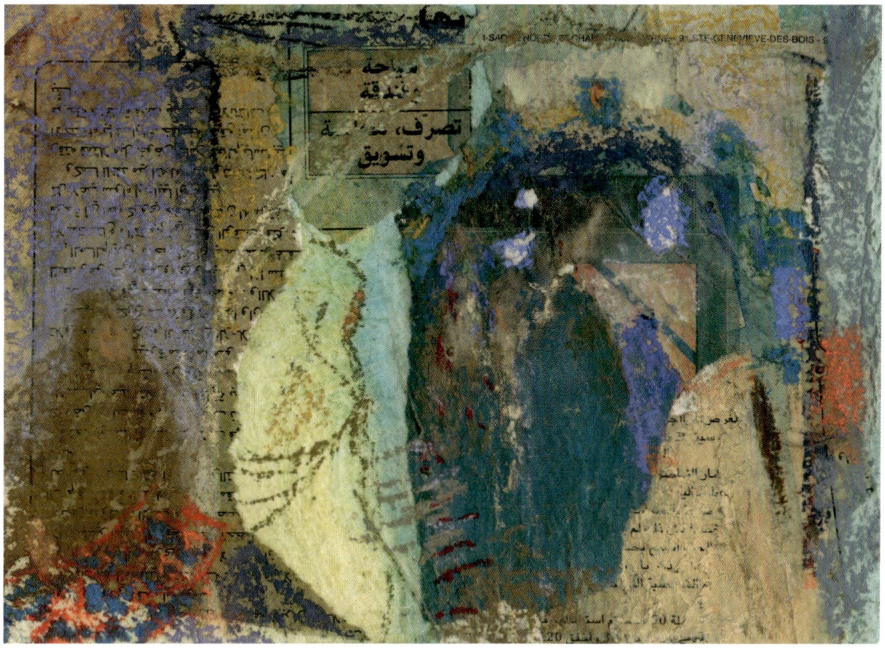

Fig. 62
Souk, Mahdia, Tunisia
1996 | collage and mixed media on paper
14 x 19 cm
private collection, France

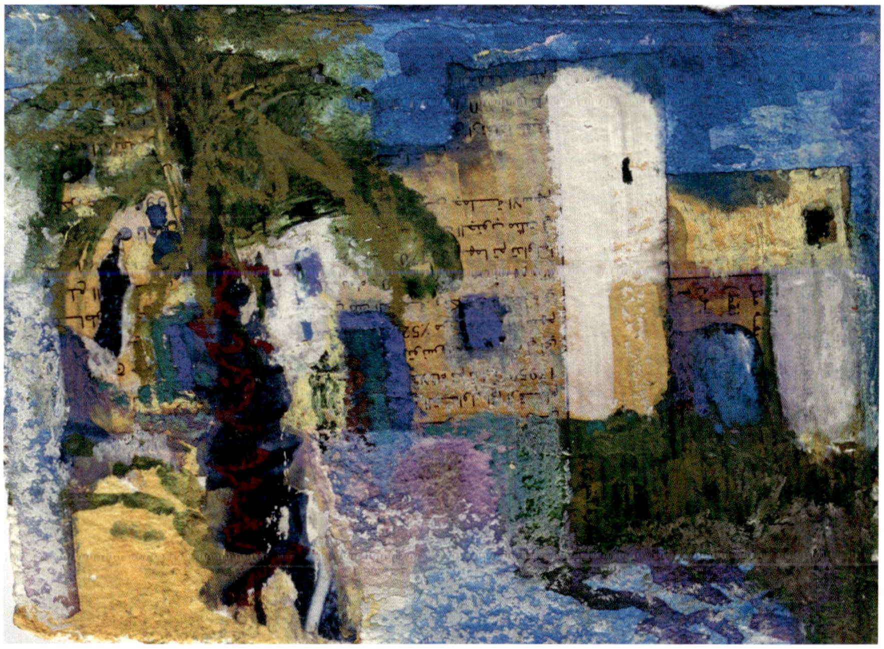

Fig. 63
Street in Mahdia, Tunisia
1996 | collage and mixed media on paper
14 x 19 cm
private collection, France

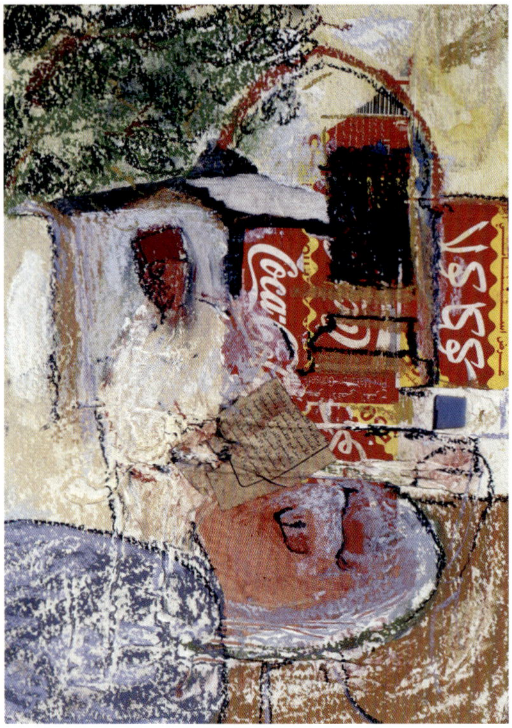

Fig. 64
Café, Mahdia, Tunisia
1996 | collage and mixed media on paper
33 x 25 cm
private collection, France

In 1996, during the couple's residence in Brittany, Prichard made three painting expeditions to Tunisia. The opportunity arose when a friend, who had been based in Tunisia during his military days, bought a house there and invited Prichard to join him on a drive down to Genoa, from which port they sailed to Sicily and from there on to Tunis. Prichard worked at Sidi Bou Said on the coast near the capital and further south at Mahdia. In the few oil paintings resulting from his visits, most notable among them *Village in Tunisia* (1996; fig. 65), Prichard approaches unfamiliar subjects with the impasto and palette-knife techniques with which his work is most often associated. He takes an entirely different approach to the scenes before him in the mixed-media paintings he produced here of mosques, souks and street cafés, which appear to have evolved as he applied and manipulated his materials: gesso, watercolours, chalk, pastel, pencil and wax resist (figs 62 & 63). His bright collages, some of which feature printed matter in cursive Arabic script along-side Coca-Cola labels, are a playful take on notions of foreign-ness and familiarity (fig. 64). East and West, ancient and con-temporary, cultural and commercial are not so much confronted as they are joyfully cancelled out in an uncanny constellation of signs and symbols. At the same time, these collages also resemble the cheerful travel journals the young family pro-duced on their journeys to Italy in 1963 and Ireland in 1968, which are a bright and wondrous assemblage of postcards, maps, bottle labels and tickets, accompanied by drawings contributed by the travellers – mementoes of paper and paste that bring home the thrill of being abroad.

Mixed-media works like Prichard's impressions of Tunisia, which were shown at the Galerie Saphir in Paris in a solo exhibition titled 'La Tunisie d'un Gallois', resist classification and thus help confront commonly held assumptions about Prichard's art, their subject matter and techniques, that have remained unchallenged. As late as 1989, for instance, Jonah Jones observed that it had not taken Prichard long to attain 'that quality' in his art that makes it distinctive and immediately recognisable:

> *'Look, there's a Gwilym Prichard,' I have often heard, for there is an unmistakable quality to them, rich paint, spontaneous brush-work, fearless colour combinations but above all, that deep sense of Celtic colour and form.*[111]

Being 'unmistakable' is a rather dubious mark of distinction as familiarity implies a lack of growth or a resistance to change. It bespeaks the apparently unique and original but at the same time suggests that stylistic originality is an effort on the part of the originator to keep copying his most representative work. 'I haven't got a formula', he says; nor does he have a 'favourite medium, as some are led to believe'. Instead, Prichard maintains, the

> *choice rests upon my feelings, and also on the spot where I happen to be at the time. The challenge and the thrill I*

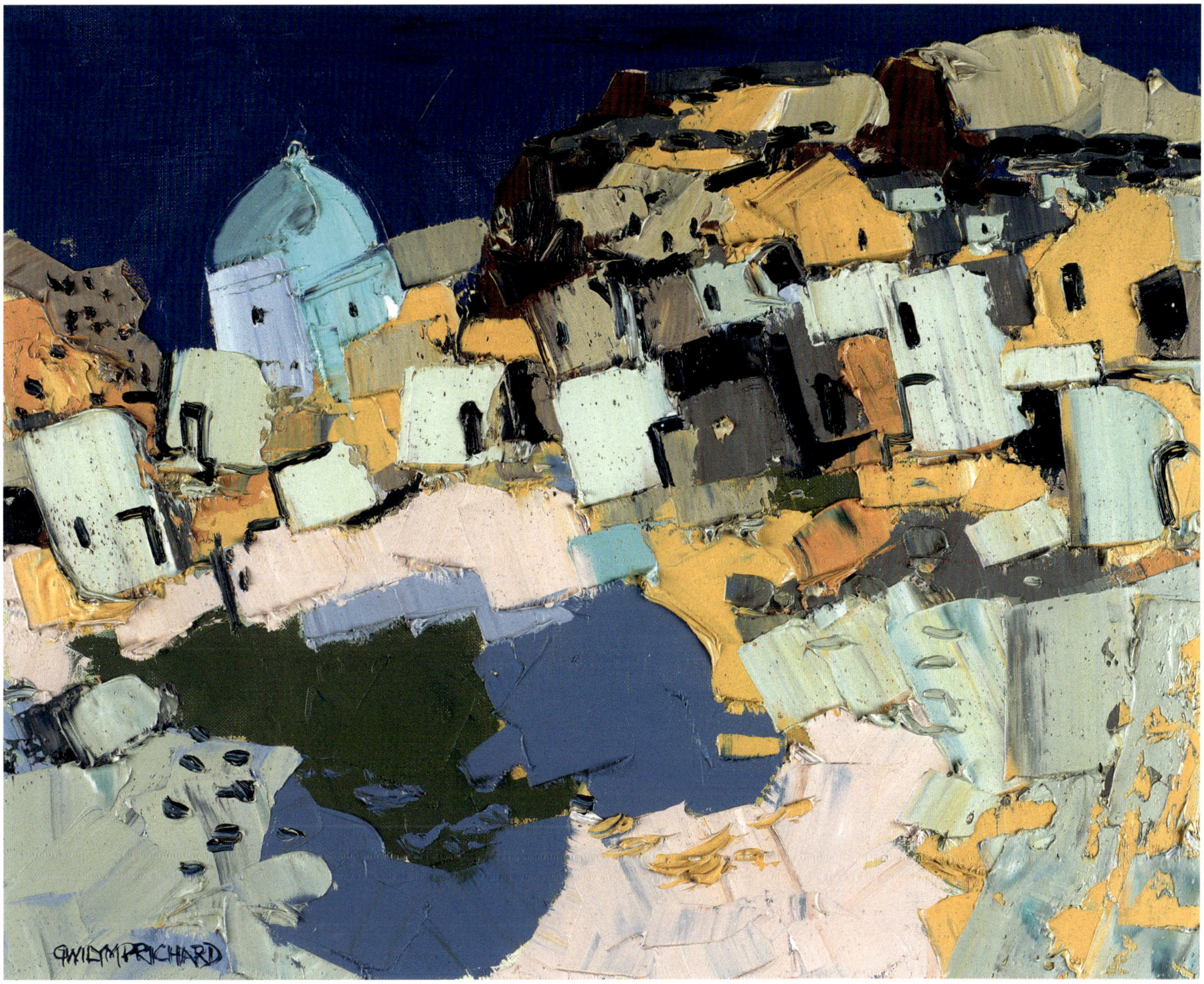

Fig. 65
Village in Tunisia
1998 | oil on canvas | 50 x 61 cm
private collection, UK

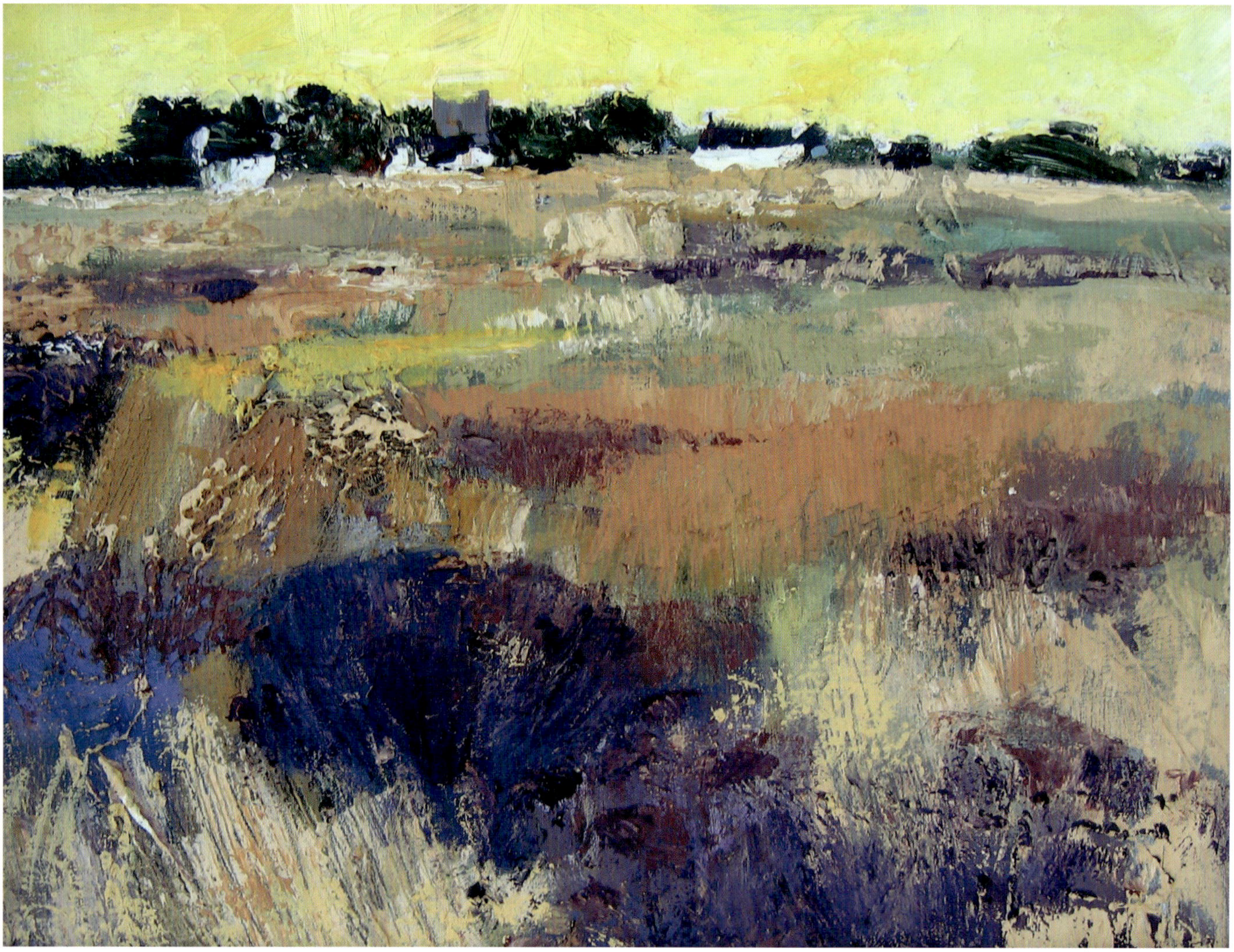

Fig. 66
Saint Armel, Brittany
1988 | oil on canvas | 24 x 33 cm
the artist

> *still experience is the uniqueness of the day and of every piece of work; nothing is repeated.*[112]

Perversely, the claim to immediate recognisability also resulted in Prichard being seen as a follower of Kyffin Williams and in Prichard's work being closely and almost invariably associated with Williams' distinctive style. And yet, the techniques of the two artists differ considerably and, even in his application of oil paint, Prichard's range is much broader and rather more experimental: he uses thinned washes that are scraped and scored, as in *Thorn Trees* (1960; fig. 70); thick, slab-like application of impastoed oils, applied with a palette knife, as in *Storm, Penmon Point* (1997; fig. 69), *Aberaeron in the Snow* (2001; fig. 71) and *Traeth y De* (2005; fig. 67); as well as sgraffito and surface attrition, as in *Cnicht* (*c.*1992; fig. 73). As Williams noted, Prichard's 'work shows traces of struggle, physical and mental. He obviously fights the picture to try and achieve the end that is always in his mind'.[113] The 'act of working the paint' is a struggle that Prichard 'enjoy[s]'.[114] His canvases are not merely responses to a landscape or visualisations of feelings evoked by a specific place; they are also a painterly celebration of the medium. 'I tend to paint in the same way as I cook,' he once explained, 'I add a bit of this and a bit of that … I like playing with the stuff!'[115] (figs 66 & 73–75). Experimenting 'with tones and textures' is to him the 'exciting part' of his work:

> *Sometimes I scrape the paint thinly onto the canvas and then ... drag thicker paint of a darker tone over the first. Again, I might scratch through the top paint to show the underpainting. I try and achieve the effect that I want without overworking the paint, otherwise it tends to 'die' or become lifeless.*[116]

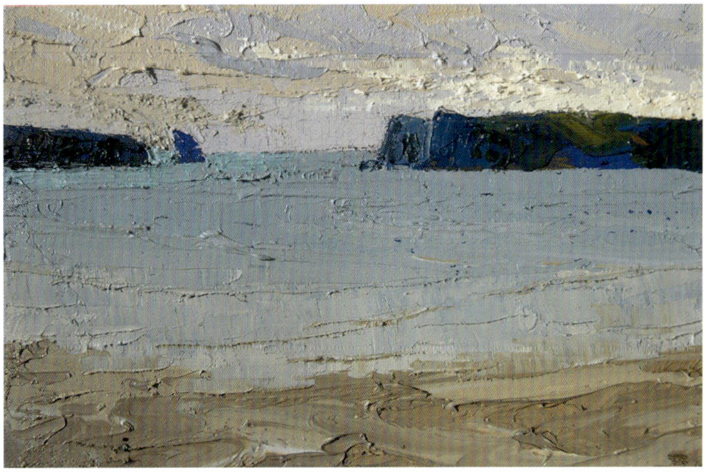

Fig. 67
Traeth y De
2005 | oil on canvas | 19 x 27 cm
private collection, UK

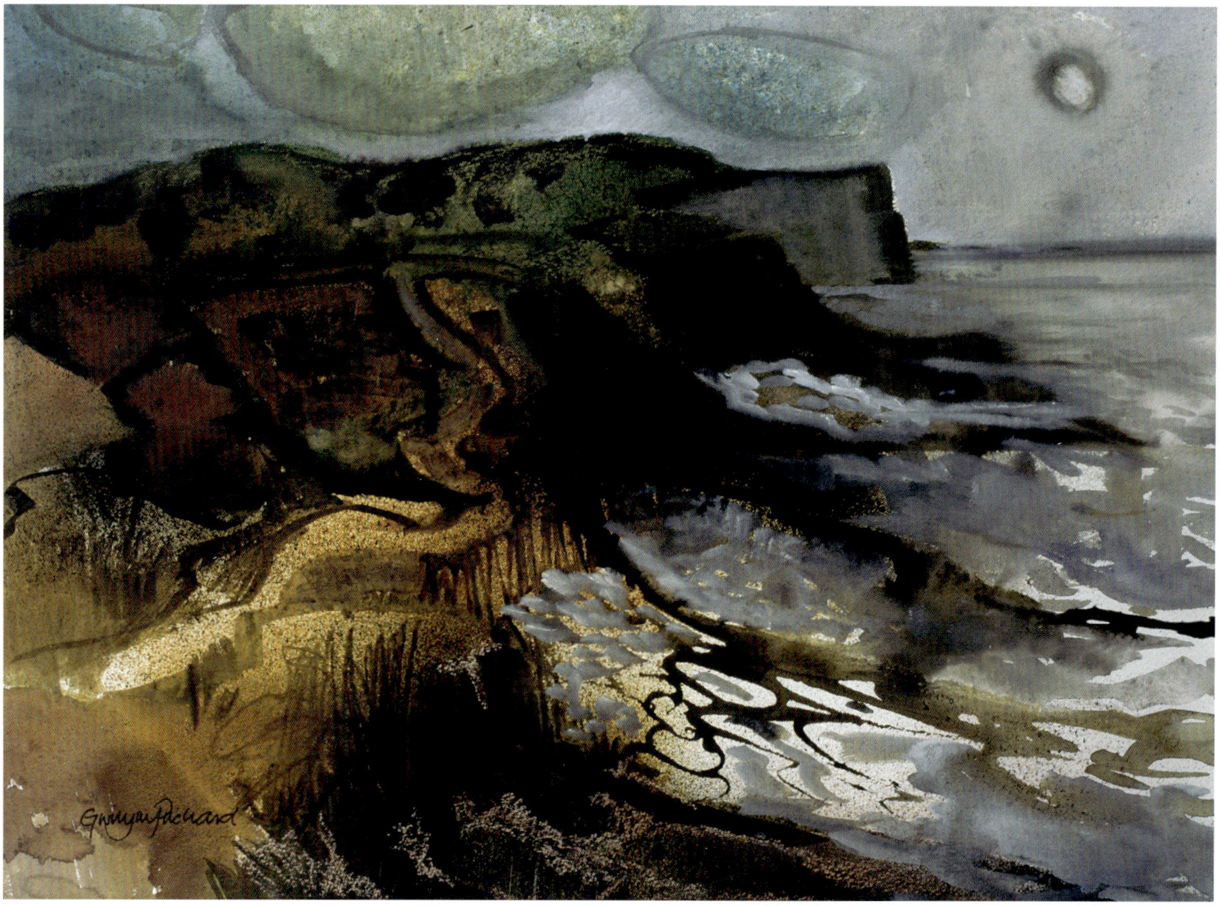

Fig. 68

Penmon

1993 | mixed media on paper | 53 x 74 cm

National Library of Wales, Aberystwyth

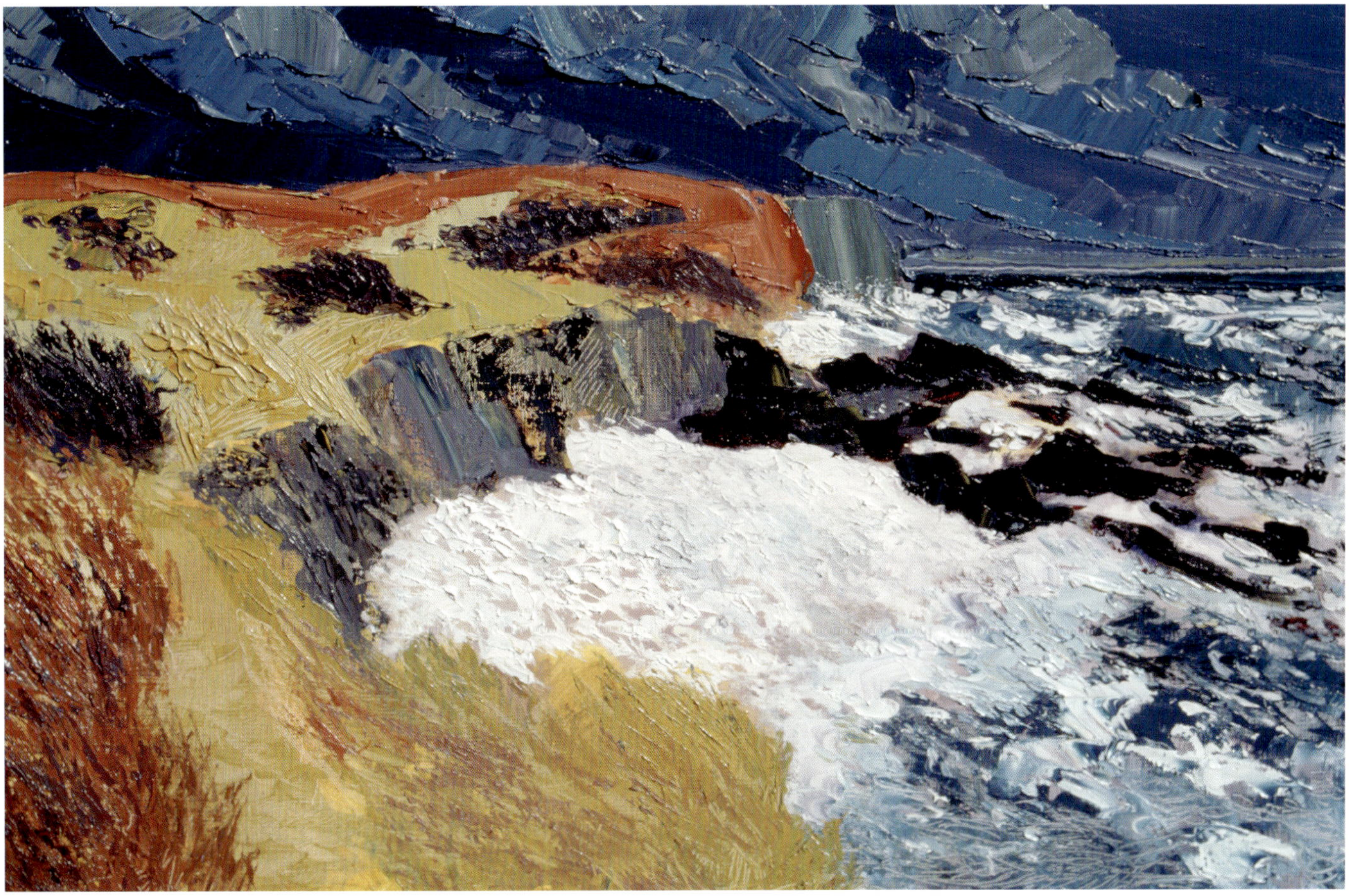

Fig. 69
Storm, Penmon Point
1997 | oil on canvas | 60 x 92 cm
private collection, UK

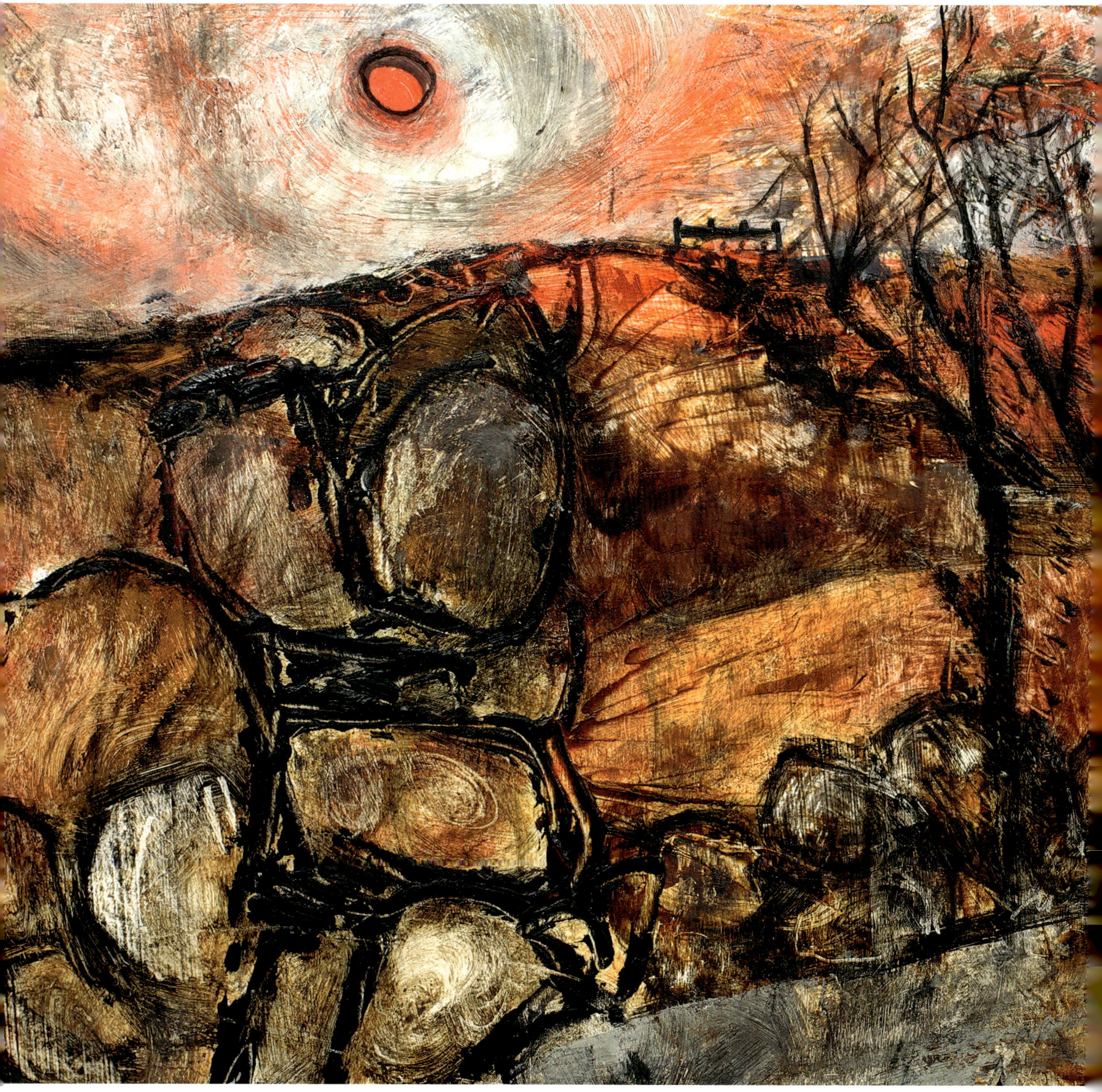

Fig. 70
Thorn Trees
1960 | oil on board | 32 x 61 cm
Aberystwyth University

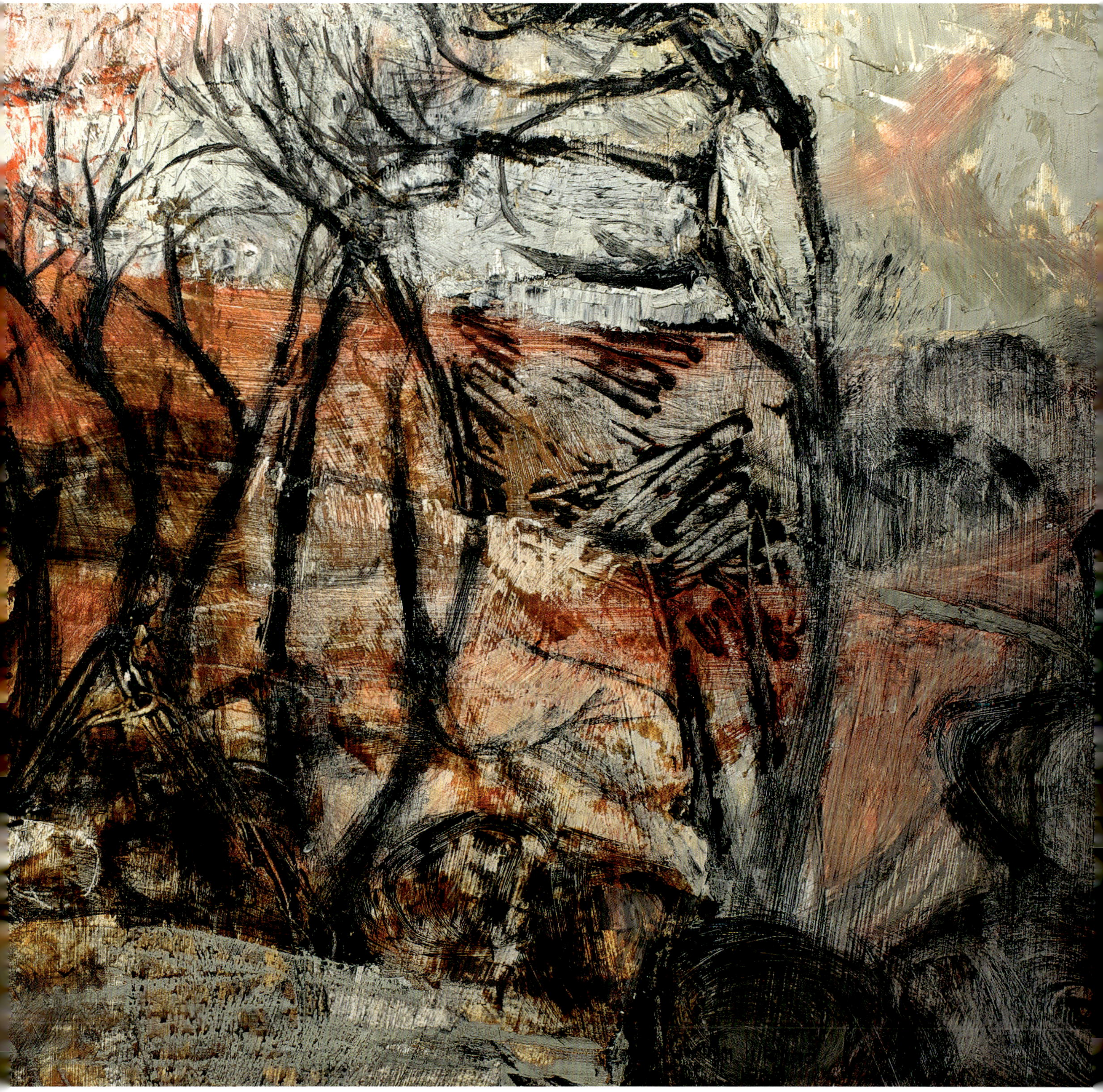

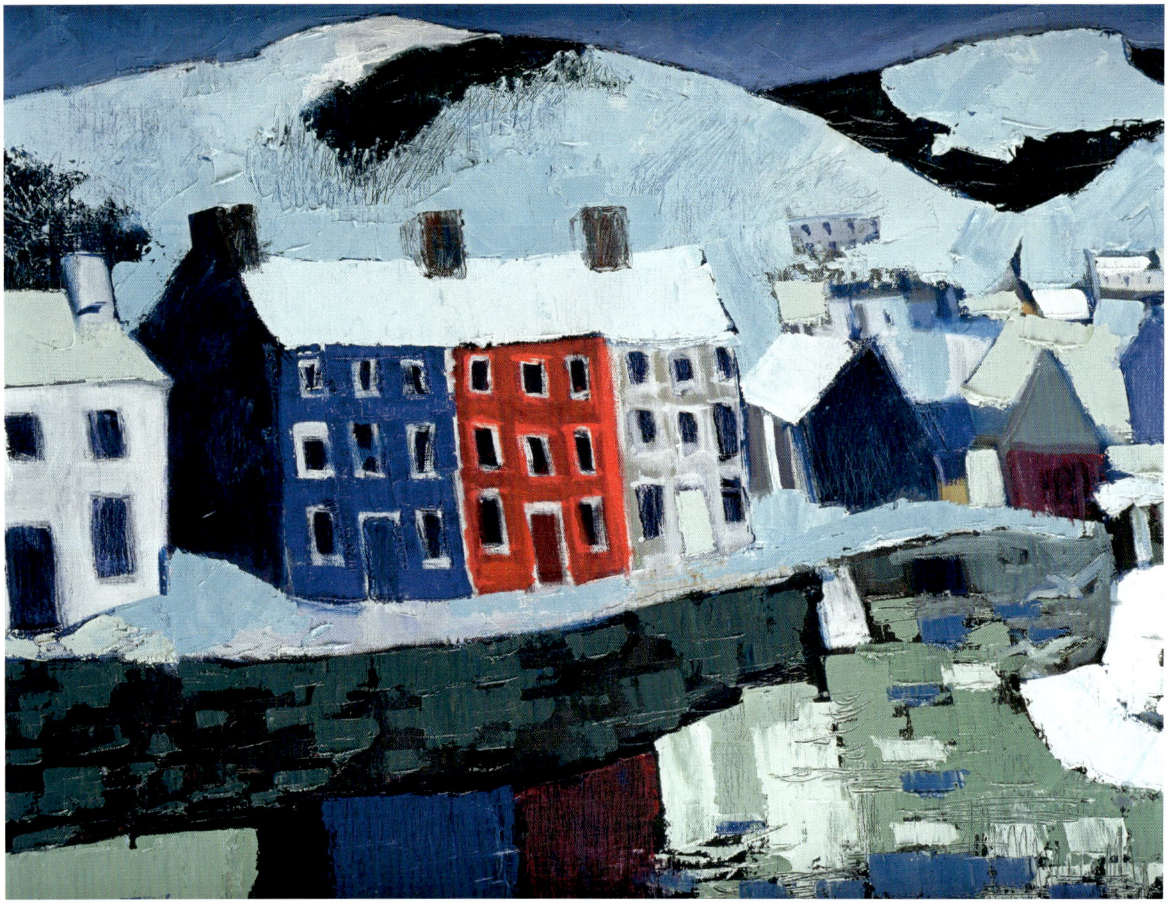

Fig. 71
Aberaeron in the Snow
2001 | oil on canvas | 50 x 65 cm
private collection, UK

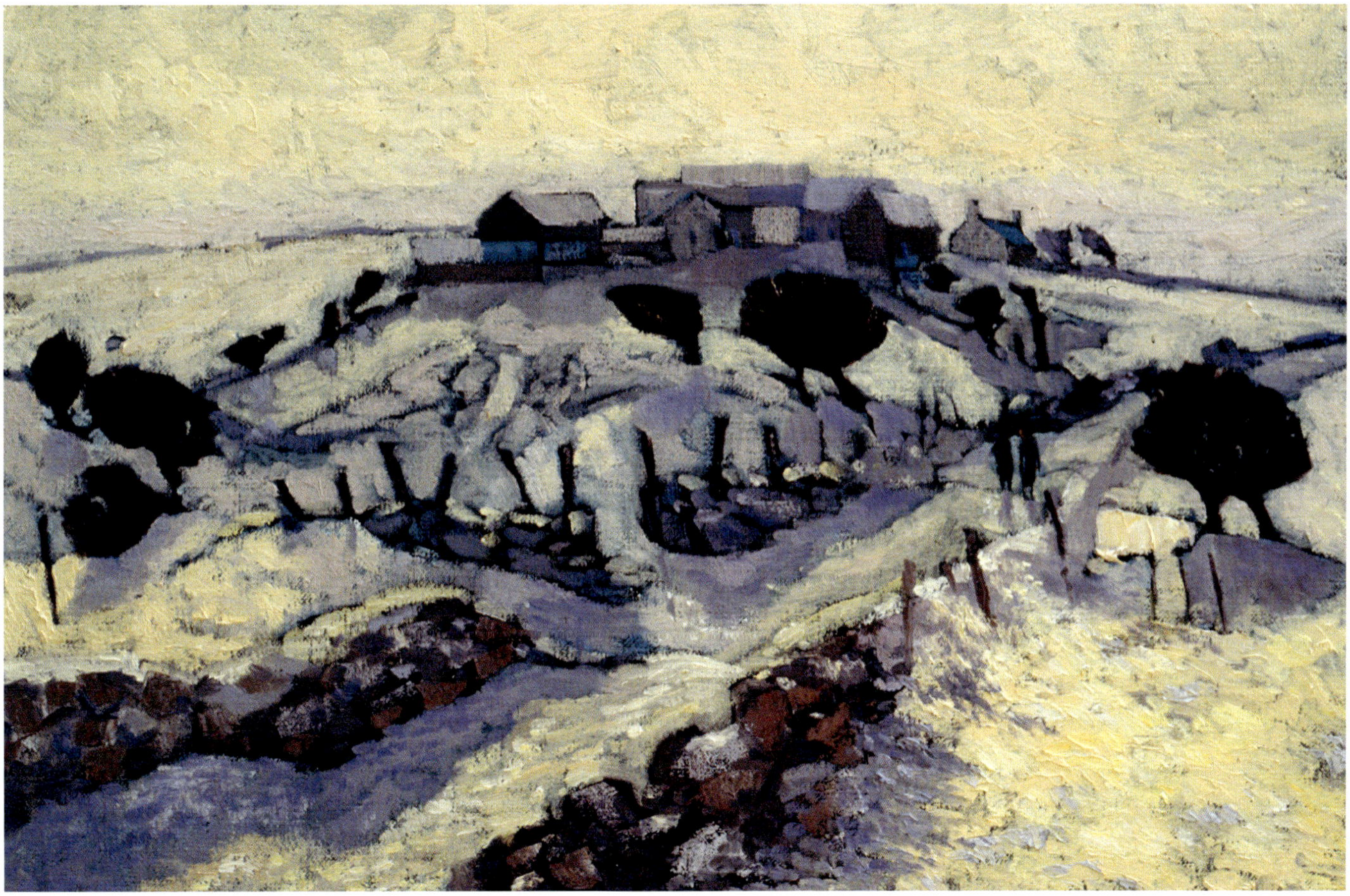

Fig. 72
Aberffraw
1988 | oil on canvas | 61 x 92 cm
private collection, UK

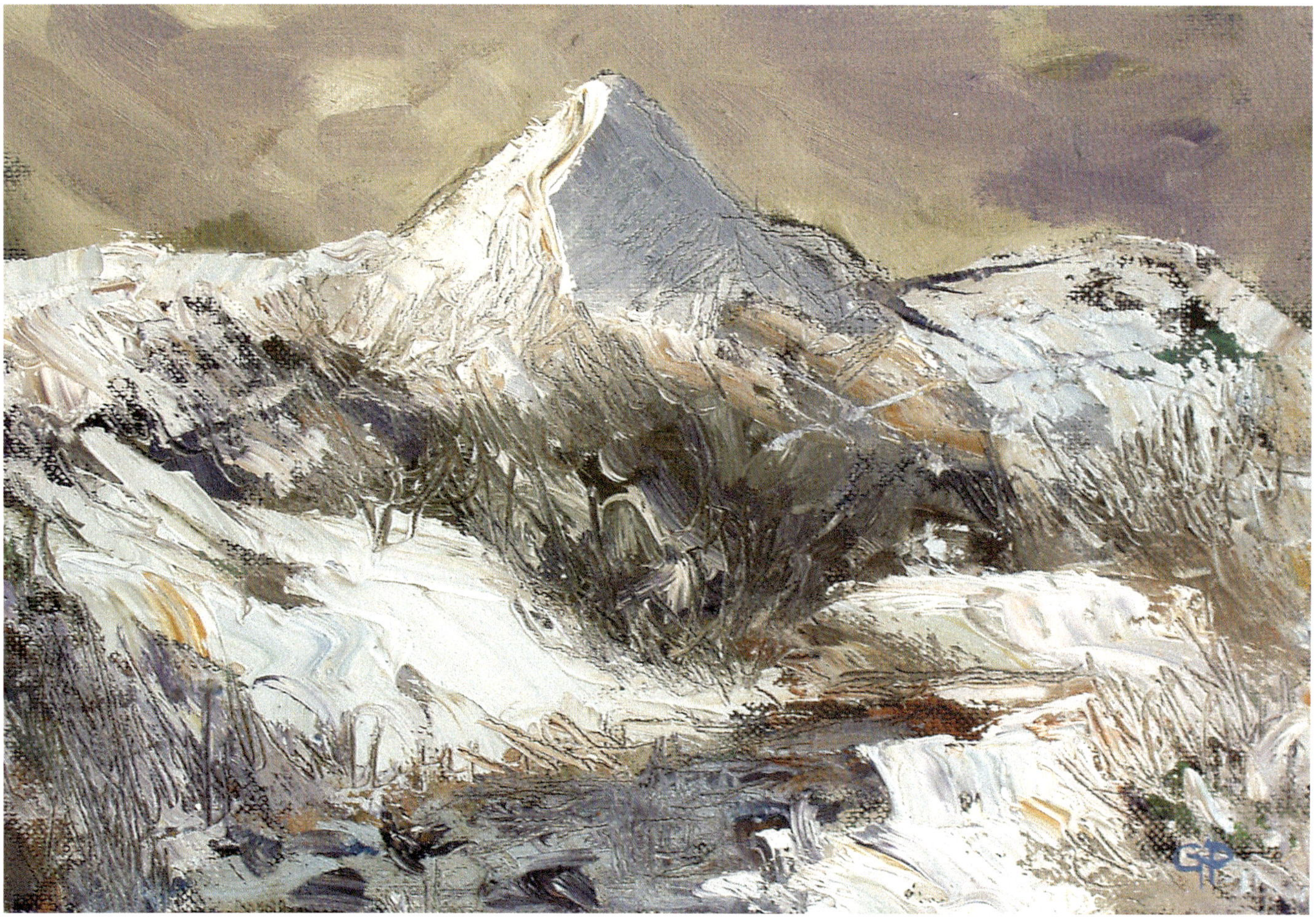

Fig. 73
Cnicht
c.1992 | oil on canvas | 38 x 55 cm
private collection, UK

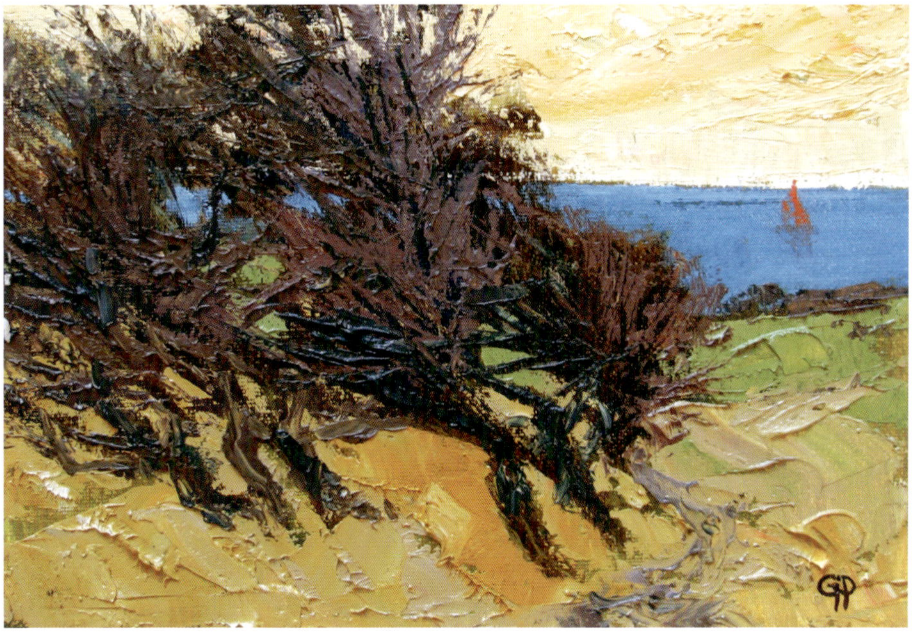

Fig. 74
Hwyl Goch
2010 | oil on canvas | 19 x 27 cm
private collection, UK

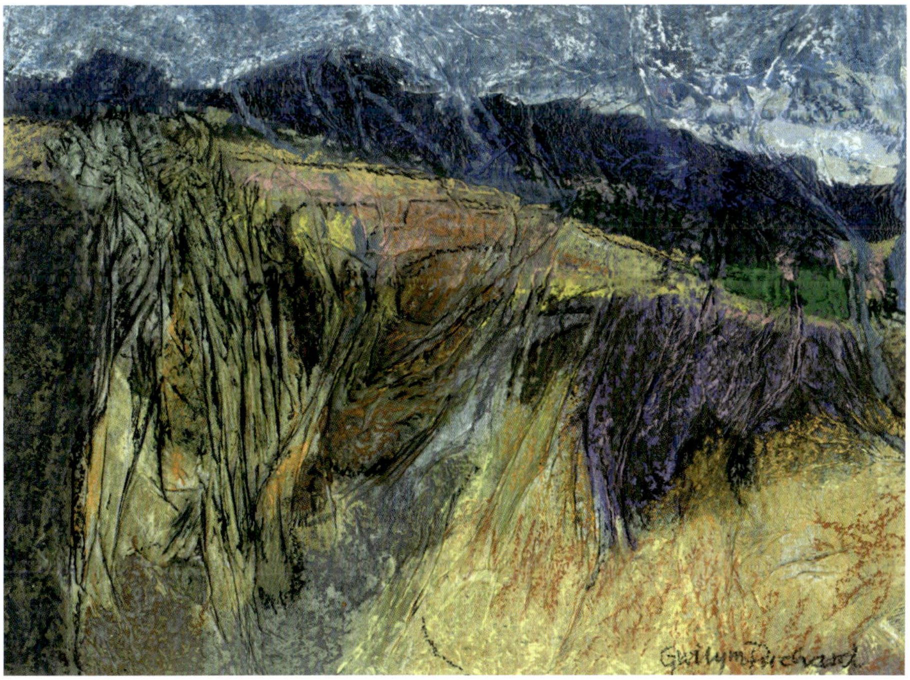

Fig. 75
Rheiniog and Thorn Trees
1996 | mixed media | 25 x 32 cm
the artist

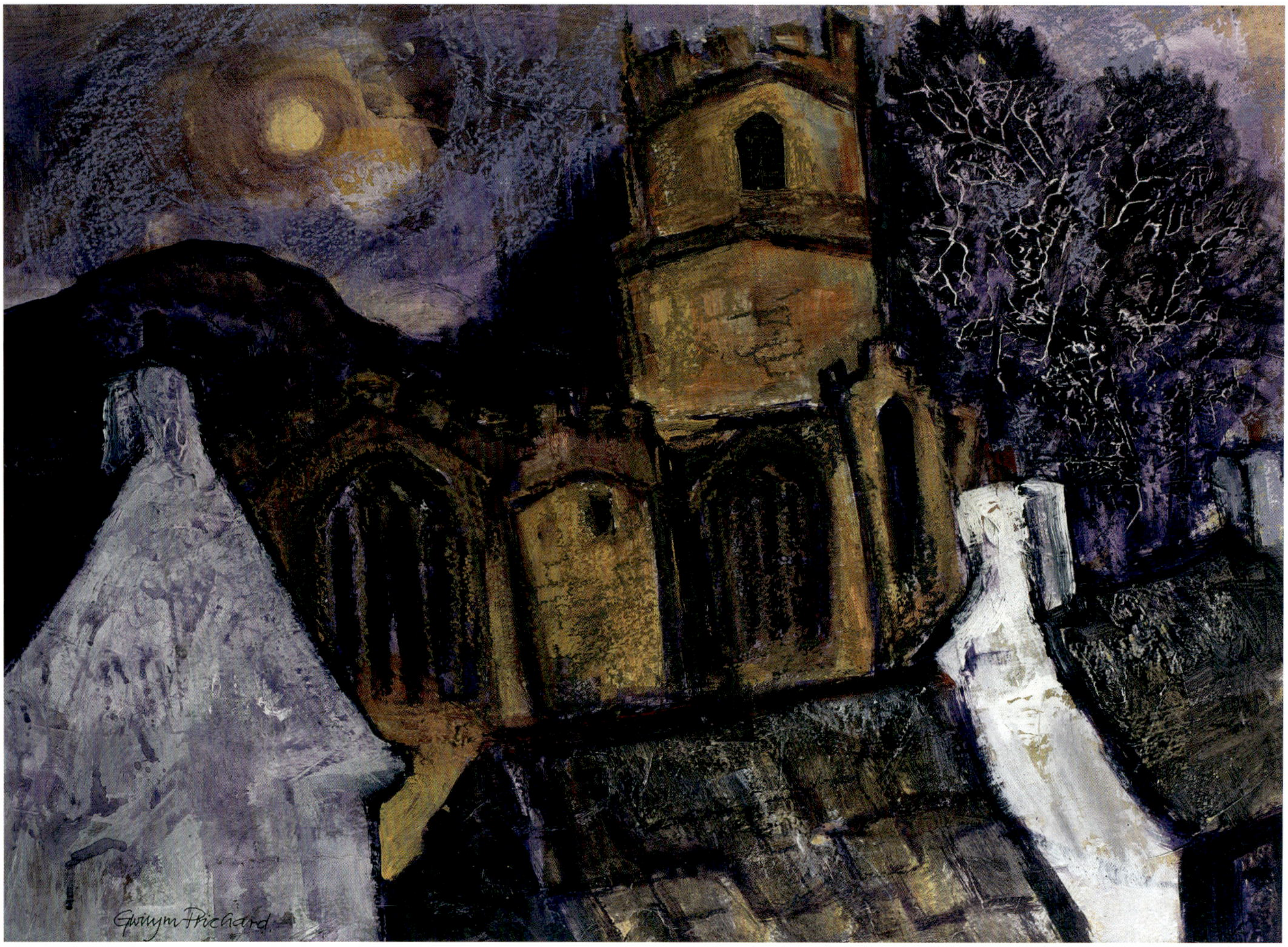

Fig. 76
Eglwys Clynnog Fawr
1990 | mixed media on paper | 64 x 75 cm
private collection, UK

To this end, Prichard remains open to the accidental, to the life and plasticity of the medium itself. '[S]omething happens' once 'you are in front of a canvas with brush and paint' – 'but not always what you want'. Manipulating the paint surface, he keeps teasing out his subjects, a process of uncovering and discovery that, for all its serendipity, is far from random. 'Scrape it off, but scrape it off intelligently', he implores:

> *[I]nstead of just cleaning it, like cleaning a mirror or some mess the cat has left about, you clean it or wash it off searching again for the painting which is underneath.*

There, artists might discover 'traces of paint' that could 'once again become part of' the composition.[117] 'The thing that I'm always afraid of is that white sheet of paper', he once declared. 'So I have to destroy that surface to start with, because to me when you have a canvas or a sheet of paper the painting is there and my problem is to find [it].'[118] '[Y]ou can see the way that I worry the paint. I'm really making it work far more to describe what I'm trying to do', he asserts.

> *I decide on vaguely the colours I'm going to use, then I splash paint over the painting and let it dribble and push it around with my fingers. And all of a sudden something happens. It's strange, but it does. If you're open, ... these 'messages' ... will suggest something ... I will then flip through my sketchbooks and usually find what I am going to paint. I will work from the sketchbook and my memory and my feelings.*[119]

Parys Mountain (1989; fig. 77), *Machlyd, Sunset* (2004; fig. 78) and *Eglwys Clynnog Fawr* (1990; fig. 76), a painting of the perpendicular gothic church of St Beuno in North Wales, are created in just such a way, from memory uncovered in the act of engaging with the media of paint and paper.

After nearly a decade in Rochefort, the long drive and overnight channel crossings to Britain were becoming rather arduous and the distance to Britain seemed greater as Williams, now a grand-mother, was anxious to be in the presence of a new generation of Pritchards growing up back in England. Yet neither Prichard nor Williams were eager to put an end to what had been a happy and productive period in both their careers. Perhaps they were, in the words of Hamlet's famous defence, 'but mad north-north-west', when they decided to buy a second property in Wales and to continue to divide their time between northwest France and the west of Britain.

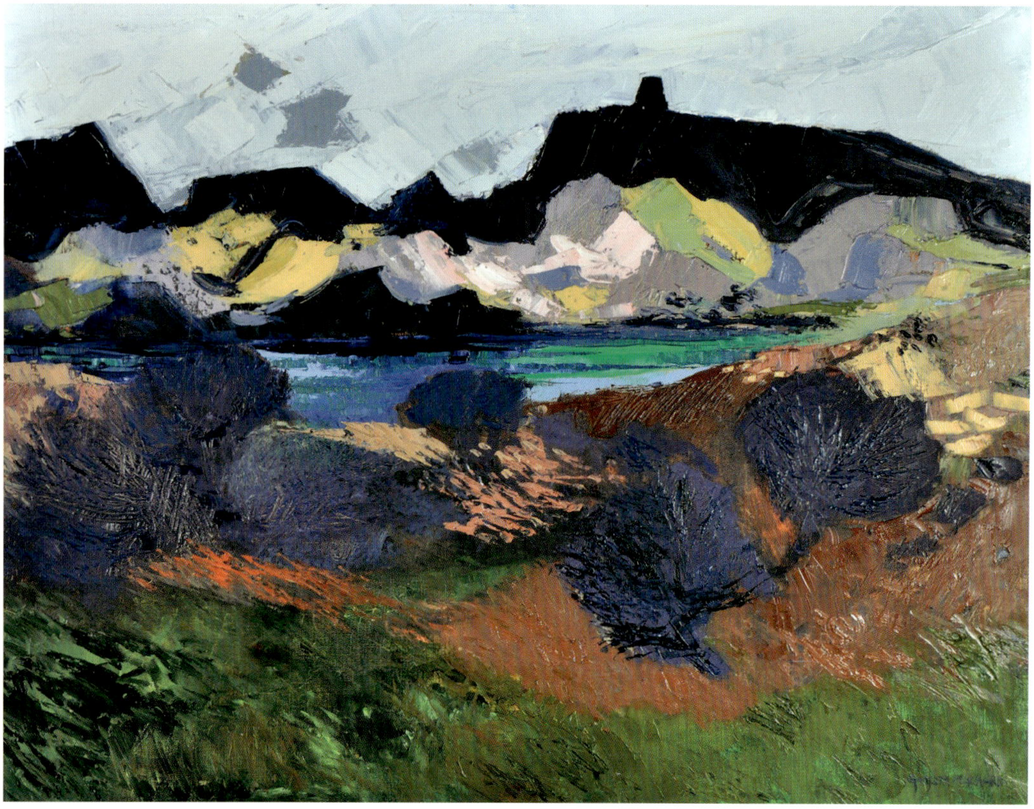

Fig. 77
Parys Mountain, Anglesey
1989 | mixed media | 28 x 38 cm
private collection, France

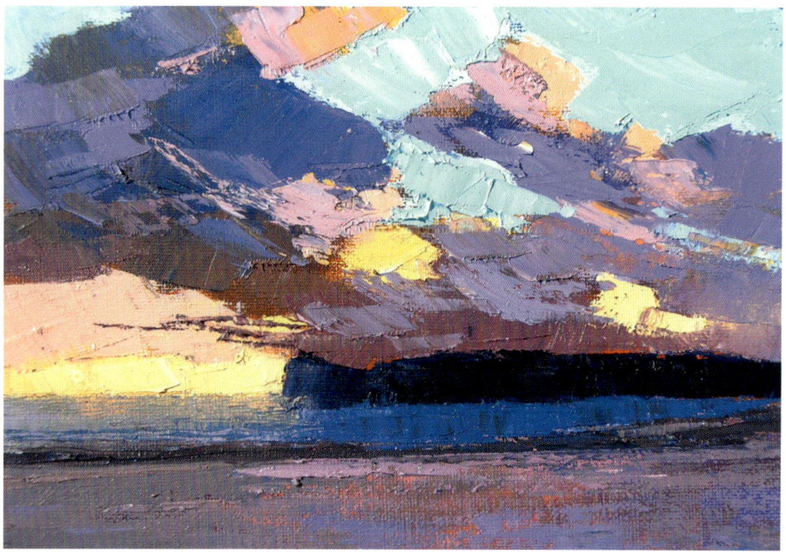

Fig. 78
Machlyd, Sunset
2004 | oil on canvas | 19 x 27 cm
private collection, UK

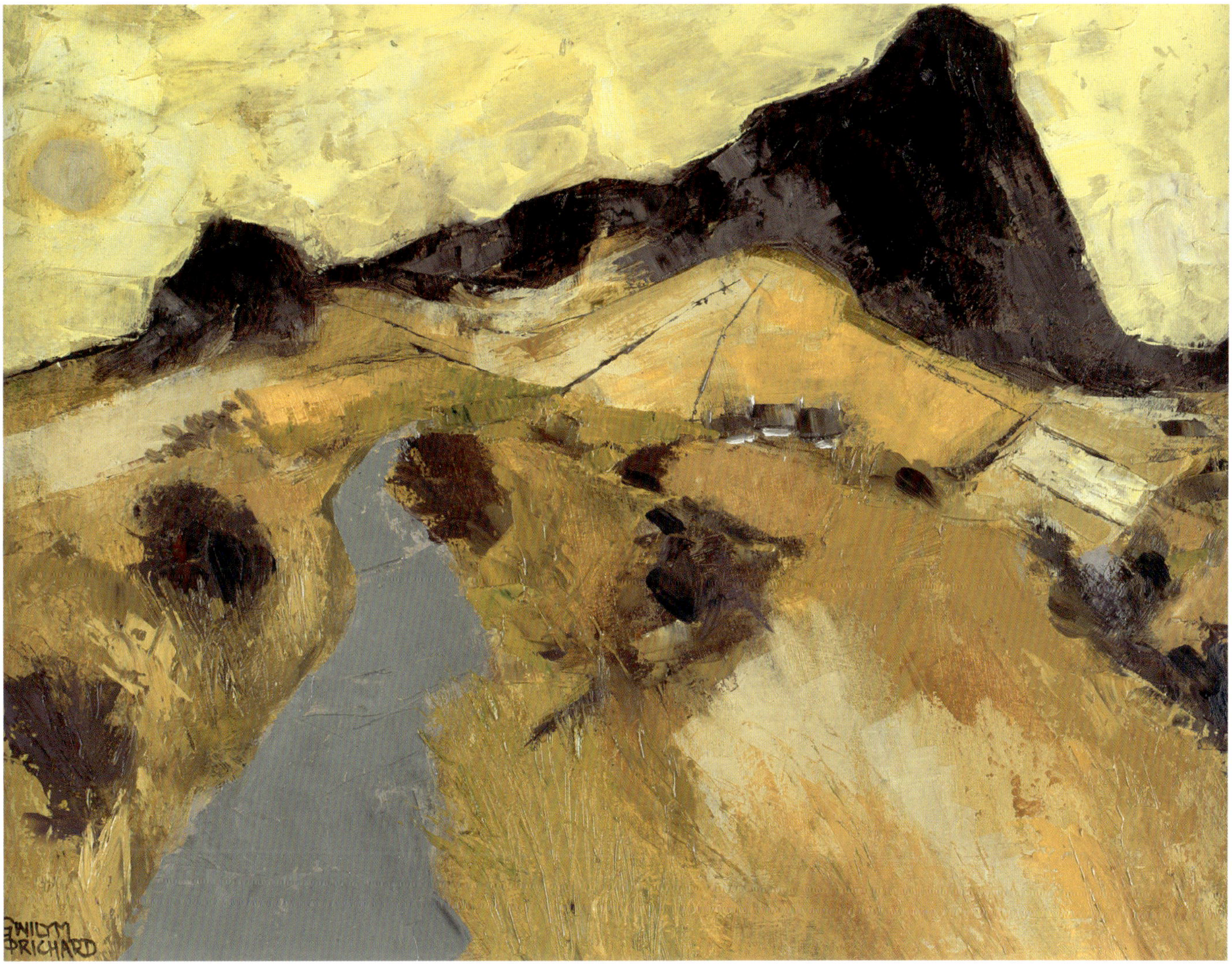

Fig. 79
Garn Llidi
1984 | oil on canvas | 41 x 56 cm
Claudia Williams

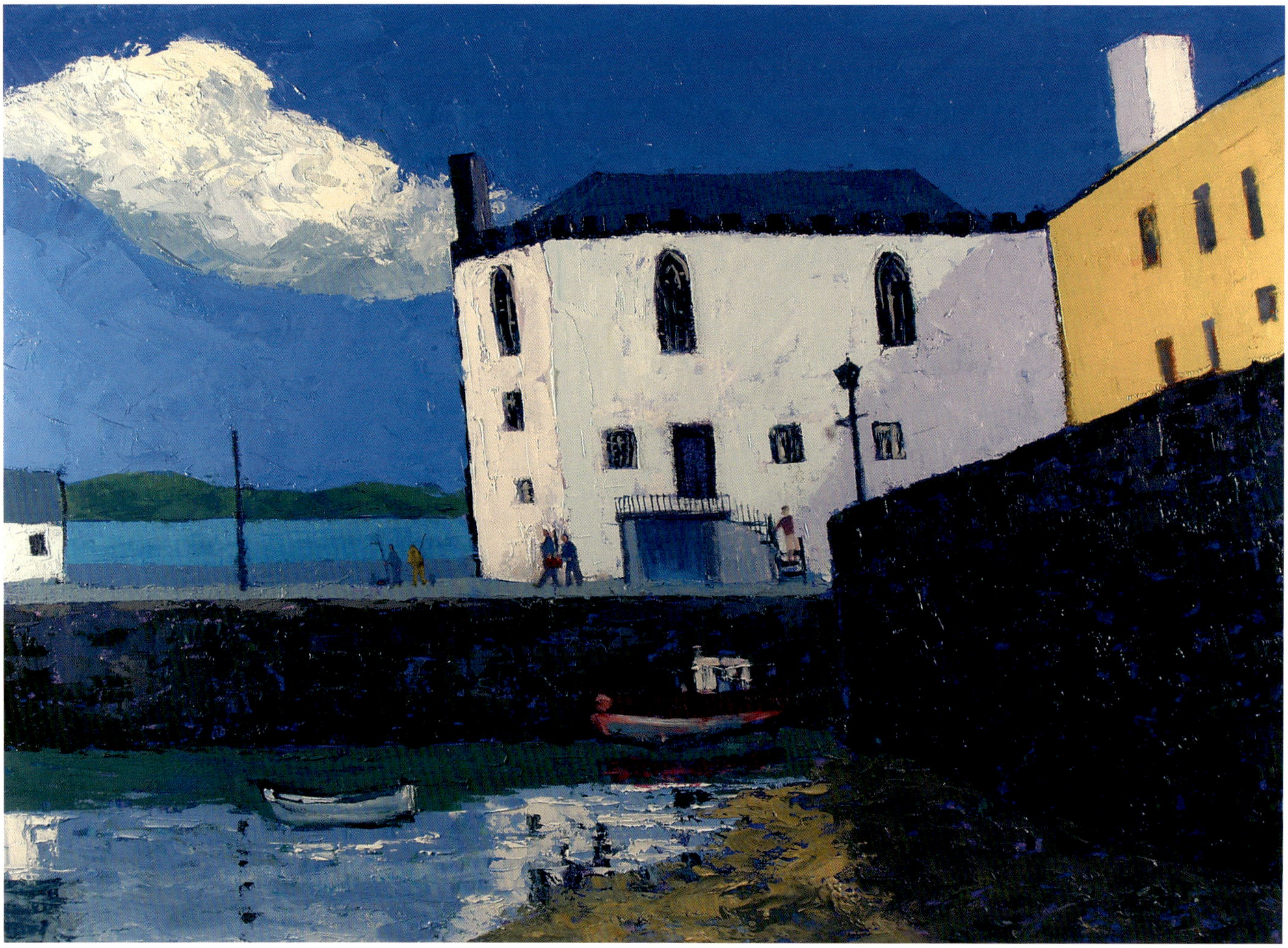

Fig. 80
Dinbych y Pysgod
2007 | oil on canvas | 60 x 81 cm
private collection, UK

'MORE TIME TO SEE AND LOOK'

'A splendid fort stands where a throng provides / Pleasure and praise, and the birds are loud', a seventh-century Welsh poet declared 'In Praise of Tenby'. 'Splendid its people taking their pleasure. / Their lively life not based on disdain, / It is not their way to be hard of heart.'[120] In the year 2000, at the beginning of a new millennium, Prichard and Williams made yet another start by moving to Dinbych y Pysgod, the 'Little Fort of Fishes'. Tenby's sandy beaches, sheltered harbour and idiosyncratic amalgam of Norman, Georgian and Victorian architecture appealed to their appreciation for Welsh-English heritage, their love of the outdoors and their passion for maritime living. Moving to the 'Little England beyond Wales', Prichard and Williams became part of a lineage of distinguished artists who have lived and worked in south Pembrokeshire, most notably among them Augustus and Gwen John.

Prichard had been here before. In April 1978, he was awarded a bursary by the West Midlands Arts Association to record the properties and land owned by the National Trust in and around St Davids, Pembrokeshire. Back then, he made drawings and watercolours of the ruins of the Bishop's Palace, the foundations of which date back to the seventh century, as well as ink and monochrome wash drawings of Bishop Gower's Great Hall, built in the twelfth and fifteenth centuries, with its distinctive parapet encircling the roof. In Pembrokeshire, he had once again felt 'at home', 'able to produce work that penetrates the landscape', paintings that were steeped in ancient history and 'charged with the atmosphere of this rather stark but warm land'[121] (fig. 79). Today, he is less concerned with penetrating the surface as he is with the surface itself – the bright façade, the broad horizon and the open sea. Tenby's clear light, along with the memory of years lived in southerly climes, have induced Prichard to paint landscapes that are vibrant rather than wild, spirited rather than severe. As Mark Lewis, assistant curator at the local Museum and Art Gallery points out, Prichard now tends to paint the

> *colourful coastline, carpeted with bright yellow sands, watched over not by dark-eyed, brooding mountains standing sentinel but by a sunlit sky, hazy and lazy with warmth. The broad horizons of blue sea and sky give him the opportunity to portray a gentler side to the Welsh landscape, with a more subtle and yet broad use of the palette knife.*[122]

There is a freshness, a geniality about Prichard's twenty-first-century canvases, in which introspection is giving way to conviviality. 'Shall I be mean, when all this light is mine?', the Welsh poet W.H. Davies once asked. 'Call for the rat, and let him share my joy, / And sit beside me here, to wash his face.'[123] In this spirit, Prichard invites us to look up into the cotton-wool-cloud-flecked sky of *Dinbych y Pysgod* (2007; fig. 80), or else takes us out to the sea, onto the rocky coastline as observed at nearby *Lydstep* (2010; fig. 83), *Y Parrog* (2005;

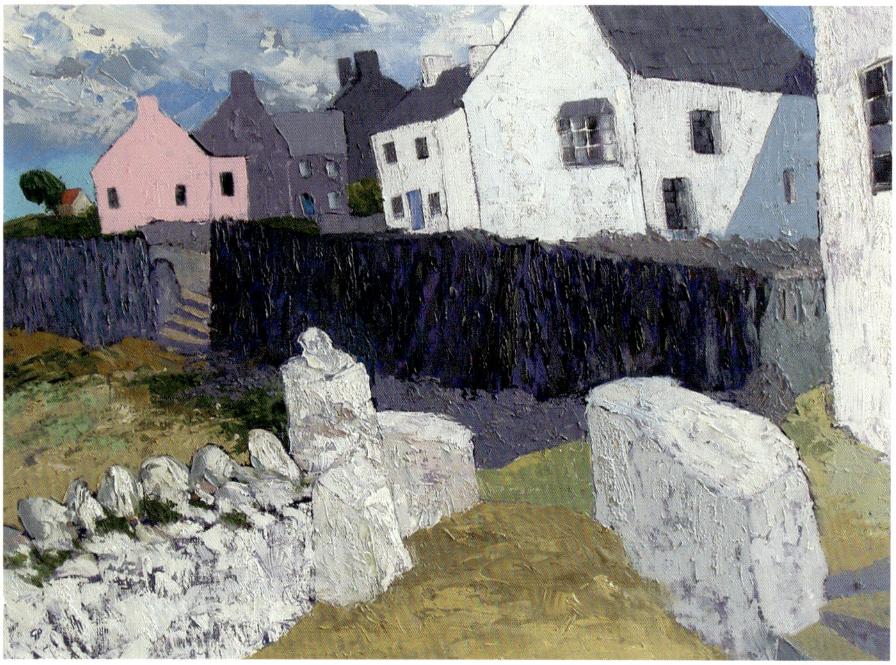

Fig. 81
Y Parrog
2005 | oil on canvas | 60 x 81 cm
private collection, UK

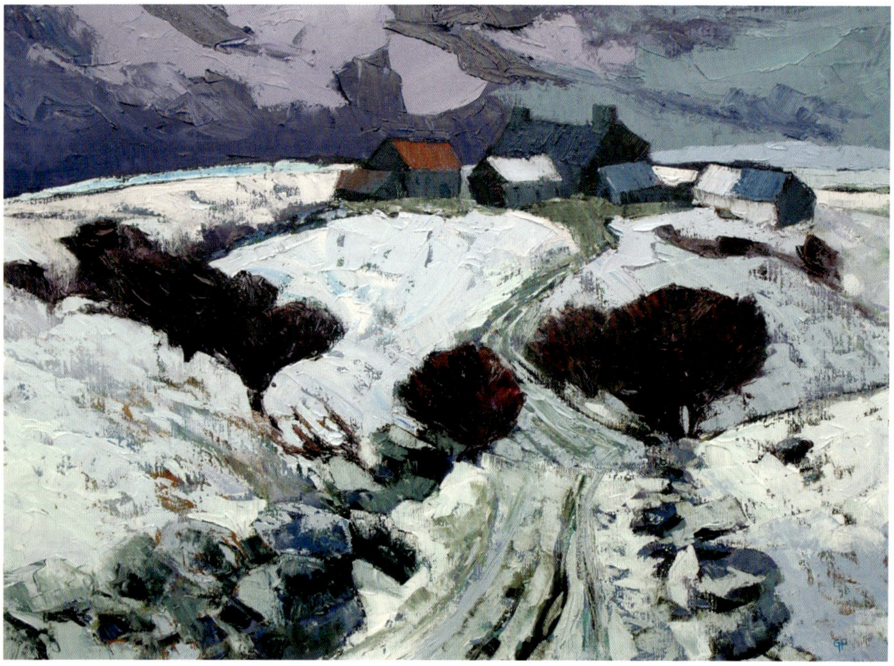

Fig. 82
Farm and Snow
2004 | oil on canvas | 60 x 81 cm
private collection, UK

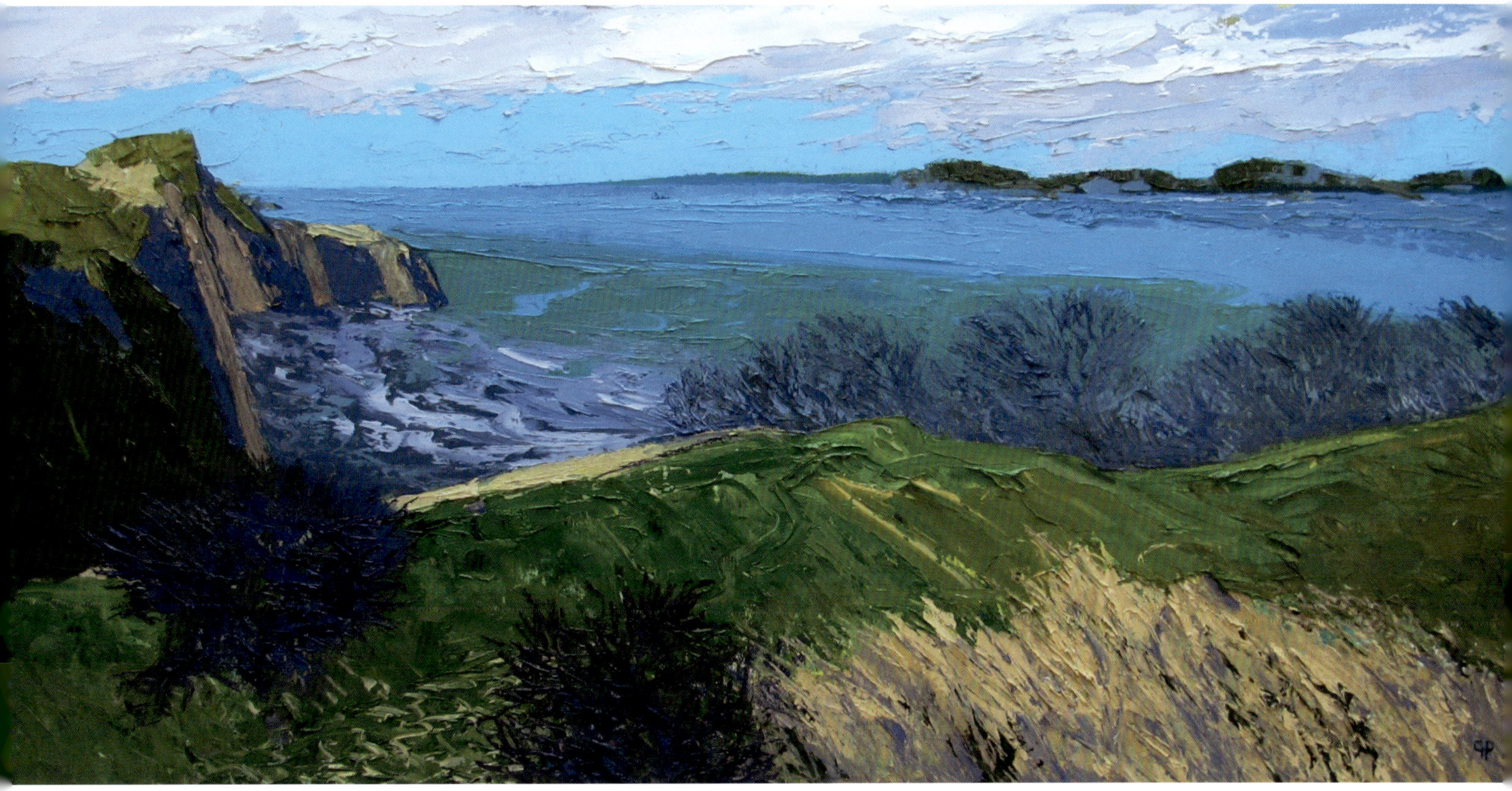

Fig. 83
Lydstep
2010 | oil on canvas | 50 x 100 cm
the artist

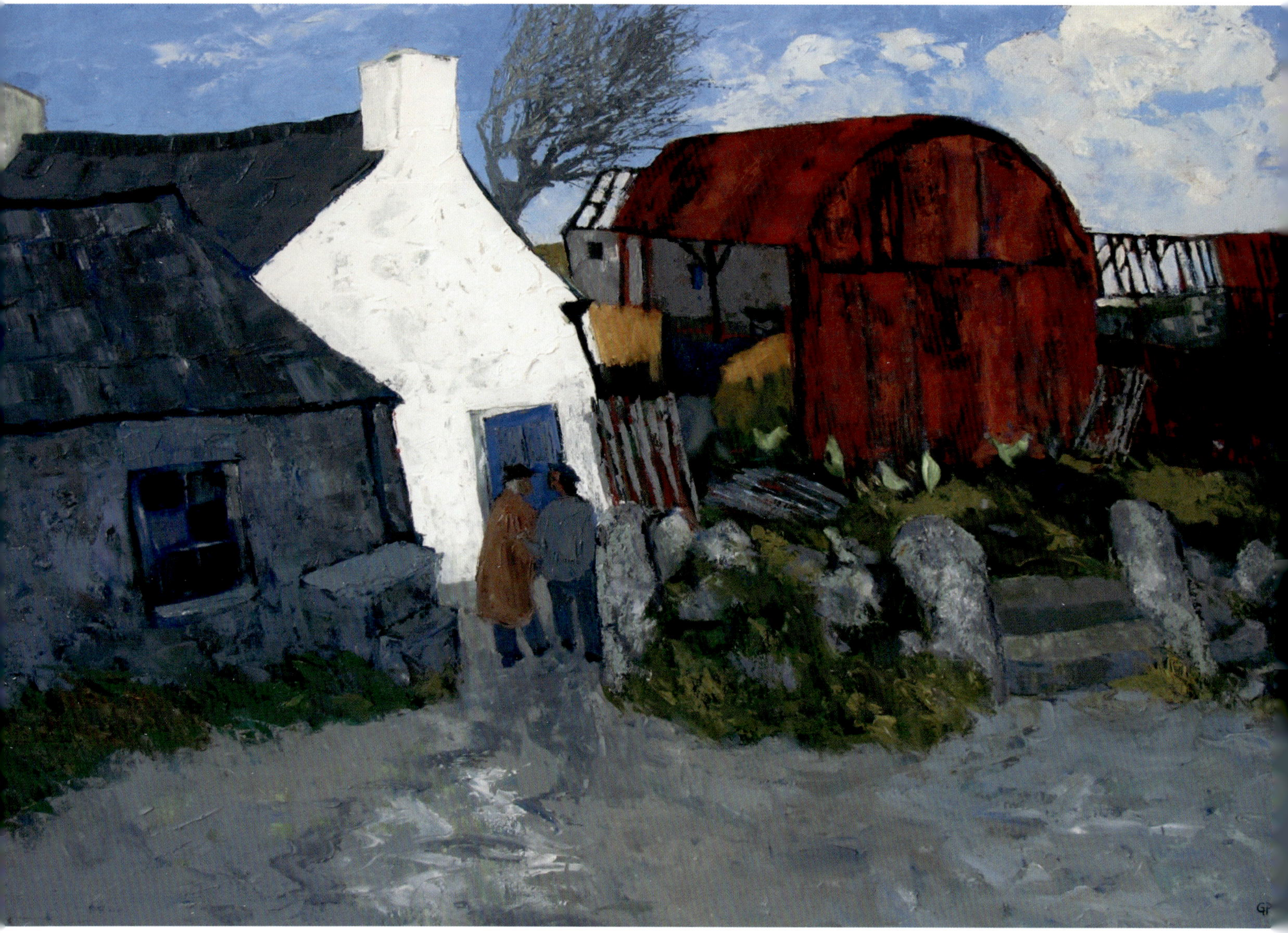

Fig. 84
Planning Permission?
2011 | oil on canvas | 73 x 100 cm
the artist

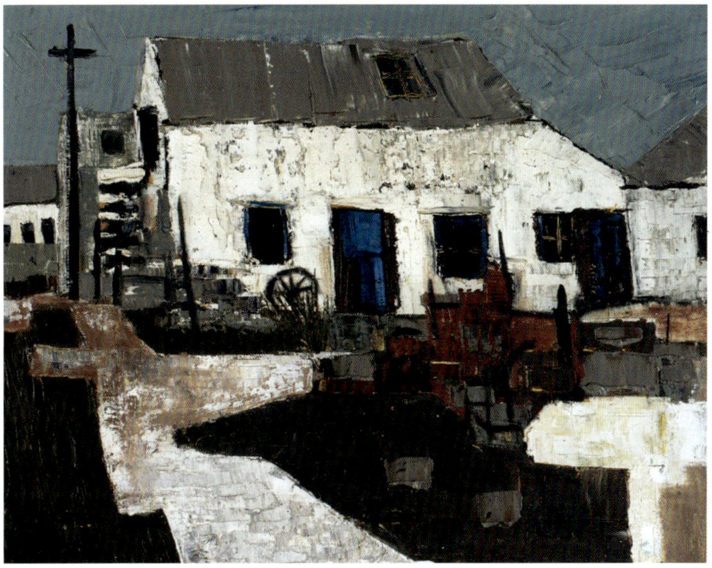

Fig. 85
Pembrokeshire Farm
1960 | oil on canvas | 46 x 55 cm
the artist

figs 81 & 93) and the beach and headland of *Poppet Sands* (2002; fig. 86). In the absence of the mountains that are the preoccupation of many of his North Wales subjects, Prichard's Pembrokeshire canvases feature the man-made mound of Tenby's Georgian townscape, as in *The Blue House* (2006; fig. 87), which presents us with the gaily painted guesthouses that follow the cliff-top contours before descending the steep incline of narrow, cobbled streets leading to the harbour beach and the jetty

That his townscapes seem more animated now is not owing to a refreshed palette alone; the figure has come onto the scene and makes its presence felt. This marks a sea change in Prichard's work whose extent becomes apparent when we compare earlier canvases like *Pembrokeshire Farm* (1960; fig. 85) to more recent ones like *Planning Permission?* (2010; fig. 84). Titles like the latter – and others such as *A Fine Day Tomorrow* (2011) or the conversational 'Have you seen them?' of *'Ydych chi wedigweld?'* (2011) – signal an increasing concern with narrative, an expressed interest in the life stories of the people as well as the history of a land or region. In fact, Prichard has always made use of figures in his landscapes; but, unless they could claim the centrality of *Ceri, Claudia and Ben at Llwydiarth* (fig. 2), they were, for the most part, 'put in just for the scale', as a means of figuring out the width of a road in relation to farm or field. Having performed the limited, liminal role he assigned to them, they were then painted out 'completely'. Yet 'nowadays', he adds, 'I like to leave them in because sometimes they amuse me'.[124] It may well be the six decades Prichard has lived in the company of a figure and portrait painter that convinced him to revisit and revise his views not only on landscape art but also

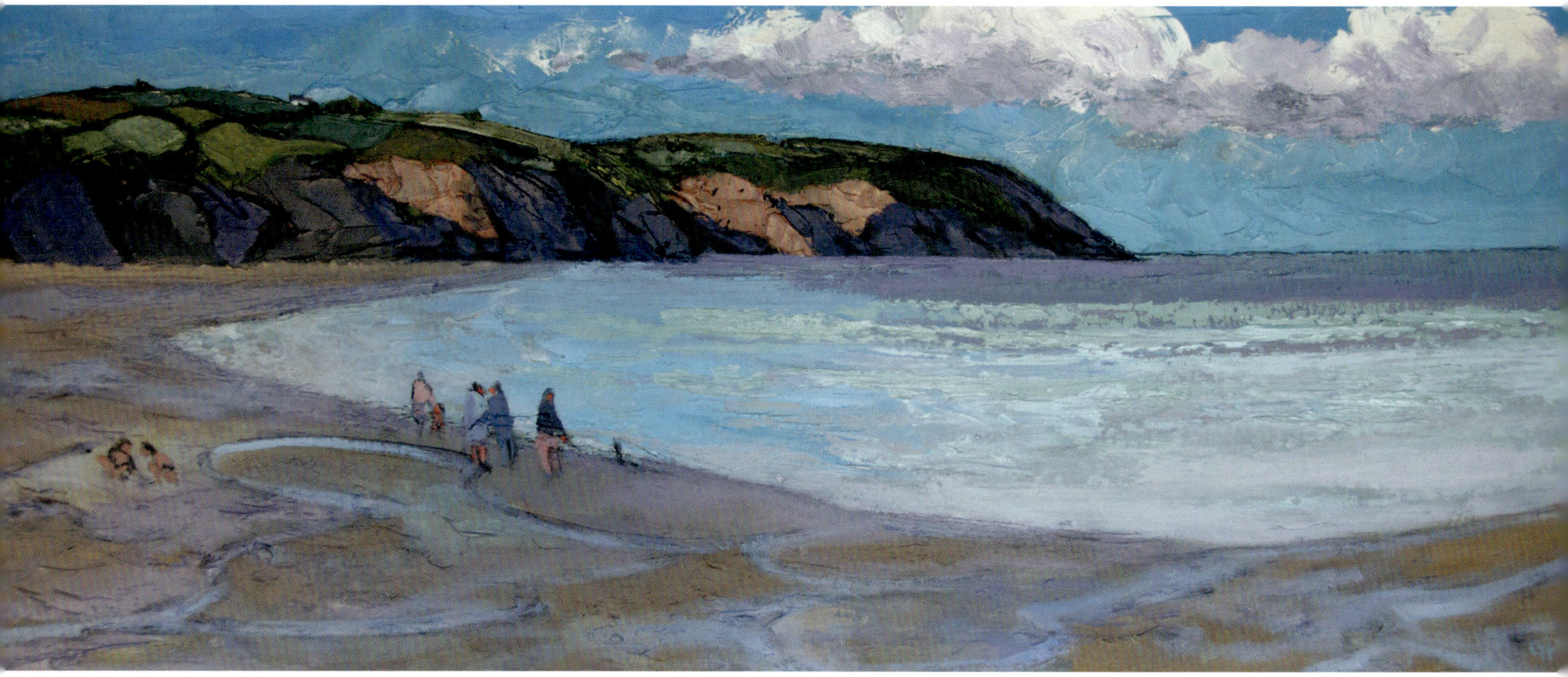

Fig. 86
Poppet Sands
2002 | oil on canvas | 40 x 92 cm
the artist

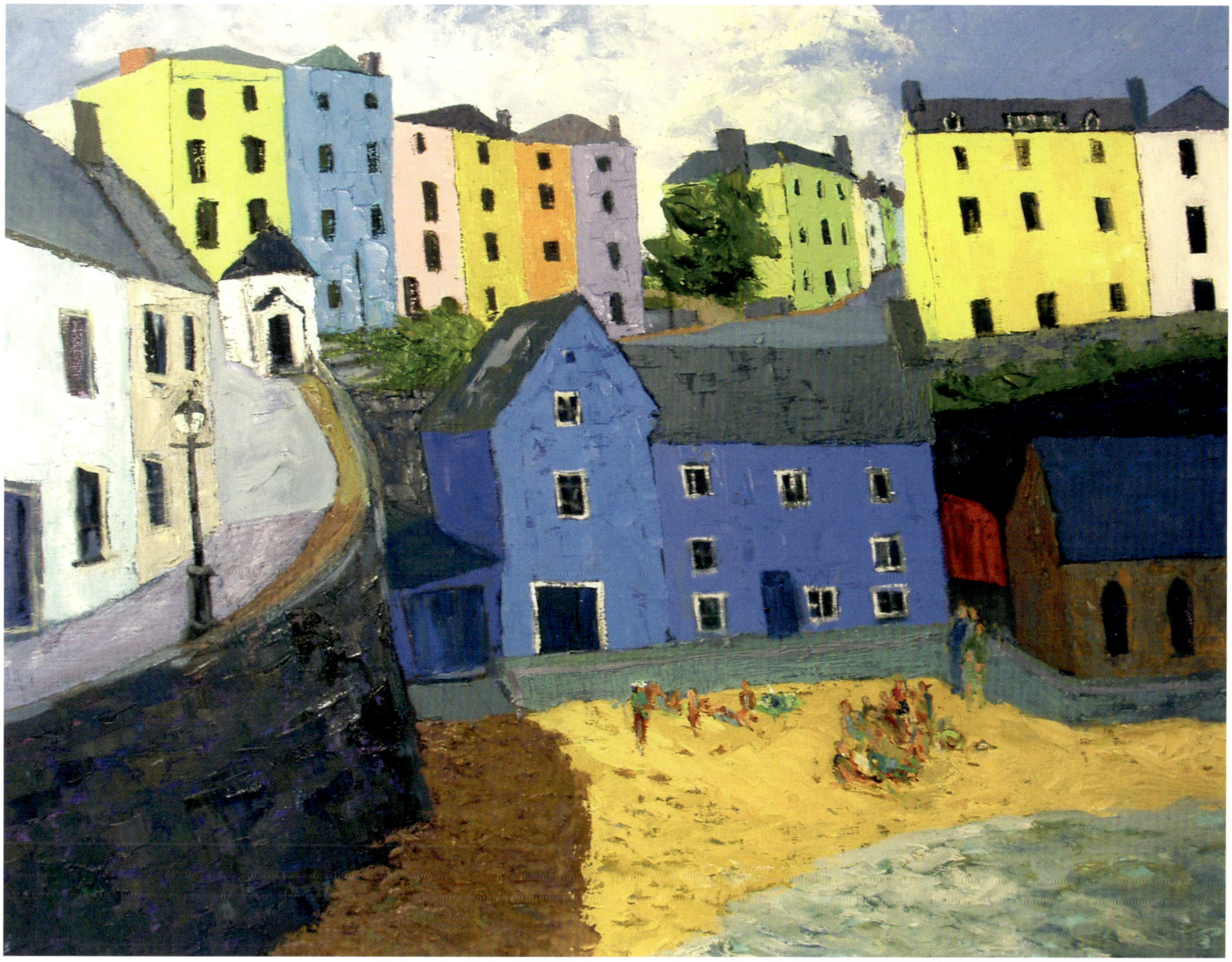

Fig. 87
The Blue House, Tenby
2006 | oil on canvas | 73 x 92 cm
private collection, UK

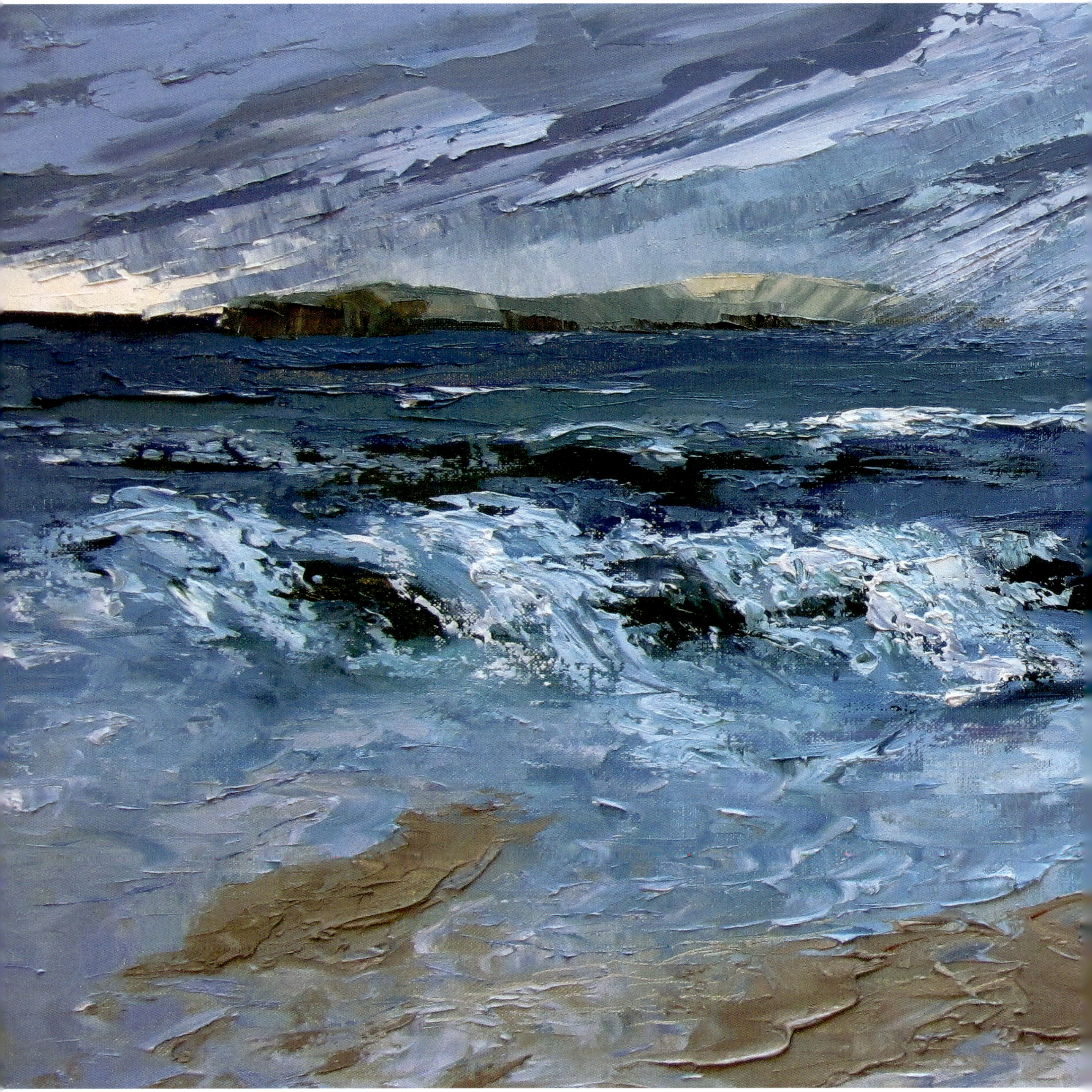

Fig. 88
Shower over Caldey
2012 | oil on canvas | 50 x 100 cm
the artist

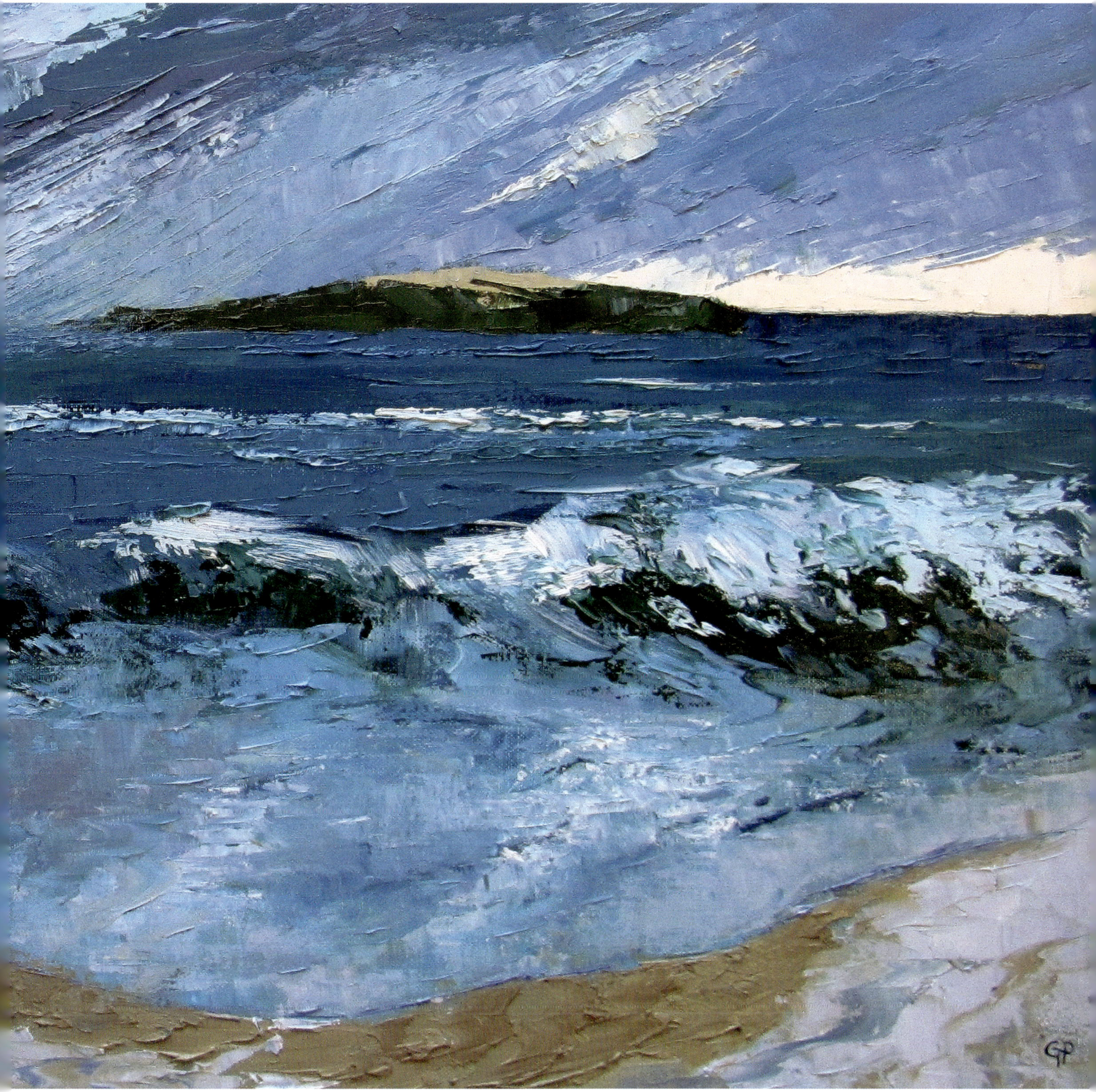

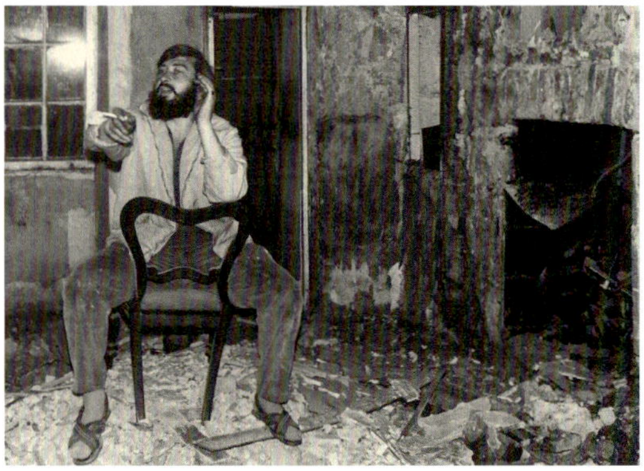

'Wipe your feet!'

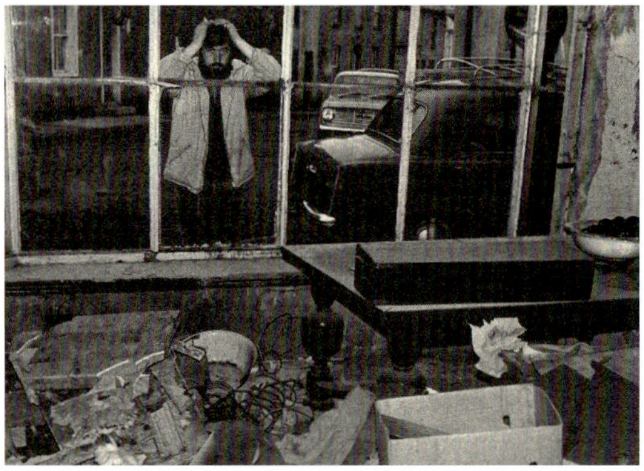

Figs 89 & 90
Gwilym, Church Street, Beaumaris 1966
photographs John Joyce

on the relative 'insignificance of man' or woman in the culturally transformed land we so often look upon as the natural world.

Even in Tenby, the artist's life has been far from settled. Between 2001 and 2009 they purchased, occupied and sold two more properties in and around town as well as a remote farmhouse in Brittany, and, to be within easy reach of their children and gallery, a house in the Cardiff suburb of Penarth that was to be their home for just nine months. In 2009, they returned to make their home in a quiet terrace of Victorian villas, away from Tenby's town centre, looking out to sea, to Giltar Point and Caldey Island (fig. 88). Throughout their life together, Prichard and Williams have moved house some two dozen times and each new home, having been someone else's old one, they had to renovate to suit their needs as a family and as professional artists (figs 89 & 90). For years, they lived frugally, did without or made do to make art. For all of that – and, perhaps, because of all that – Prichard has kept on with his life's work. He does not wait for the right moment when he can work in the rain. He does not wait for the one view when there is so much else to see. Asked whether he has 'to wait for … inspiration', he replies: 'if you got to wait, you may be waiting a lifetime. It may never come'.[125] The last few months have not been very productive', Prichard wrote in September 2012; he has had two operations for cancer, followed by a course of chemotherapy. 'At one time I could finish a painting *plein air*, but not now.' By November, however, he was once again camping outdoors to paint the nocturnes with which he has been experimenting of late (*St Catherine's Rock*, 2012; fig. 91); and, as the year drew to a close, he went off in his camper van on a trip to Brittany to purchase canvases. 'Painters don't retire,' he says, 'they just keep on going. What else is there to do if I didn't paint?'[126] However much he may have slowed down, he also takes 'more time' now 'to see and look'; and the fact that he needs more time to compose is something Prichard attributes to having become 'far more critical' of his work.[127]

'A poor life this, if full of care, / We have no time to stand and stare,'[128] declared W.H. Davies, whose years as a hobo poet suggest that wandering around with one's mind open and standing still to let the eye do the travelling are not mutually exclusive modes; nor is either one more productive than the other. As an artist who 'drifted into painting', Prichard has never stopped looking, has always stopped to look – to be amazed, puzzled and intrigued. What better way to prevent that stare from becoming vacant, that standstill from ever being mental, than life in a state of purposeful drifting? And so, whether he is surveying the sea at Tenby or casting a critical eye on some of the canvases he has produced over the years, Gwilym Prichard carries on what has carried him this far: a 'lifetime's gazing'.

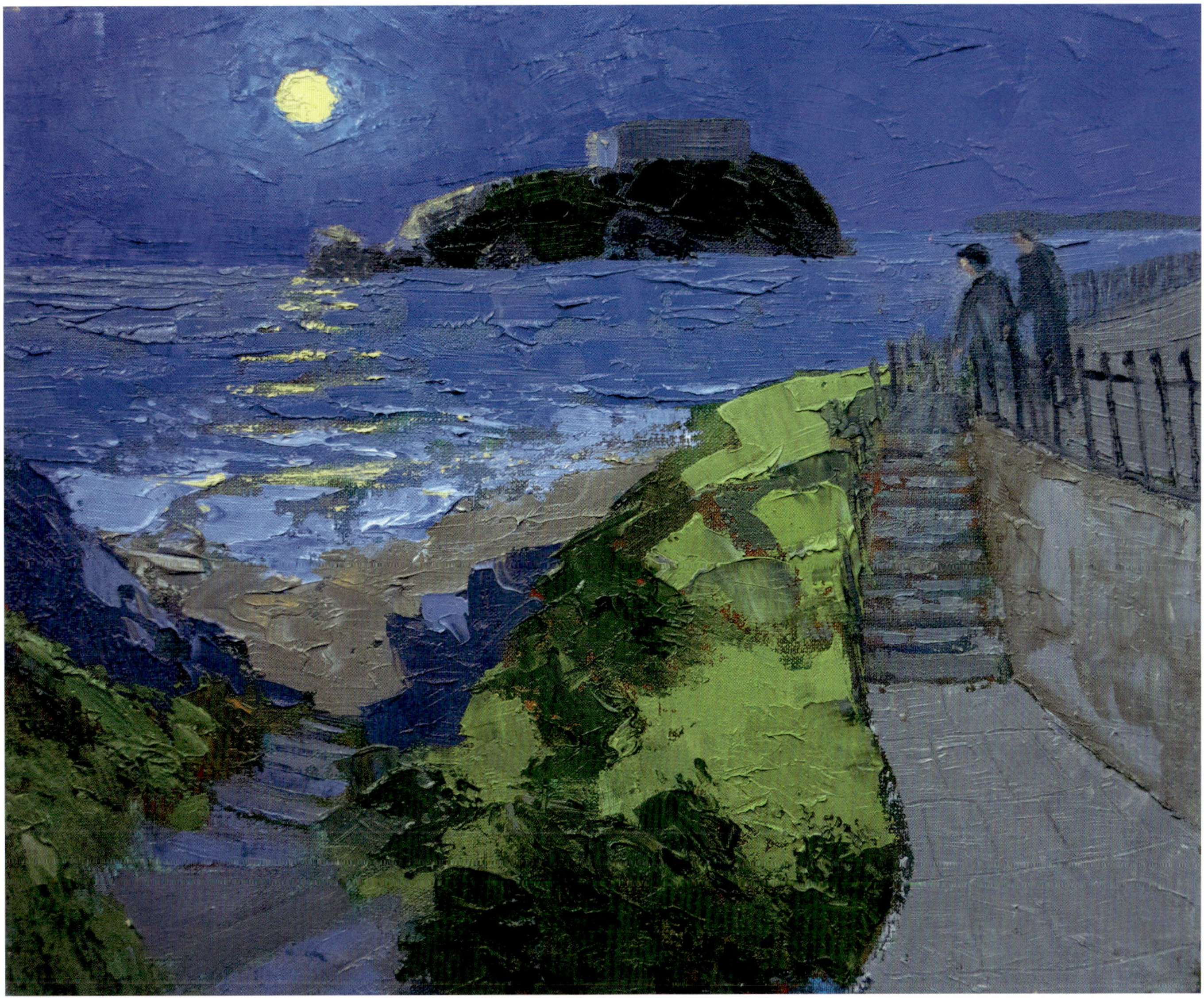

Fig. 91
St Catherine's Rock and Moonlight
2012 | oil on canvas | 46 x 55 cm
the artist

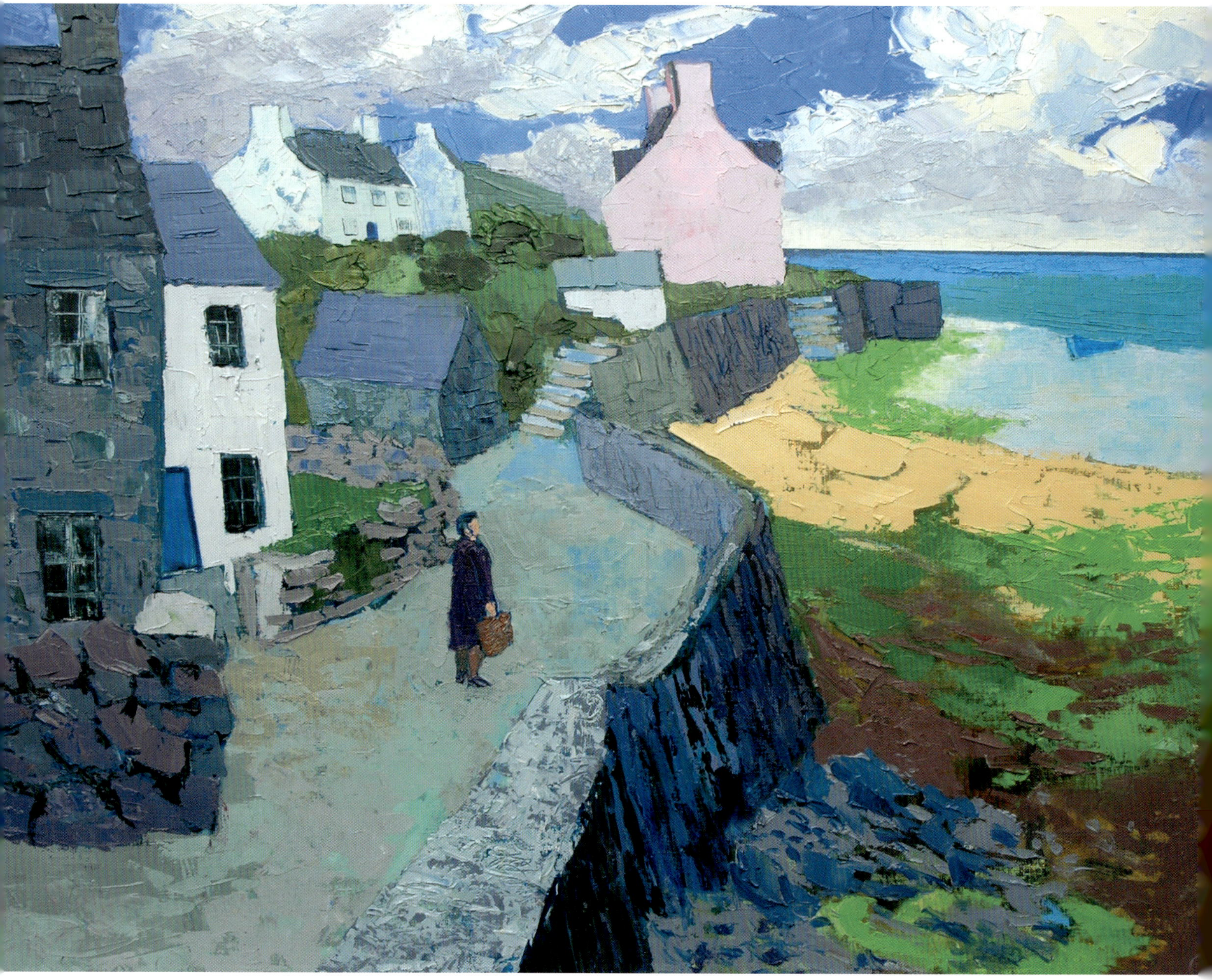

Fig. 92
Going Shopping
2004 | oil on canvas | 73 x 93 cm
private collection, UK

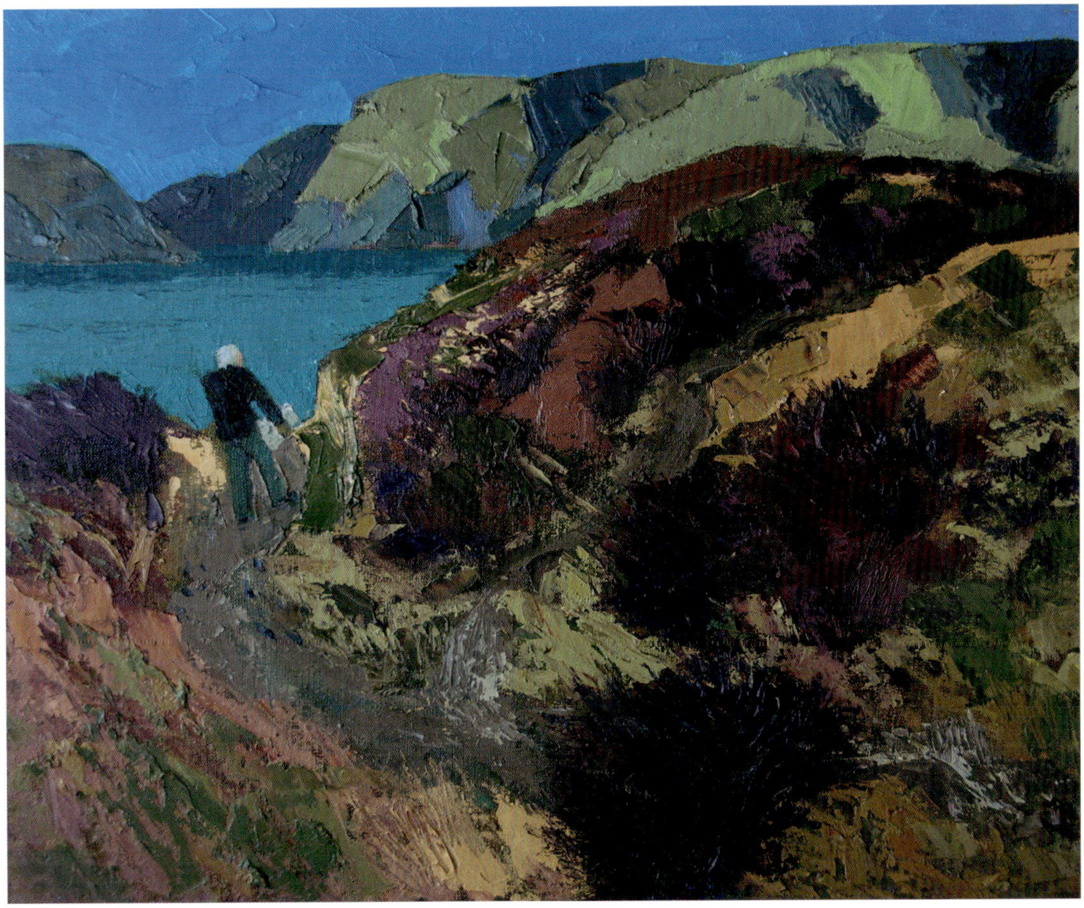

Fig. 93
Going Sketching
2012 | oil on canvas | 50 x 65 cm
the artist

NOTES

1. Bell, *The Artist in Wales* (London: Harrap, 1957), 19–20.
2. Robert Frost, 'The Road Not Taken', *Broadview Anthology of Poetry*, 2nd ed. (London: Broadview, 2009): 380.
3. The *cracach* is a community's social elite. Prichard, undated letter to the authors, Sept. 2012.
4. Hughes, *A Wanderer in North Wales* (London: Phoenix, 1949), 12–13.
5. Thomas, *Song at the Year's Turning* (London: Hart-Davies, 1955), 72–73.
6. Prichard, 'Gwilym Pritchard', *Gwilym Pritchard*, exhibition. cat. (London: Heal's Art Gallery, 4–19 Oct. 1974).
7. Prichard, interview by Ian Skidmore, BBC Radio Wales, spring 1995; recording, private archive, Prichard and Williams, Tenby.
8. St Michael's has since been demolished. Prichard, undated letter to the authors, Sept. 2012.
9. Prichard, undated letter to the authors, Sept. 2012.
10. Jones, 'The Art of Gwilym Pritchard and Claudia Williams', *Anglo-Welsh Review* 11.27 (1961): 37–9, 37; Jones, 'Gwilym Prichard', *Paintings and Pottery*, exhibition cat. (Swansea: Ceri Richards Gallery, Taliesin Arts Centre, Univ. College of Swansea, 21 Apr.–5 May 1989).
11. Prichard, 'Gwilym Pritchard', Heal's, 1974.
12. Jones, 'The Art of Gwilym Pritchard and Claudia Williams', 37.
13. Williams' life and art are discussed in a companion piece to this volume by Heuser and Meyrick (Sansom, 2013)
14. Prichard, undated letter to the authors, Sept. 2012.
15. Williams, 'My Autobiography', unpublished ms., edited by the authors; private archive, Prichard and Williams, Tenby.
16. Prichard, undated letter to the authors, Sept. 2012.
17. Williams, interview by Ian Skidmore, BBC Radio Wales, spring 1995; recording, private archive, Prichard and Williams, Tenby.
18. Vincentelli, *Gwilym Prichard, Claudia Williams: Recent Paintings*, exhibition cat. (Mold: Oriel Theatr Clwyd, 26 Oct.–24 Nov. 1985).
19. Prichard, undated letter to the authors, Sept. 2012.
20. Pennant, *Pennant and His Welsh Landscapes*, ed. Gwyn Walters (Newtown: Gregynog, 2006), 107.
21. Williams, 'My Autobiography'.
22. Qtd in Meyrick, *Gwilym Prichard* (Aberystwyth: Nat. Library of Wales, 2001), 4.
23. Jones, 'The Art of Gwilym Pritchard and Claudia Williams', 39.
24. Perspex, 'Glimpse of the Arts in Wales', *Caernarfon and Denbigh Herald and North Wales Observer*, 27 Nov. 1959: 10.
25. Rennell, 'Gwilym Pritchard', *Liz Sherburne, Gwilym Pritchard* (London: Heal's Art Gallery, Oct. 1975).
26. 'Anglesey Brothers Will Discuss Their Interest in Art on Radio', unidentified newspaper clipping; private archive, Prichard and Williams, Tenby.
27. Zobole, interviewed by Tony Curtis; in *Welsh Painters Talking* (Cardiff: Seren, 1997), 170–171.
28. Zobole, qtd in Tom Cross, 'Ernest Zobole', *Two Painters: Brenda Chamberlain, Ernest Zobole*, exhibition cat. (Cardiff: Welsh Committee of the Arts Council, 1963); Giraldus Cambrensis, *Itinerary through Wales* (Newtown: Gwasg Gregynog, 1989), 80–81.
29. Clausen, *Six Lectures on Painting* (London: Methuen, 1904), 96.
30. Meyrick, *Gwilym Prichard*, 11.
31. Susanna Goodden, *At the Sign of the Fourposter: A History of Heal's* (London: Heal's, 1984), 61–3.
32. K. Williams, 'The Artist and His Work: Kyffin Williams on the Work of Gwilym Pritchard', *Anglesey Bulletin of the Arts*, Sept. 1961.
33. Jones, 'The Art of Gwilym Pritchard and Claudia Williams', 39; Williams, 'An Appreciation', *Gwilym Pritchard: Paintings and Drawings* (Oxford: Lincoln College, 6–13 Feb. 1968).
34. Prichard, interview by Ian Skidmore.
35. K. Williams, *Gwilym Pritchard*, exhibition cat. (London: Heal's Art Gallery, 14–19 Sept. 1973).
36. Prichard, 'Gwilym Pritchard', Heal's, 1974; Prichard, 'Landscape Painting in Wales', *Artist*, Aug. 1978: 21.
37. Petts, Foreword, *Thirty Welsh Paintings of Today* (Cardiff: Arts Council of Great Britain, 1954), 2.
38. Bell, *The Artist in Wales*, 180–81.
39. Bell, qtd in Petts, Foreword, *Thirty Welsh Paintings of Today*, 3.
40. Lord, *The Visual Culture of Wales: Imaging the Nation* (Cardiff: Univ. of Wales Press, 2000), 404–405.
41. Prichard, *Gwilym Pritchard: Paintings of Wales/ Tom Cross: Drawings of Italy*, exhibition cat. (Cardiff: Howard Roberts Gallery, 4–25 May 1963).
42. Prichard, 'Landscape Painting in Wales', *Artist*, Aug. 1978: 23.
43. Prichard, *Gwilym Pritchard: Paintings of Wales/ Tom Cross: Drawings of Italy*.
44. Prichard, *Gwilym Pritchard: Paintings*, exhibition cat. (Builth Wells: Wyeside Arts Centre, 4–23 Oct. 1979).
45. Prichard, 'Landscape Painting in Wales', *Artist*, Aug. 1978: 22.
46. Qtd in Meyrick, 16.
47. Thomas, 'Welsh Landscape', *Song at the Year's Turning*, 63.
48. Prichard, Wyeside, 1979.
49. Prichard, 'Gwilym Pritchard', Heal's, 1974.
50. Prichard, 'Artists Abroad', interview by Nicola Heywood Thomas, *Primetime*, 3 Jan. 1995, HTV Wales.
51. Rowan, *Art in Wales: An Illustrated History 1850–1980* (Cardiff: Univ. of Wales Press, 1985), 122.
52. Richards, 'Alun Richards', *Artists in Wales*, ed. Meic Stephens (Llandysul: Gomer, 1971), 55–66, 66.
53. Prichard, undated letter to the authors, Sept. 2012.
54. Jones, 'The Art of Gwilym Pritchard and Claudia Williams', 39.
55. Rolston, 'Does Aesthetic Appreciation of Landscapes Need to Be Science-Based?', *British Journal of Aesthetics*, Oct. 1995: 374–86, 379–80.
56. Bell, *The Artist in Wales*, 158.
57. Prichard, 'Landscape Painting in Wales', 16.
58. Prichard, undated letter to the authors, Sept. 2012.
59. Jones, 'A Sense of Place', *Gwilym Prichard: Oil Paintings, Water Colours, Drawings* (Aberystwyth: Aberystwyth Arts Centre, 24 June–24 July 1982); Hopkins, 'Pied Beauty', *Gerard Manley Hopkins* (Oxford: Oxford UP, 1986), 132–3.
60. Prichard, undated letter to the authors, Sept. 2012.
61. Frances Davies, 'Finding the Colour of the Jewels', *Cambria* 6.1 (2003): 50–51, 51.
62. Thomas, 'The Small Window', *Collected Poems 1945–1900* (London: Dent, 1993), 202.
63. Williams-Ellis, *An Artist in North Wales*, pictures by Fred Uhlman (London: Elek, 1946), 13.
64. Piper, *British Romantic Artists* (London: Collins, 1942), 7.

65. G. Jones, *A Prospect of Wales* (London: Penguin, 1948), 30–31.
66. K. Williams, 'The Artist and His Work'.
67. Prichard, undated letter to the authors, Sept. 2012.
68. J. Jones, 'Gwilym Prichard', *Paintings and Pottery*.
69. K. Williams, 'Kyffin Williams', *Artists in Wales*, ed. Meic Stephens (Llandysul: Gomer, 1971), 18.
70. K. Williams, *Gwilym Pritchard*, Heal's, 1973.
71. Prichard, 'Landscape Painting in Wales', *Artist*, Aug. 1978: 21.
72. Qtd in Prichard, Wyeside, 1979.
73. Rennell, 'Gwilym Pritchard'.
74. Croft, speech, 19 Mar. 1976, Hereford City Art Gallery, opening the 'Exhibition of Paintings and Drawings by Gwilym Pritchard and Claudia Williams'. For an account of Croft as an art patron in the 1930s and 1940s, see Anna Müller-Härlin, 'Rebellious and Supportive', *Exile and Patronage* (Berlin: Lit, 2006): 45–54.
75. Williams, 'My Autobiography'.
76. Prichard, 'Landscape Painting in Wales', *Artist*, July 1978: 16–18, 16.
77. Prichard, 'Artists Abroad'.
78. Prichard, 'Landscape Painting in Wales', *Artist*, July 1978: 16; Herrick, 'Delight in Disorder', *Broadview Anthology of Poetry*, 2nd ed. (London: Broadview, 2009), 39.
79. Prichard, 'Landscape Painting in Wales', *Artist*, July 1978: 16.
80. Prichard, 'Gwilym Pritchard', Heal's, 1974.
81. Prichard, 'Landscape Painting in Wales', *Artist*, July 1978: 16.
82. K. Williams, *Across the Straits* (London: Duckworth, 1973), 158.
83. Prichard and C. Williams, 'From Gwredog Isaf to Santorini: December 1984–March 1985', *New Welsh Review* 60 (2003): 35–42; 40, 39.
84. Prichard and Williams, 'From Gwredog Isaf to Santorini', 35.
85. Williams, 'My Autobiography'.
86. Williams, 'My Autobiography'
87. Prichard and Williams, 'Gwredog to Greece Journal '84–'85', 11 Dec. 1984; unpublished ms.; private archive, Prichard and Williams, Tenby.
88. Prichard and Williams, 'From Gwredog Isaf to Santorini', 36–7.
89. Prichard and Williams, 'Gwredog to Greece Journal '84–'85', 17 Dec. 1984.
90. Prichard and Williams, 'Gwredog to Greece Journal '84–'85', 22 Dec. 1984.
91. Prichard and Williams, 'Gwredog to Greece Journal '84–'85', 26 Dec. 1984.
92. Prichard, sketchbook, 'Wales-Venice 1984': 17 Feb.; 19 Feb., 28 Feb., 10 Feb. 1985; unpublished ms., private archive, Prichard and Williams, Tenby.
93. Prichard, sketchbook, 'March–April 1985', 11 Feb. 1985.
94. Prichard and Williams, 'Gwredog to Greece Journal '84–'85', 16 Dec. 1984.
95. Prichard and Williams, 'Gwredog to Greece Journal '84–'85', 22 Dec. 1984; Prichard, sketchbook, 'Wales-Venice 1984', 24 Feb. 1985.
96. C. Williams, interview by Ian Skidmore.
97. Williams, interview by Ian Skidmore.
98. Prichard, sketchbook, 'March–April 1985'; 22 Mar. 1985; [19] Mar. 1985.
99. Williams, 'My Autobiography'.
100. Prichard, sketchbook, 'March–April 1985', 23 Mar. 1985.
101. Prichard, interview by Ian Skidmore.
102. Qtd in Meyrick, 25.
103. Williams, 'My Autobiography'.
104. Prichard, 'Artists Abroad'.
105. K. Williams, Foreword, *Gwilym Prichard: Recent Works*, exhibition cat. (Aberystwyth: Nat. Library of Wales, 17 July–11 Sept. 1993).
106. Alain Favelle, 'Gwilym Prichard', *Gwilym Prichard: Recent Works*; these comments, translated by Melanie Owen, originally appeared in Favelle's article 'Prichard Coeur Breton', *Presse-Ocean*, 4 May 1993.
107. Prichard, interview by Ian Skidmore.
108. Prichard, interview by Ian Skidmore.
109. Hopkins, 'Penmaen Pool', *Gerard Manley Hopkins*, 123–5.
110. Qtd in *Gwilym Prichard: Recent Works*.
111. J. Jones, 'Gwilym Prichard', *Paintings and Pottery*.
112. Qtd in Flo Brady, 'Gwilym Prichard Yn 80', *Y Faner Newydd* 56 (2011): 28–35, 31. Qtd. in Hywel Harries, 'Gwilym Pritchard', *Cymru'r Cynfas/Wales on Canvas*, ed. Hywel Harris (Talybont: Y Lolfa, 1988): xxi–xxii, xxii.
113. K. Williams, 'The Artist and His Work'.
114. Prichard, 'Gwilym Pritchard', Heal's, 1974.
115. Prichard, interview by Ian Skidmore.
116. Prichard, 'Landscape Painting in Wales', *Artist*, July 1978: 16–18.
117. Prichard, 'Artists Abroad'.
118. Prichard, interview by Nicola Heywood Thomas, *The Arts Show*, 27 Apr. 2011, BBC Radio Wales.
119. Prichard, 'Artists Abroad'.
120. Anonymous, 'In Praise of Tenby', *Oxford Book of Welsh Verse in English*, ed. Gwyn Jones (Oxford: Oxford UP, 1977), 7–9.
121. Prichard, 'Landscape Painting in Wales', *Artist*, July 1978: 17.
122. Lewis, 'Return of the Native: Mark Lewis Meets Landscape Artist Gwilym Prichard', *Pembrokeshire Life*, Jan. 2002: 14–15, 15.
123. Davies, 'A Bright Day', *The Oxford Book of Welsh Verse in English*, ed. Gwyn Jones (Oxford: Oxford UP, 1977), 146.
124. Prichard, interview by Nicola Heywood Thomas, *The Arts Show*.
125. Prichard, interview by Nicola Heywood Thomas, *The Arts Show*.
126. Prichard, interview by Nicola Heywood Thomas, *The Arts Show*.
127. Prichard, undated letter to the authors, Sept. 2012.
128. Davies, 'Leisure', *Songs of Joy and Others* (London: Fifield, 1911), 15.

CHRONOLOGY

1931 | Gwilym Arifor Pritchard is born March 4th, the second child of Rhoda and Hugh Ivor Pritchard of Llanystumdwy near Criccieth, Caernarvonshire. Gwilym has an older brother, Arthur Pritchard (1927–1993).

1942 | Attends Portmadoc Grammar School.
1948 | Begins National Service training as a radar engineer. Contracts rheumatic fever and spends much of 1949 in hospital in Swindon.

1950 | Begins a two-year art teacher training course at Normal College, Bangor.
1953 | Takes a diploma course at Birmingham College of Art where he mostly practises ceramics and weaving.
1954 | Marries artist Claudia Williams. Birth of their son John Ceri Herington Pritchard. Moved into a council house at Pencraig, Llangefni, Anglesey. Appointed crafts teacher at Llangefni County Secondary School where Prichard taught weaving, pottery and other crafts for eleven years.
1955 | First exhibited at the National Eisteddfod in Pwllheli, where runner up for the Gold Medal for Fine Art.
1956 | Birth of second child Benjamin Jerome Ward Pritchard.
1957 | Bronze Medal at the Anglesey Arts Association exhibition for his painting *Feeding Seagulls*.
1958 | Moves to Old Bank House in Beaumaris, Anglesey. At the Royal Cambrian Academy awarded the Saxton Barton Memorial Prize for his painting *Anglesey Landscape*.
1959 | Elected Associate Member of the Royal Cambrian Academy. *Cwmpas*, a film on the work of Prichard and Williams by Nan Davies broadcast by the BBC, November 13.

1962 | Converts to Roman Catholicism.
1963 | Birth of third child Justin Hugh Pritchard. Elected Full Member of the Royal Cambrian Academy.
1965 | The couple adopt a baby girl, christening her Clare Vézélay Pritchard.
1965 | Co-founds Gwynedd Artists Association, a professional splinter group of the North Wales Group. Sells Old Bank House and moves to Rearsby near Leicester to teach at Ratcliffe College.
1966 | Returns to Anglesey and buys a derelict junk shop in Church Street, Beaumaris. Takes post as Head of the Art Department at Friar's School, Bangor – a position he holds until 1973.
1968 | Moved to Rhos Cottage at Penmon Crossroads near Beaumaris.

1973 | Admitted to the Max Glatt Drug and Alcohol Detoxification Unit in Southall, London. Relocates to Weobley, Herefordshire in the Welsh marches.

1974 | Relocates to Norton Canon in Herefordshire. Commissioned by Lt. Col. Colvin Chamberlain to visit Northern Ireland and produce two large paintings for the Royal Artillery, then serving in Belfast.
1978 | West Midlands Arts Association bursary to record the National Trust area in and around St David's, Pembrokeshire.
1979 | Returned to north Wales to live at Bryn Môr, Llanddona Beach near Beaumaris.

1980 | Moves to Gwredog Isaf, a smallholding near Caernarfon. Commences occasional teaching commitments at the Extra Mural Department of the University of Wales, Bangor, St Gerrard's Convent and as tutor at Plas Tan-y-Bwlch, Maentwrog. Drops the 't' in the spelling of his family name after seeing an exhibition catalogue with works by a namesake.
1984 | Sells Gwredog Isaf and journeys with Williams to the Greek island of Skiathos.
1985 | Three weeks on Santorini before heading north through Italy, stopping en route to paint for days at a time, and settling in Provence for a year where they rented an old farmhouse north of St Maximin la Ste Baume in Var.
1986 | Heading northwards, they came to Vannes in the Golfe de Morbihan on the southern coast of Brittany. Here they bought a small house on the Rue Jean-Jaurès near the harbour and lived in the town for four years.

1991 | Discovered the mediaeval hill town of Rochefort-en-Terre. Moved into a former boulangerie on the Place de L'Église. Founded, with others, the Rochefort School of Creative Arts. Returned to Wales at regular intervals to teach on short courses at Plas Tan y Bwlch and to paint in Snowdonia.
1992 | Welsh medium television S4C broadcast 'Llun, Lliw a Lle' in its series *Hel Straeon*, a 25-minute documentary about Prichard's work at the time of the couple's move from Vannes to Rochefort-en-Terre.
1995 | Together with Williams, awarded the Silver Medal by the Academy of Arts, Sciences and Letters in Paris. In May, BBC Radio Wales broadcast *Travelling Together*, a 30-minute interview with Ian Skidmore. HTV Wales broadcast 'Artists Abroad' in its *Primetime* series, a 30-minute television documentary charting the couple's life in Brittany.
1996 | Three visits Tunisia. September painting in Belle Ile.
1997 | Travelled throughout Brittany on painting expeditions. September painting in Lesconil.
1998 | BBC Radio Wales broadcast *Beti ai Phobl*, a 30-minute interview with Beti George.
1999 | After nearly a decade in Rochefort-en-Terre, bought Osborne House in Tenby. The couple shared their time between Rochefort-en-Terre and Pembrokeshire.

2000 | Sold house at Rochefort-en-Terre.
2001 | Relocated to Tenby, moving to a larger house and studio in Tenby. National Library of Wales, Aberystwyth stages a major retrospective exhibition researched and curated

by Robert Meyrick. Welsh medium television channel S4C broadcast *04 Wal* featuring an interview with the couple in their new Tenby home.

2003 | With Williams, made Honorary Fellow of Bangor University.

2007 | In October, moved to Penarth near Cardiff. In December, returned to Pembrokeshire to live with friends near Tenby.

2008 | In August, left Penarth. Stayed with friends at Jameston for four months. In December, moved to Jaffreyston.

2009 | In April, moved to present house in Tenby.

2011 | BBC Radio Wales broadcast 30-minute interview by Nicola Heywood Thomas for *The Arts Show*, 27 April.

2012 | In May, HTV Wales broadcast *Gwilym and Claudia*, a 30-minute television documentary by Trevor Fishlock.

2013 | Interviewed by Cathy Courtney, Project Director of National Life Stories 'Artists' Lives' oral history project based at the British Library, London.

SELECTED EXHIBITIONS

Solo (*), two-person with Claudia Williams, and selected group shows. The number of works exhibited has been indicated in brackets where the information is available.

1952 | Portmadoc Arts and Crafts Exhibition (4)
1955 | Portmadoc Arts and Crafts Exhibition (4); Royal National Eisteddfod of Wales, Pwllheli (1)
1956 | Royal National Eisteddfod of Wales (2); Arts Council of Wales 'Contemporary Welsh Painting and Sculpture', National Museum of Wales (1)
1957 | Royal National Eisteddfod of Wales, Anglesey (3); Portmadoc Arts and Crafts Exhibition (4); Arts Council of Wales 'Contemporary Welsh Painting and Sculpture', National Museum of Wales (2)
1958 | Royal National Eisteddfod of Wales (3); Portmadoc Arts and Crafts Exhibition (5); 'Festival Exhibition', Howard Roberts Gallery, Cardiff (4); Society for Education through Art, National Museum of Wales, Cardiff (2); 'Artists Working in Wales', Portmeirion (12); 'Welsh Names in Painting', Howard Roberts Gallery, Cardiff (10); Arts Council of Wales 'Contemporary Welsh Painting and Sculpture', National Museum of Wales, touring Swansea, Aberystwyth, Wrexham and Newport (2); 'Contemporary Welsh Painting', Howard Roberts Gallery, Cardiff (4)
1959 | Bangor Arts Festival – with CW and Anthony Stevens (41); 'Autumn Collection of Paintings', Howard Roberts Gallery, Cardiff (2); Society for Education through Art, National Museum of Wales, Cardiff (2); Arts Council of Wales, 'Young Welsh Artists', National Museum of Wales, Cardiff, touring Aberystwyth, Swansea and Wrexham (2); Royal Cambrian Academy of Art, Conwy (5); Society for Education through Art, National Museum of Wales and London; 'Wales through the Eye of the Artist', Howard Roberts Gallery, Cardiff (2); Royal National Eisteddfod of Wales, Caernarfon (2); Royal West of England Academy, Bristol (3); 'Paintings and Drawings by Welsh Artists', New Art Centre, London; Howard Roberts Gallery, Cardiff – with CW, Jonah Jones and Selwyn Jones; New Art Centre, London

1960 | Royal National Eisteddfod of Wales (2); Bradford Art Gallery; Society for Education through Art, National Museum of Wales (2); New Art Centre, London (5); North Wales Group; 'Summer Exhibition', Howard Roberts Gallery, Cardiff (9)
1961 | 'Spring Exhibition of Paintings and Drawings', Howard Roberts Gallery, Cardiff (5); Arts Council of Wales 'Contemporary Welsh Painting and Sculpture', National Museum of Wales, touring Bangor, Aberystwyth and Swansea

(1); Society for Education through Art, National Museum of Wales, Cardiff; 'Modern Welsh Painters', Hereford Art Gallery (2); Bangor Arts Festival; Howard Roberts Gallery, Cardiff; North Wales Group
1962 | New Art Centre, London*; Royal Cambrian Academy of Art, Conwy (2); Society for Education through Art, National Museum of Wales, Cardiff; 'Contemporary Welsh Paintings', Shrewsbury Art Gallery (2); 'Summer Exhibition', Howard Roberts Gallery, Cardiff (3); 'Autumn Exhibition', Howard Roberts Gallery, Cardiff (1); North Wales Group
1963 | Howard Roberts Gallery, Cardiff – with Tom Cross (30); Royal Cambrian Academy of Art, Conwy (2); Society for Education through Art, National Museum of Wales, Cardiff (2); Royal National Eisteddfod of Wales (3); Bangor Art Gallery – 6-man show (16)
1964 | Blue Coat Chambers, Liverpool – with CW (23); Royal Cambrian Academy of Art, Conwy (2); Old Town Hall, Criccieth – with CW and Kyffin Williams (35)
1965 | Howard Roberts Gallery, Cardiff*; Gwynedd Artists Association, Wrexham; 'Centenary Exhibition', Royal Cambrian Academy of Art, Conwy (2); Bangor Art Gallery – with CW; 'Spring Exhibition', Howard Roberts Gallery, Cardiff
1966 | Heal's Mansard Art Gallery, London (31)*; University of Wales, Gregynog Hall*; 'North Wales Artists', Albany Gallery, Cardiff
1967 | 'Paintings and Drawings', Tegfryn Gallery, Anglesey*
1968 | 'Paintings and Drawings', Lincoln College, Oxford (31)*; Heal's Mansard Art Gallery, London (26)*
1969 | 'Recording Wales – Chapels', Arts Council of Wales – touring (1); 'The Possessors – Paintings in Welsh Collections', Howard Roberts Gallery (3)

1970 | Heal's Mansard Art Gallery, London (23)*
1971 | 'Drawings', Tegfryn Gallery, Anglesey – with CW; Tegfryn Gallery, Anglesey*
1972 | Heal's Art Gallery, London (36)*
1973 | Heal's Art Gallery, London (25)*
1974 | Heal's Art Gallery, London (44)*; Anglesey Central Library, Llangefni – with CW (31); Albany Gallery, Cardiff
1975 | Heal's Art Gallery, London – with Liz Sherburne; Albany Gallery, Cardiff – with CW
1976 | 'Recent Paintings, Drawings and Portraits', Hereford Art Gallery – with CW (38); Tegfryn Gallery, Anglesey – with CW; 'Drawings and Paintings', Mid Wales House Gallery, Newbridge-on-Wye – with CW (GP–30, CW–21); 'Christmas Exhibition', Albany Gallery, Cardiff
1977 | 'Recent Paintings and Drawings', Old Mayor's Parlour, Hereford*
1978 | 'New Works', Tegfryn Gallery, Anglesey – with CW (75); Royal Cambrian Academy of Art, Conwy (5); University of Wales, Gregynog Hall – with CW
1979 | Royal Cambrian Academy of Art, Conwy (5); Tegfryn Art Gallery, Anglesey – with CW; 'Gwilym Prichard: Paintings', Wyeside Arts Centre, Builth Wells (47)*;

'This Native Land', Welsh Arts Council – Mostyn Art Gallery, Llandudno and touring

1980 | University of Wales, Swansea (44)*; Royal Cambrian Academy of Art, Conwy (6)
1981 | 'Paintings and Drawings', Tegfryn Art Gallery, Anglesey – with CW (47)
1982 | 'Oil Paintings, Watercolours and Drawings', Aberystwyth Arts Centre (104)*; Royal West of England Academy, Bristol; 'Places and People', Holyhead Library 1982 – with CW (GP–83, CW–11); 'Welsh Landscape in Oils', Albany Gallery, Cardiff
1983 | 'Gwilym Prichard', Framed, Worcester (39); 'Recent Paintings', Oriel 31, Welshpool*; Royal West of England Academy, Bristol; 'Wales 1983' The Welsh Group – Cardiff, Aberystwyth, Llandudno and Mold
1984 | Royal West of England Academy, Bristol
1985 | 'Recent Paintings', Turner House, Penarth – with CW (46–GP, 40–CW); 'Recent Paintings', Oriel Theatre Clwyd, Mold – with CW (46–GP, 40–CW); Royal West of England Academy, Bristol
1986 | Salon D'Art Contemporaine, Brignoles, France
1988 | Forum International, Nantes – with CW and Ceri Pritchard; Oriel Plas Glyn-y-Weddw, Llanbedrog*
1989 | Beaumaris Festival, Beaumaris Town Hall – with CW; 'Paintings and Pottery' Ceri Richards Gallery, University of Wales, Swansea – with CW and Ben Pritchard

1990 | Halle de Kéranguen, Crédit Agricole Banque, Vannes*
1991 | Galerie Moyen-Avenard, Nantes*; Espace Gauguin, Pont Aven*; Oriel Plas Glyn-y-Weddw, Llanbedrog*
1992 | Espace Gauguin, Pont Aven*, Galerie Saphir, Dinard and Paris – with CW; Attic Gallery, Swansea*
1993 | Galerie Moyen-Avenard, Nantes*; Galerie Saphir, Dinard and Paris – with CW; Galerie Vanhove, Quimper*; Espace Gauguin, Pont Aven*; 'Recent Works' National Library of Wales, Aberystwyth (53)*
1994 | Espace Gauguin, Pont Aven; Galerie Saphir, Dinard and Paris – with CW; Galerie l'Atelier, Angers*; Kunsthandel Kooring, Amsterdam
1995 | Galerie Moyen-Avenard, Nantes; 'Travelling Together', Oriel Ynys Môn, Anglesey – with CW; 'Travelling Together', Attic Gallery, Swansea – with CW (GP–40, CW–25); 'Un Gallois amoureux de la Bretagne', Galerie Saphir, Dinard*
1996 | 'La Tunisie d'un Gallois', Galerie Saphir, Paris*; 'Summer Exhibition', Martin Tinney Gallery, Cardiff – with CW; The Fort, Ste. Marine, Quimper – retrospective with CW, Ceri and Ben Pritchard
1997 | Martin Tinney Gallery, Cardiff – with CW; Galerie Moyen-Avenard, Nantes*; Galerie Saphir, Paris; 'Recent Paintings', Attic Gallery, Swansea – with CW (GP–28, CW–30)
1998 | Galerie Moyen-Avenard, Nantes; Galerie Saphir, Dinard*; 'People and Places', MOMA Wales, Machynlleth – with CW; 'Recent Work', Tegfryn Gallery, Anglesey*

1999 | 'New Paintings', Martin Tinney Gallery, Cardiff – with CW (27)

2000 | Galerie Moyen-Avenard, Nantes – with CW; Galerie Saphir, Dinard*; 'New Work', Attic Gallery, Swansea – with CW (41)
2001 | 'Recent Paintings', Martin Tinney Gallery, Cardiff (53)*; 'Travels Abroad' University of Wales, Aberystwyth, School of Art (25)*; National Library of Wales, Aberystwyth – retrospective, touring
2002 | 'The Return', Tenby Museum and Art Gallery – with CW
2003 | 'New Paintings', Martin Tinney Gallery, Cardiff (57)*
2004 | 'Back in North Wales', Tegfryn Gallery, Anglesey – with CW
2005 | 'New Paintings', Martin Tinney Gallery, Cardiff (72)*
2006 | '75th Birthday Celebratory Exhibition', Martin Tinney Gallery, Cardiff*; 'The Welsh Connection', Scottish Gallery, Edinburgh
2007 | 'New Paintings', Martin Tinney Gallery, Cardiff *
2009 | 'New Paintings', Martin Tinney Gallery, Cardiff (73)*

2011 | '80th Birthday Celebratory Exhibition', Martin Tinney Gallery, Cardiff*